I0224081

THE DOUBT PROJECT

The Doubt Project

A Crisis of Faith, the Battles, and the Answers

Devin Squeri

The Doubt Project: A Crisis of Faith, the Battles, and the Answers
© 2025 by DeWard Publishing Company, Ltd.
P.O. Box 290696, Tampa, FL 33687
www.deward.com

All rights reserved. No portion of this book may be reproduced in any form without written permission from the publisher.

Cover by

Reasonable care has been taken to trace original sources for any excerpts and quotations appearing in this book and to document such information. For material not in the public domain, fair use standards and practices were followed. Should any attribution be found to be incorrect or incomplete, the publisher welcomes written documentation supporting correction for subsequent printing.

Printed in the United States of America.

ISBN: 978-1-947929-39-5

To
my wife Paige

my foundation, whose unwavering love and support gave me
strength to persevere through the darkest days

And to
Allen Hainline

who patiently listened to my fears and wild multiverse rants,
gently guiding me toward a path of understanding.

Without you both, I would never have made it; you saved
my soul, and I am forever in your debt.

Contents

*Acknowledgements*t

My heartfelt thanks to Allen Hainline, my wife Paige, and Matt James for their invaluable help in editing this book, and to Luke Barnes for his dedicated work on the fine-tuning chapter, Casey Luskin on the chapter on evolution as well as Jonathan McLatchie for setting me straight on the reliability of the Gospels.

Their insights and efforts have greatly enhanced the work. Any remaining errors are entirely my own.

ONE | *Onset of a Crisis of Faith*

Maybe it was because I was rapidly approaching my 50th milestone birthday, but whatever the reason was is immaterial, what is important is that it was the moment that Peter Pan was killed. He did not peacefully die in his sleep; it was more akin to being shot in the head, run over, eviscerated, burnt, blown up, the gatherings put into a howitzer and fired into outer space. In an instant the bottom fell out and the underpinnings of my life were knocked away. Yes, it was that quick

In a heartbeat, I became aware that I was getting older and therefore, would eventually, inevitably and undeniably, succumb to death. Yeah, I know, the gray hair, the little wrinkle lines and the random aches and pains from hard physical work, such as raking a few leaves, should have prepared me for this realization, but hey, I still thought of myself as a young man. The door to the secret room where I had locked away all the questions and uncertainty about God was thrown open wide, and the rush of doubt and fear overwhelmed me. Frankly, I panicked. The seeds of distrust that I had hidden away had hatched and grown into savage creatures, empowered by despair and defeat. Once freed, their eager assault was immediate and intense, quickly overwhelming my defenses, my crash had come.

The realization that no matter how much time I have left, even if it's another 50 years or even 500, is not even a blink of the cosmic eye was staggering. I came to face that no matter how long our lifespan is, it is trivial compared to the infinity that we will spend, or not spend, in the afterlife. What had never earned a second thought had now become my main priority; my sole focus was on trying to understand what is the truth about God. Thoughts of God and eternity monopolized my time, work became secondary, and free time disappeared in the quagmire of worried contemplation. I was terrified that if what I feared was true and Christianity was empty, then I was doomed to just disappear in a few short years, and there is absolutely nothing that I can do about it. Nothing at all. All my thoughts and dreams, memories and love of my family, the sum of what I spent my life building, and the entirety of my consciousness simply ceasing to exist. Think about yourself just being gone. Not in an empty space. Not in pain or just a floating mind. Gone. Imagine the time before you were born, how you didn't exist; what if we returned full circle and disappeared into nothing?

I was in a state well beyond terror. Each tick of the clock reinforced the futility of fighting against a fate that you are powerless to prevent. Devin Squeri may be imperfect, but I desperately don't want to simply vanish. My future was set in stone. I couldn't work, buy, or plead my way out of it.

I was completely overcome with despair and became fixated on the reality that if there is no God, then everything is meaningless. It is not that I was so church oriented that I no longer have any direction, or that I would be missing an important part of my life, it is literally without meaning. We live for a few short years and regardless of what we do, no matter what we accomplish or accumulate, it has no significance at all. If there is no God, you and I matter as much as an insect that lived 5,000 years ago and just as bad, our children mean just as little—and again, there is absolutely nothing that we can do about it. What can possibly be achieved to leave a lasting mark? Build a giant company? Fleeting. Earn 50 billion dollars? Hollow. Save 500 orphans from a fire? Shortly forgotten. Write a book? Immaterial in the grand scheme of the cosmos.

Whatever it is, it doesn't matter. Since it's utterly pointless and futile, it stands to question why even try? How little is remembered of even the most accomplished individuals that lived 200 years ago? How about 2,000 (well, except that guy)? For perspective, how about we fast forward 50,000 years. Do you really have the fantasy that anything that you, your family, your grandkids, your grandkids' grandkids possibly did will matter to the universe or even be remembered in future generations? I know it's possible, but I also know that's merely wishful thinking. Zero point zero chance. If there is

> "Nothing is so important to man as his state: nothing more fearful than eternity . . . . It is a monstrous thing to see a man in this state of indifference, when the certainty of death, judgment, and eternity is so near."
>
> ***Blaise Pascal*** *(Pensées, verse 195)*

no end game, no point, no lasting impression, the question becomes, why bother? Still holding out hope? Our universe is heading for a heat death so that in a few short trillion years there will be nothing but diffused molecules in cold space with no light or heat, and believe me, they won't care.

The next few months were a downward spiral, an uncontrollable tailspin. I fell into a severe depression where it was a major struggle to get out of bed. Many days, the only time I could marshal the strength to rise was when my children were returning home from school because I desperately did not want them to see me in that state. In the first three weeks, I lost eight pounds. I found no joy in any of the things that I used to, and any happy times were quickly overtaken with the remembered horror that we would all soon disappear. My wife, who will forever have my gratitude, was my rock and my lifeline. I truly don't know what would have happened without her. She is a woman of steadfast faith, of which I have always been extremely jealous. She never pressured me to simply blindly believe or to put my doubts aside, cope and move on. Instead, she was always a bastion of support and encouraged me to spend whatever time I needed to find the answers I was seeking. She would do the heavy lifting for our home and family while I figured myself out. She is patient beyond belief and ever present with her loving encouragement. Calling her my rock is almost literal; she was strong, unyielding and supporting but also, and just as importantly, a solid place where I could marshal my strength and have solid footing to raise myself up from.

I vividly remember one day being in my walk-in closet changing clothes when I started deeply contemplating the nihilism and futility of it all. I had the very distinct feeling of looking into a vortex of nothingness. As I explored the idea further and further, I felt like I was being sucked in, falling into the depths of the void. I reached a point where I had to rip myself away or risk being lost. The shock and fear of that moment still reverberates like it happened a moment ago, and I do feel as if I barely escaped. I reached the moment where things became unsustainable. I don't know if it was that my mind saw that it was losing the battle and I was at the edge of the abyss, barely hanging by my fingertips, or as in the wise words of Popeye the Sailor, "I hads all I could stands, and I can't stands no more." Whatever the reason, I did the bravest thing that

I have ever done in my life; I turned around and faced my terror. I decided that I was going to finally ask my questions and deal with what came. The cold acceptance that if things went as I feared, faith really was a house of cards and that I couldn't believe, I would have to find a way to make peace with it and live my life as best as I could. At this point, I was so certain of the conclusions that I began investigating how the prominent atheists found meaning in their lives without God. Whatever fruit came, I would accept the result and work through the aftermath as best as I could.

If God is not there, I was spending a completely inappropriate amount of time on spiritual matters. The seconds of my life are a finite quantity and eventually, we are destroyed. What we were turns to dust and is forgotten, having zero lasting value. If we try to balance a finite resource, time, to be equated in worth to activities that will eventually turn to nothing, then there is nothing that you can do that is equal in worth to the immense value of time. Since every second of life is so precious, I needed to make the most of them as best as I could—and clearly church and praying to an empty God was not making a good use of it. If we are offering prayers to a vacuum, then even the little bit that I do was way too much and must be discarded.

However, if God is there, then I was not spending nearly enough time and not being devoted to the level that I should be. If there is an afterlife as professed by Christianity, then the value proposition shifts dramatically. In this scenario, there is an unlimited amount of time. As there is some level of value in listening to a bird sing or taking a walk (even if you assign a trivial value to it, it is still greater than zero), and there is an infinite number of seconds, then it is an incredibly good investment to relax and enjoy the world around you. Investing something that you have an unlimited supply of to gain an even moderate value is a pretty easy decision. In this paradigm, I am able to relax and take real joy in simple things.

Then if atheism leads to a place where life is meaningless and despondent nihilism, but theism leads to peace and hope, why don't you just believe and be done with it? Seems pretty simple. The problem is that I cannot simply force myself to believe something without the confidence that it is true, and after thinking on it, I don't feel that I would choose that, even if I could.

If God created me and did all the things described in the Bible, then He deserves my steadfast devotion and dedication. My ego had trouble accepting that God is so far above me that I should serve and worship him. A much more comfortable idea is that our relationship is that of respected peer or even a trusted adviser, but the final authority is reserved for me; admitting that I am not intelligent enough even to know the words to describe how much more massively great He is than I am does not sit well. I acknowledge that a part of my skepticism is being able to accept that, and therefore I would need to humble myself before Him. If there really is a soul and an afterlife, then I need to invest my time wisely. Eternity is a long time, doing whatever is needed to make sure that you end up where you want to be is obviously a good trade. I fully realize that this is not the proper way to view this; if you are a believer, then you should be acting in a moral and generous manner as a way to conform to God's word because of your love for God, not to earn yourself into the afterlife. My mindset is clearly the tail wagging the dog.

After decades of smoldering, the push and pull of my questions and doubts had reached a critical mass. My personal cold war between the Christian and the naturalistic worldviews had suddenly gone hot.

Hot or cold, I could no longer be lukewarm.

TWO | *A Brief History of (My) Time*

While my foundation collapsed in an instant, the erosion that led to that moment occurred over a lifetime. I was born and raised on Long Island, New York. To those unwashed masses unfamiliar with NY geography, that is down by New York City (or "the City"). My dad grew up in 1930s Little Italy, NY and frankly, was a bit of a street kid, but had a basic Roman Catholic upbringing—what do you expect from a NY Italian? My mom, a good Irish woman, is from western Pennsylvania and was raised Protestant. What is more important is that I was raised as a Roman Catholic, attended Sunday school, held on Wednesday afternoons of course, and completed all of the Catholic sacraments that were available up through high school. There are seven sacraments in Roman Catholicism, and I had accomplished all that were age appropriate. Additionally, in the Boy Scouts, I earned the Catholic medal, *Ad Altari Dei* and, when I was in High School, and taught Sunday school to third grade boys. Boy, I sounded good on paper! I felt that I was a good Christian and was going above and beyond the prescribed path, but in my heart of hearts I knew that I had no understanding of my faith or deep connection to God. Conversely, over the years, doubts had crept in that seemed impossible to reconcile. I hoped that "our side" had these issues well in hand, and the only reason that I was not aware of the answers was simply due to my ignorance.

What I do remember, vividly in fact, was having some very disconcerting questions and thoughts starting in my early teens. I have a science and math-oriented mind with an (un)healthy dousing of NY skepticism, more than a dash of sarcasm, and a strong willingness to question. When applied to Scripture, the loaded questions demonstrating the failure of Bible stories, eternity, heaven and hell and many others, came easily. It terrified me that in the back of my mind, I absolutely knew that if I asked these questions, the answers would have been unsatisfactory—after all, how could they not be? A person living in the stomach of a fish for three days, oh come on! I didn't think that there was any way that a rational person could take this seriously. If I was honest, I felt that Bible and Christianity was not just a house of cards, but a house of cards made of fine glass.

I consciously decided that I would not examine religion too closely as it was an illusion that I was unwilling to shatter at that time—and yes, it actually was a conscious decision. I was young; death was a fact of life but not a fact of *my* life. I knew that if I asked hard questions on the authenticity of the Bible, miracles, prayer, evolution, eternity, and a host of other topics, that veil would forever be pierced, and there would be no putting the genie back in the bottle. I would have to finally face the facts and be left with the reality that God really was just the "opiate of the masses" and my spiritual pockets were empty. I knew it was a placebo, but my time on Earth was seemingly unlimited; getting old and dying was a reality that I knew would happen to me, but in a blind disconnect, I didn't believe that it would happen *to* me. Best to kick that can down the road.

In my early church learning, I received some basic "facts" with no basis besides "the Bible says so" and participated in ceremonies with the jingling of bells, incense, and rhetoric in a long dead language, all of which did nothing for me. I always felt at some internal level that it was probably true, but I prize logic and rational thought, feelings don't count for very much to me when making decisions. Facts and evidence are solid ground to build a belief system from; feelings are easily manipulated by family, society or even wishful thinking.

My family were C and E Christians—going to church on Christmas and Easter—and the extent of tithing and Biblical living was putting $20 in the plate on the holidays. Needless to say, the family religious experience was sparse, but I think it was also somewhat typical. There was no prayer at dinner or regular church service, I had never even heard of a Bible study until I moved to Texas—and while I sit here and write, actually trying to recall the Bibles influence on me when I was growing up, I realize that what I had always warmly reminisced as the large, leatherbound family Bible, as I think about it now, was actually an old dictionary. I guess we didn't open it much. The closest thing we got to a sermon at home was my father yelling "Jesus Christ!" and while that was a frequent occurrence, I don't really count that as spiritual guidance.

It's not as if my father was dismissive of or scorned religion, I think that he actually held it in high regard, but just not something that he was directly involved with. It seems like he did what he thought he was supposed to do and believed as much as he thought anyone could—and I am sure that he considered himself a Catholic and a Christian. But, in fairness, he also used to say that if the priests were so sure of God, why were they afraid to die? The point is that I do consider myself as having a Christian upbringing and, ironically enough, I think religion was important to my dad and family, but it certainly was not a regular part of our lives.

I lived the next 30 years of my life with a tentative relationship with God. While I still had not dealt with the doubts and questions, I feel that I did believe at some real level. Furthermore, I was a weekly church goer and the regular usher on aisle 3 at the 10.45 service. While I did not understand the born-again crowd, I reached the point that I could say "Jesus" out loud without feeling absurdly awkward. I knew that some level of faith was present, but it was a hesitant and detached one, one that paled in comparison to that of the true believers. Sterile or clinical is probably a good way to describe it. I regularly wondered if I believed "enough" to pass the test to get into heaven.

More and more frequently, I would get emotional during worship music or service. My wife thought that it was sweet that I could be so vulnerable, but I secretly knew what my tears represented. Instead of a joy and closeness to God, they were from agonizing frustration driven by the desire for peace being prevented by the very real doubts and fears. It was as if my body was split, and the two warring hands had grabbed onto opposite sides and were pulling apart. It was the unstoppable force fighting against the unmovable object, and I was caught in the middle. Then came the crash.

At this point, I was in a pretty bad state. Probably clinically depressed, not sleeping, overly emotional and despondent. Fast slipping into nihilism. I had no interest in exposing my wife to how low and fragile I had become. She has never been judgmental, but I was supposed to be the man and be a source of strength. We are taught from an early age to not show weakness and exposing this to my wife was a shame that I was not willing to endure. She was of steadfast faith; how would she react to her husband having heretical thoughts and quickly verging on atheism? As there could not be any acceptable answers to my doubts, would I ruin her relationship with God and drag her down with me? Better to handle this alone.

That this was a self-imposed standard, my wife never had these kinds of expectations.

After failing to push this aside or "handle it myself" as men are taught to, I went to a local church and was directed to a couple's pastor to help with my doubts. I know he was trying to help, but the only advice that I received was to "take 40 days and pray on it with my wife." As you can imagine, when you are having doubts that God exists, the advice to pray on it doesn't really help very much.

Seeking further spiritual help, I visited multiple local churches but it was clear to me that they were not prepared for these types of questions. Advice such as "pray on it," "decide to believe," "you can't understand the mysteries of God," or any of the other suggestions hurt more than helped. I felt that if the spiritual leaders had no reply to the skeptic's demand for answers and evidence, then those answers and evidence probably didn't exist.

I became so despondent that I wrote a letter to the head pastor at my church in November. I am not going to include the text, but I feel that it is important to highlight the interaction. This church, as well as the others, and especially their leadership, is filled with what I truly believe are good people trying to do the right thing. I really do believe that they wished to help but it was abundantly clear that they were woefully unequipped to deal with it.

When someone is having a crisis of faith and ready to walk away from God, it should be the pastoral version of the Super Bowl, Game Seven of the World Series, and the Heavyweight Title Fight all in one. I know that it's a bit presumptuous for the doubter to say this, but I would think that dealing with the person falling away would be the absolutely most important thing to the church and should be treated as such. I can only speak for myself, but especially after these interactions, I felt very alone, lost, and overwhelmed.

I hoped for, but did not really expect a local church member to be able to address the specifics of my doubts as they are scientific in nature—mostly regarding the conflict of empiricism / materialism vs. the Christian worldview. But honestly, I did expect more than emails taking weeks to be returned and the sum of the advice being that there are mysteries with God or to pray with your wife with zero follow up. I did expect someone to have taken the walk with me and/or to point me to resources where I could find answers. I highlight this not to air grievance, as I have noted that they meant well. What I am trying to convey is that the local church may not be prepared for questions.

Belief in God, and the natural extrapolation of what happens after you die, is the most important question that I have ever faced, and as I had no confidence in any answer, I started researching the major areas of my doubt. The new atheists' push to frame faith as blind faith and promote the idea that belief in God is diametrically opposed to "science and reason" has had great success. It has had a profound effect on society, and specifically, on me. I was surprised to find how many other people, both online as well as church attending Christians that I know personally, have many questions as well. The topics of concern were varied, but many were centered, like mine, around the conflict between science and faith. I point this out because there are people, like my wife, whose level of certainty is unshakable, but there are also many people with questions and doubts.

Since then, I have spent well over two years obsessively reading, listening to podcasts, watching videos and documentaries, and attending meetings that express both the Christian apologist's and the atheist's viewpoints. I needed to do the work and evaluate both sides in as fair and unbiased way as possible and see which side made the most sense. While I will agree with one position to a larger degree than the other, and therein lies my opinion, I feel that I should be able to express the counter arguments as well. Not understanding the points and counterpoints risks forming an ill-considered belief based on desire, not evidence. In short, giving consideration to both positions should make your level of certainty stronger, not weaker. I have always made it a point not to stake out a position on an issue until I feel that I have enough information, pro and con, to feel a high level of certainty. Historically, there have been many times when people were surprised because I was presented with new evidence, reevaluated my position, and reversed myself. What people had assumed was a hardheaded stubbornness (or maybe being a know it all) was instead a decision based on facts that may be changed, but only with new data.

When I dissected the core of my skepticism, I became aware that it started with my problems reconciling evolution vs. Genesis and the Bible, and science vs. religion in general. It also included the vacancy of any factual evidence to support the Bible, namely that the apostles weren't just a naïve and superstitious lot that fell in with a charismatic leader and were prone to primitive mysticism and exaggeration. When I started digging, I found that, if truth be told, the issues extended to the believability of Bible stories, the supernatural, miracles, multiple religions all claiming truth, natural evil, and (what I learned was termed) the hiddenness of God. Yeah, pretty much the gambit. Go big or go home.

My goal for this writing project is twofold. First, it is to finally force me to clarify what I feel are legitimate issues and what are sound bites said for effect, but without any real depth or merit. After about 20 weeks of intensive study, I went through an overload phase where I had a vast amount of data—facts, figures, rationale, and other information but just couldn't process them into a coherent conclusion or even understand where my objections still resided. I was so swimming in information and reasoning, pro and con, that I didn't understand how God could possibly exist but simultaneously, also didn't understand how God could possibly not exist.

I needed a way to bridge the logical and emotional sides of my mind, and I am cautiously optimistic that this will be that catalyst. Committing ideas to tangible form makes it real—at least psychologically, and I need to let these competing ideas coalesce and finally, hopefully, decide what I believe.

I have also come to realize I have some intellectual leanings toward a default materialist view where reality is comprised of only our physical world, therefore belief in God requires proof. As such, the God paradigm is making the truth claim and so, puts the burden of proof on the theism side, which is a much more difficult position. Logically, I recognize that there is no reason that theism should be the only one held to the standards of evidence. Atheism is certainly making a truth claim as well and fully promoting a worldview, therefore it should be held to the same standard. Unfortunately, most of the time that does not seem to be the case.

Many of the atheist arguments that I have encountered seem shallow and, frankly, often logically incoherent. However, there are also a few showstoppers that, if true, would be a poison pill to theism. If it was an unbiased comparison and you simply said which one has more evidence and more reasoning, I would easily say the Christian worldview—but the challenge for me is that my standard for beleiving in Christianity is so much higher.

For example, if 75% of atheist's claims were demonstrably false, it would not weaken the atheist worldview to me. However, if 25% of the Christian claims, or even 10%, were shown to be demonstrably false, then I think my ability to believe the Christian worldview would be shattered. Would the Bible hold any weight if it were determined that 5% of the meaningful content, not silly typos or word substitution nonsense, was proven to be incorrect? Now I know that it could be argued that this would only prove that the Bible is not the inspired word of God or not infallible, but that is a very slippery slope. If it's not 100% accurate, then what percentage of error can I allow and still believe that it is true? Can I then just take anything that is shown to be false and simply say, well that part is made up, but the rest really is the true word of God and keep going? Under those conditions, any writing can claim to be divine truth, and if you simply discard each part as it was proven to be erroneous, it would technically be right. As such, I stand by the claim that if any part of the Bible was proven to be false, while not a mortal wound, it would be a grievous one to me. Even one error would significantly degrade my confidence in any of it. Yes, I admit a different set of standards.

Now, not to jump too far ahead, but since the door was opened, I also accept that there must be a reasonable expectation of evidence. Going back in time to witness the miracles of Scripture is impossible, no one that I know was there when Jesus was preaching, nor can I perform experiments on God or interview the apostles, so I need to rely on the proven methodologies used today to determine believability of historical documents and witnesses. I will not repeat the fallacy that I have seen from many atheists to justify their lack of faith, setting impossible initial conditions and then, amazingly enough, reach the conclusions that they expected at the start.

The idea that obtaining 100% certainty that God either exists or doesn't is a fool's errand, as this is a level that unobtainable for anything beyond knowing that you personally exist. But for me to truly believe, I do need to get to a very high level of confidence and then allow the earned trust to bridge the gap.

It is important to note that I carefully considered if my admitted self-interest in there being a God and an afterlife resulted in a bias that had skewed my analysis. After constant self-reflection, I have concluded that this is not the case. I have always prized truth above all else and have gotten pretty good at recognizing, and then compartmentalizing and filtering out my feelings, especially when there is an issue that I want or fear to be true. Additionally, I feel that if I were to deceive myself, even unintentionally, there would always be that whisper in the back of my mind quietly reminding me that I really do know the truth, even if I don't admit it to the world. That is hollow consolation, and that kind of behavior has never been a comfort to me, and therefore, has no appeal. I don't claim to be the epitome of detached, unbiased thinking, but I do claim that in areas where the danger of these pitfalls is clearly apparent, I can be vigilant and clinical in my thoughts. Sticking your head in the sand doesn't stop the oncoming train.

The second reason for this writing is to honestly and openly expose the journey of finally asking the questions, the emotional hardships of the journey, and the progress that has been made in finding what I believe is the truth. I hope that by honestly exposing my crisis of faith, it may help someone else who was or is in my position. People hide these crisis events out of guilt and shame, but they are real, not as uncommon as many would like to think, and they are, in my experience, devastating. Feelings of being utterly lost and adrift were somewhat expected but what surprised me was how devastating the feelings of being totally alone were.

When I looked around, it felt as if everyone else was secure in their faith and I was separated, a pariah on an island of doubt. Maybe it was depression, maybe it was absorbing the futility of it all, maybe I was so threatened that I retreated within myself, maybe I simply felt distanced from God, whatever it was, I felt completely disconnected from everyone and everything. The feelings were so overwhelming that I could not clearly identify any specific problem, and therefore, could not communicate what was wrong. As soon as one objection flashed across my mind, another would appear and attack from a different direction, even before I could grab hold of the first. Imagine trying to solve a problem, going through the pain of reorienting yourself with its details, but before any progress is made, a new topic arises and consumes your thoughts, forcing you to start over. I could assess the uncertainty, having just enough time to continually feel the doubt and hopelessness of the topic, but not enough time to make any progress or gain any new understanding. I started calling this phenomenon "spinning"; as I would start to wrestle with one issue but before any progress was made, I would spin off to another. It was a cycle of endless mental flailing, and it was truly exhausting.

I also felt—and feel—a tremendous amount of guilt and, to be honest, fear. I do feel guilty in questioning and my mind knows that's irrational, but I feel it nonetheless. Is it that I am fighting the natural belief in God that is imbued in us at creation or possibly finally acknowledging the possibility of something that I admit I dread? Maybe I feel guilty for challenging the status quo and potentially causing upheaval for my family? At this point, I don't know. I do know that I can only equate it to the guilt that you feel as a small child when you know that you're doing something wrong, but you don't know exactly what. Some will view this as proof that I already know that God exists and am erecting barriers to belief; I acknowledge this possibility as well.

Part of the fear in this instance is not the fear of the abyss, although that is very real as well; it is the fear that if God exists, then how doomed am I for even questioning Him. I do take some solace in few items that suggest that God understands that we will question and have need of evidence. First, as noted, the apostle Paul says to love God with all your mind. If we were to blindly believe, I do not think that they would have taken the time and precious space to note this. Also, Jesus said to the people that even if they will not believe what He said, at least to believe the miracles that He performed. He understood that people needed evidence. Finally, Thomas his apostle, even after seeing Jesus perform miracles, living with him, and hearing him preach, still would not believe his fellow apostles' testimony that Jesus rose from the dead. If Thomas can experience all these things firsthand and doubt so much that he rejected the sworn testimony of the resurrection and still not lose God's love, maybe there is hope for me.

In no way am I an authority of apologetics, theology, or the Bible. If anyone else ever reads this, they will probably be able to point out a litany of items that I missed or should have said. While I am sure that this is true, that is not the point. There are many fine works by people who are much more thoroughly versed in these topics than I am. If someone is reading this who is going through what I went through, and to some real degree still going through, I do want you to know that you are not the only one who has experienced this and most importantly, you are not alone. The reality is that there are well thought out, and often compelling, answers. You may or may not find them persuasive, but they exist well beyond "because the Bible says so." You will probably find, as

I did, that most of my areas of concern were not original and have actually been debated previously, sometimes for centuries.

Some of the ideas presented will be original thoughts and so, may very well be half baked. I have decided to not edit out these examples as I feel that it is important to display the types of odd questions that come to mind; they are not necessarily present to make a persuasive argument for their merit.

It is now December, and I have been dealing with this conflict for about 20 months. I had many of my questions answered satisfactorily, but along my travels, I also encountered new objections that needed inspection. The feeling of dread has slowly abated, and I almost felt like myself for the first time about a month ago; it has been a long hard road. What has not gone away is the feeling of impending doom. Every day that passes, it is one day closer to my end. If I go three hours without at least a momentary thought in the direction of mortality or the reality of the afterlife, it is a marathon run.

I envision myself on a long, narrow ledge extending out over the abyss. There is a wall that pushes out, slowly but indomitably every second, driving me back and back, closer and closer to the end of the ledge. Every second, the screw turns slightly and the wall advances. No matter how I push and strain against the wall, no matter my position, it keeps moving ever forward. My safe footing is becoming less and less. Maybe my ledge is 20 years long, maybe 40, maybe two days, I do not know. I know that beyond the ledge is the abyss and every night I think about how the ledge is smaller than the day before.

This is a walk through my (ongoing) journey to find the truth.

| *Facing the Demons of Doubt*

I remember when I was in the fourth grade and my brother clued me in as to how you could always pass the tests in catechism (Catholic Sunday school). He said, just answer "because God loves you" and they will never mark you as wrong. Amazingly enough, he was absolutely correct! And while it was nice to ace every test on God and Christianity that was thrown my way without having to study, or even think, it brought me to the conclusion that religious education was really a very shallow thing. Since parroting rote platitudes seemed to be of sufficient depth to satisfy an assortment of questions seemingly critical to the theology of Christianity, I logically concluded that this whole thing was merely a thin, flimsy veneer on reality and therefore, I had better not scratch too hard! It very much felt like there was an unspoken agreement, they would sign off on me being a good standing member of the flock and in return, I didn't look under the covers too hard.

While I do not think that my religious schooling sent me in the direction of atheism, I do think that instead of giving me faith, it bolstered and emboldened my doubts. The lack of depth reinforced that there were no real logical or evidential reasons to believe, beyond that it said so in the Bible; it was an authority unto itself and was beyond question. I truly understood the situation to be that the Bible stood alone, and you could either believe it or not—and that was that. Why do you believe the Bible stories? Because the Bible says so! Circular references answer nothing, even when relating to God.

I don't consider Sunday school as having failed for not fully instilling all the biblical stories or evidence for God to a teenage boy in New York. The truth is that I was much more interested in girls and booze. I was far from a hoodlum, but my objectives at that time were hanging out and drinking with my friends and especially in meeting girls, not hearing about the authenticity of the Bible. What I do consider a failure, is even after completing years of classes, I was never exposed to the idea that everyone has doubts, that it is normal and natural, and even more important, the evidence for belief is out there. Instead, I had the accumulation of my questions, bottled up by the mindset that you didn't discuss these issues or subjects, and if you did, there were no good answers to them anyway.

For me, it took a long buildup of the forces of skepticism and fear to overcome the inertia of keeping quiet and hoping it would somehow go away. Once they did, outwardly vocalizing my questions gave them life; they were now real. I immediately felt marked with the stigma of one of the faithless. I disdain hypocrisy but the feeling was ever present, especially as I ushered at church or talked to my children about God.

There is a strong natural impulse not to ask questions or show uncertainty on any topic, but it is especially prevalent regarding faith. Exceeding the pressure to keep quiet and not just internalize them is not a trivial threshold. My guess is that an overwhelming percentage of people who step out and ask questions have some serious level of uncertainty. In my case, the pressure continually built over decades until, like the buildup of the continental plates pressing against each other, it was just a matter of time until there was an earthquake. I think this quiet buildup of pressure is very common in church today. The final effect can either become internal and manifest as a personal, hidden, and quiet falling away from faith or, as for me, an overwhelming tidal wave of doubt.

After reaching the critical mass and acknowledging my doubts, answers like "you have to have faith" are powerless. In fact, I find them maddening. I don't know about anyone else, but I don't have a "faith switch" that I can simply flip on and suddenly have it. I can't simply decide to believe. In order to extend your faith to the topic in question, you have to have a foundation to draw from, right? I can see how existing belief could be extended to any areas of doubt, but this solution fails miserably when the person is lacking that confidence to start with. Why would you and how could you extend it to another area? If the well is dry, it's going to be very hard to water the crops.

I found myself getting very frustrated, and a little angry, that this life-changing event was met with advice that is better left for a fortune cookie. As another line of answers intended to satisfy my doubts not only came up empty but instead reinforced that there really were no logical or evidential reasons to believe. I decided to take matters into my own hands, and no matter what the cost, I would find the answers that I was looking for.

Early in my truth seeking, I had also heard a somewhat famous evangelist, when questioned about some difficult problems with Scripture, reply that God uses foolish ideas to trick the wise. My jaw hit the floor. It seemed like their position was that any perceived logically incoherent or nonsensical verses in Scripture aren't a proof that it's simply a bunch of imperfect human authored stories embellished over the ages; they are instead a clever tripwire to defeat intellectual thinkers…. talk about a cringewor-thy statement! With friends like these, you don't need enemies!

Blaise Pascal was a famous French mathematician, physicist, inventor, philosopher, and Catholic theologian. For those out-side of the science circles (where all the cool guys hang), he is so famous that the computer language Pascal is named after him. He also created what is famously referred to as Pascals Wager in which he says that no one can prove that God exists. If God exists, the believer gains everything and goes to heaven but the unbeliever loses everything and goes to hell. On the other hand, if God doesn't exist, the believer loses nothing and the unbeliever gains nothing. Therefore, there is everything to gain and nothing to lose by believing in God.

My take on this was, go ahead and believe even if it doesn't make sense—you have nothing to lose and everything to gain. If the odds are one in a million that the Bible is true and God exists, then you have a one in a million chance of a good afterlife if you believe—which is better than the odds of zero in a million if you don't. While logically true, instead of being compelling for faith, this instead feels like a detriment to me. If that's the best reason that a famous Catholic theologian offers for belief, I'm in trouble.

I do need to note that a friend of mine added that this is not Pascal's main argument, it is really only a personal reflection. He was an avid apologist and after many years putting forth rationale and reasons for faith, he decided to compile it into manifesto of sorts named *An Apology for the Christian Religion* (from the Greek *Apologia* meaning defense of, not as in "I am sorry"). Its intention was to move skeptics and freethinkers to the Christian faith. Un-fortunately, he died before it was completed and all we are left with are his notes—some thousand ideas, theories, maxims and philosophical insights, which were published as *Pensées* translated to "thoughts" with Pascal's Wager being one of them. It is not put forth as an argument for Christianity or even God's existence, but simply an argument for why belief in God is rational.

I have heard many times that seeking evidence for belief in God smacks of heresy as, if you have faith, then you don't need evidence. Some also say that faith comes from the Holy Spirit and not from any worldly knowledge; if you were pre-ordained to believe, then the Holy Spirit would reach out to you. Faith comes from a movement of the soul and then conversely, no one has ever been converted or established belief due to logic, reasoning or evidence. There was a time when I feared that I simply wasn't one of God's chosen people. I heard the Good News of Jesus, and I was missing something inside that would allow the Holy Spirit in to give me the experiential belief. I had my chance, and I still doubted. No matter what I did, no matter what I learned, I would always be on the outside looking in.

Spoiler alert: this is completely false! In what I believe is a distorted theology, some promote that God has foreordained who were to be the ones to believe and therefore saved, and the rest of us are just chaff for the fire. If you don't believe it, then you simply weren't chosen, and no amount of evidence or logic is going to change that. The same people who promote that God loves all his children. I see a tragic irony in a belief that a God who loves us can have created a population pre-determined to not believe and therefore be damned to spend an eternity in hell. In my opinion, this makes absolutely no sense and seems to be contradictory. What I am left with is that there are many intellectually lazy people; it's enticing to just believe based on feelings, not entertain and evaluate counter arguments and, at the same time, feel the cultish self-righteousness of being one of the cosmically special people who do not need any reasons to believe.

It seems that for many of the true believers, there is a lack of evidential knowledge because they feel that it is unnecessary. If you already have a foundation of faith from experience or emotion, I can understand why someone would not feel the need to seek further. After all, when you're already in the end zone, you stop running. Also, being able to have a compelling, evidence-based conversation on Christianity, especially considering that the person to which you were speaking would probably be a skeptic or at the very least someone with serious questions, is a daunting task. Speaking from firsthand experience, the material is voluminous and spans numerous disciplines. To exacerbate this challenge, I did find that while it is good that the internet makes all voices somewhat equal, and it is good that everyone has a platform, it is also problematic as every crackpot with a digital bullhorn promotes themselves as an authority—and they are usually the loudest and most assertive ones. Having to filter out extreme theories or statements that are presented as absolute fact, but after investigation are completely fallacious, is taxing. Furthermore, having to sideline more pleasurable endeavors to prioritize learning the justifications, and then investing in mental cycles to be able to give coherent reasons for your faith to a hostile audience probably isn't very appealing. It's a lot of work.

This led to my perception being, and I think for many other people as well, that you could either be a logic-based, inquisitive thinker who demands reasons and evidence for acceptance of an idea *or* you could be a faithful believer in God. They were mutually exclusive; it is an *or*, not an *and*.

Maybe in years gone by when the Bible was inaccessible, the church was the center of the community, and societal pressure kept people quiet, then the blind faith arguments may have won the day but in modern America, that dog don't hunt (did I mention that I moved to Dallas, Texas?). I am sure that the general clergy has a large workload and maybe learning all of the actual reasons for faith would be too much. Maybe they are feelings/experience based and, as they would be devout followers, can't empathize with people with significant doubts and the need for a factual basis for faith. Maybe they believe that the only path to belief is through the Holy Spirit. I don't know. I do know that the church is having a major falling away as people are confronted with "evidence" for why God doesn't exist—and that you don't need Him anyway! As people have not been taught any solid foundation for the reasons for faith, when challenged by some reasonable—and also some very absurd—counterpoints, their faith easily falls away. 75% of Christian teens fall away from their faith after high school, yeah, it's that bad.[1] In fairness, I do not know specifically what the definition is for "falling from their faith." Is it permanent or do they come back when they grow out of the "drink so much that you throw up on your shoes" stage? Either way, I will bet that some very real, non-trivial percentage lose their belief due to the "intellectual" atheists' arguments.

While I knew that blind faith was not for me, I had no idea that there have been great thinkers discussing and debating areas of skepticism since the first century. Interestingly enough, I have found that while my ego likes to think of myself as having original and brilliant thoughts but all of my questions—and many others—have been discussed for almost 2,000 years. As noted before, the classical term is Christian apologists but I think J. Warner Wallace, a cold case detective and former atheist, has a more appropriate modernization of the term in "Christian case making."

I have always felt, for all subjects, that any argument is within bounds to question, and falsehoods will dissolve like shadows under a bright light. This should be no different. When I started digging into this massive beehive, I learned is that it actually says in the Bible, "come, let us reason"[2] and "test everything, and hold onto the good[3]." The apostle Peter said "always be prepared to give an answer to everyone who asks you the reason for the hope that you have"[4]. Jesus said to love God with all your heart, soul, and mind. This doesn't sound to me like the Bible is telling me to blindly believe. Instead, it seems to say to examine, test, and evaluate to make sure that what I hold onto is "good."

I was startled to learn that the Greek biblical word "Pistis" is translated to the word "faith" in modern Bibles, but it does *not* mean blind wishing, it means active trust. Think about that for a second. I have heard persuasive arguments why the term "faith," which has been corrupted so badly over the years by antagonists as well as by self-inflicted wounds, to be almost synonymous with blind acceptance, may be better suited to be replaced by the word trust. Let me clarify that I do not feel like I am someone to judge or are hierarchically superior to God, but I do think that God would want us to understand His reasons and intentions and not just be mewling sheep.

> "I do not feel obliged to believe that the same God who endowed us with sense, reason and intellect had intended for us to forego their use."
>
> *Galileo Galilei*
>
> ("Letter to the Grand Duchess Christina")

One of the challenges that I faced in deciding whether I could believe in God, miracles, the Trinity, and similar concepts was coming to grips with my understanding of what "knowing" truly means. I always just assumed that we knew a tremendous number of things. The reality is that we truly "know" very, very few things—it is an entirely reasonable argument to say that you only know that you exist and everything else is a belief. Bear with me on this and don't shut down because it sounds nuts. I know that the Earth is round, the coffee is hot, the dog is snoring (again) while he sleeps under my desk. But, what do I actually know? How do I know that the Earth is round? Have I circumnavigated the globe? Even if I did, how do I know that I didn't travel in circles that seemed to trace a sphere? Have I been to outer space and viewed it from afar? No to all of these. Even if I did experience all of these, how do I truly know that this isn't artificial stimuli created by electrical impulses being transmitted to my brain such as was imagined in the popular movie *The Matrix.*

There was another movie titled *The Truman Show* where a baby was bought by a corporation for the purpose of making a "whole life" reality show. His entire life was fake—parents, friends, adversaries, every single person he saw or knew were all played by actors, he existed in a giant movie set where everything was scripted down to the most minute detail. His life was a 24/7 reality show on TV, but not real at all. Even with all the evidence, is it possible that I am wrong and that I am actually living in some elaborate *Truman Show* (or *Matrix*) and the Earth is not round? While ridiculous, the actual answer is technically yes.

It's theoretically possible that the Earth is some shape other than spherical, but I doubt it so much that I can confidently say that I absolutely believe that the Earth is round. The reason for my belief is due to the evidence presented from people and sources that I trust. I have looked at the consensus, I verified the positioned mathematical calculations, the logic is sound, and the measurable scientific evidence is abundant and compelling. None of the pieces of evidence for the Earth being round contradicts each other. Also, I have evaluated the counterarguments and have tried to uncover any reason why it would benefit someone to push a false narrative of a round Earth and fool me. I have weighed all of these and concluded that I believe that the Earth is round, there is so much evidence that I have a very, very, very high level of certainty.

While this is a bit of a silly example, it really does illustrate a very important point. Even with things that you are certain about, you are only "certain" because you have multiple avenues of evidence and no strong arguments against the idea; but even so, you really never know 100%. There is an overwhelming body of evidence for belief in the Earth being round and very little against, so I have reached such a strong position of trust and belief that it's round that I say that I "know" it to be true. The truth is that I don't *know* it at all, I just have an *extremely* high level of confidence. The only thing that you can say for sure is that you exist; everything else just has levels of certainty. Coffee is hot? How do you know that there are not probes in your brain that are electrically stimulating the correct nerves so that you have the sensation of "hot" or some elaborate hallucination—or even that there is coffee, a cup, a desk, even a world around you. I hope you have a very high level of certainty to all of these things, but what is the actual level of confidence for someone to go from considering something to be possible or probable to knowing something to be true?

I have always wanted, or even needed, to have a 100% certainty that there is a God and that the Bible is true. Unfortunately, with the realities listed above, 100% is not something that can ever be achieved. This may seem like it should be a detractor for belief, it isn't to me. It makes belief possible as I realize that nothing holds up to the expectation for absolute certainty.

God is not something that we can put in a test tube and run experiments on—as much as I wish it were so. We have no machine that can detect that God exists—or, for that matter, conversely, there is no machine or experiment that can prove that God does not exist. So, now we're in a shade of gray—where in the gradient of certainty does the evidence for God lie and is it sufficient for belief?

So, now I accept that I need to evaluate all the evidence for and against, and decide for myself if there is enough evidence, logic, and experience to give me the confidence so that trust will bridge the *possibility* of God to a belief or trust *in* God. I had heard an analogy that you can look at faith in God like a physical chair. Someone can describe the chair, define the materials used, explain the construction process, the engineering and mathematics, show examples of how it had been proven to be able to carry the load without fail, but until you really put your weight on the chair and experience its ability to do all that it says, it will be a detached and clinical understanding of the chair. You will never truly know.

I know that in the scenario where there is no God and we are only matter and energy, everything is meaningless. If I do foolish things, it really doesn't matter. Logically, it follows that if I were to give over and "sit" in the chair and surrender to God and it comes up wanting, I can always get up and walk away. Since things are meaningless and nothing actually matters, there is nothing lost by trusting, except maybe a little bit of my dignity—which doesn't exist anyway because I am nothing more than matter and energy! Conversely, if it is everything advertised, it would be the best thing to happen to me in my life. With all of that said, why is it that I can't seem to give over and see, even though it seems to be the most logical and rational course of action? I do feel a calling (whether self-created or inherent), so what is it in me that can't let go? I do know that some part of it is that I am afraid of losing my objectivity and I truly want to understand the truth—but that is not the whole story.

Side note, I believe that the evangelist noted previously was using a bastardized application of 1 Corinthians 1.26–31 "but God has chosen the foolish things of the world to shame the wise, and God has chosen the weak things of the world to shame the things which are strong." Side note to the side note, someone has said to me that it is very dangerous to look at one line of Scripture by itself as the meaning can only be determined in context. Even without context, this does not say that foolish things in the Bible are there to shame the wise to dismiss errors or inconsistencies; it's clearly referring to worldly things where what arrogant people view as their strength will be used against them.

FOUR | *The Choice of Worldviews*

A worldview is simply the lens through which we see, well, everything. It is formed by all of our experiences, thoughts, and interpretations of past events. Going forward, it directly affects the way that we interpret current events, the decisions we make and the ideas we support.

A Christian worldview is one in which God exists, Jesus is God incarnate, and He died on the cross for the forgiveness of our sins and was resurrected. The Bible is authoritative and the inspired word of God. Our morality and moral compass were imbued by our Creator and there are a set of guidelines and a code to which we should adhere, known as the moral law. Because it is established by God, it is universal and eternal. We are loved and are important to our creator, will rejoin Him in the afterlife and the events on this planet and reality are temporary. We were given free will to do as we choose, and we make our own decisions to do good or evil.

My problem with the people who say that they subscribe to the Christian worldview is pretty typical; they're often a hypocritical bunch. If Christians believe in their hearts, then their behavior should reflect biblical teaching. I get that people are broken, imperfect beings, but I think that the level of intentional sin is telling. Let's face it, many of the same people who vocally promote this worldview are the same people who are having affairs, divorces and, in my experience, not at all morally superior. Honestly, it seems to me that not all that many really embrace the tenants of Christianity. Yes, I know that the authenticity of the Bible and existence of God can't be decided by how the "followers" act, but if these are the people who supposedly truly believe, and they constantly behave in a way that belies that code, then think it's reasonable to conclude that they don't really believe in their hearts and it's all a social side show. I recently heard a good analogy, these people were trying to buy spiritual fire insurance— only to be used in case of an emergency to keep you out of the flames! Since the supposed acolytes act like they don't truly buy in, then for me, it gives rise to doubt that there really is something to this. It is my perception that while the United States is roughly 70% Christian, I would bet that maybe 20%—30% are really believers and the rest are social Christians going through the spiritual motions.

Before anyone starts screaming that this is not fair or factual, I never said it was. Remember, I said that the point of this is to expose what I went through and give transparency to my perceptions. I recognize that my personal experience is really not exhaustive and may be completely inaccurate.

My upbringing and the lack of engagement in church or church life resulted in never forming bonds or connections that would support faith. It is entirely possible, if not probable, that my lack of personal experience with true believers, such as those who would be heavily involved with church or charities, has left an unspoken underlying assumption that they do not exist. I also recognize that, statistically, Christians have much higher percentages of adoptions, volunteering, and charitable giving than any other group. To fill the spiritual void, most of my opinions on this are, admittedly, formed by media, especially television and movies, as well as other external social influences which I would never deny carry a very significant bias.

I am open to reevaluating when I get more data—and I do hope that I am wrong. To those who were raised in the church, did mission trips, volunteered, etc. and see a different side, lucky you. No really, I am happy for you, but just realize that there are many of us who are on the outside looking in.

The other option for me is the atheist worldview, in which there is no God and there is nothing besides nature. Said differently, the only things that exist are matter, the stuff that things are made of, and energy. Molecules in motion! That sounds simple enough that it's easy to read and pass over but let me explain what I realized are the ramifications of that pithy one liner. Human beings are simply the result of random mutations that happened over time and are simply "moist machines." Over generations, we have refined our behaviors to react in certain ways with the goal of propagation of the species. If something helps the organism survive, the animal lives to reproduce and that trait is passed down to future generations. If it's something that is detrimental, it would lessen the probability of survival and would be killed off, removing the mutation from the gene pool. (Note that I will be using naturalism and materialism somewhat interchangeably. While there is difference in nuance, I do not feel it is of import in this context.)

Let's say organism "A" and "B" are identical except that "A" has a mutation. As "A" and "B" are competing for the same food and in higher-level organisms, shelter, and mates, and if the mutation in "A" gives an advantage over "B," then "A" will be more successful in obtaining the food, shelter, mate, etc. and "B" will perish. However, if the mutation is detrimental, as almost all are, "B" will win out and "A" will perish. We are simply the product of a galactic DNA cage match. Ok, that sounds plausible for the physical self, but what about the human mind.

Behaviors and decisions would have to be created and refined through the same process as there is no guidance besides survival. The reason that you act a certain way is simply through a logic tree—a highly complex logic tree, but a logic tree nonetheless. You have no free will; you are just a giant biological computer program. If we could understand the logic tree thoroughly enough, it would be entirely possible to input a set of stimuli as to elicit a specific behavior 100% of the time. Like a machine, if I do x things in sequence, I will always get y output—the machine has no true decision-making capabilities and no free will to choose between options. It is purely a "If x condition, then do y" situation. *If* I leave my dirty socks on the floor right next to the hamper, *then* my wife rolls her eyes and shakes her head. I know empirically that this works! (More on libertarianism, determinism, and compatibilism later)

In this scenario, there is no God; this is an idea created to soothe the discomfort of knowing we are mortal and will be deleted at the end of our time. As there is no God, there is no moral code or benchmark; therefore, each individual may decide for themselves what is good and right, and everyone had their own version of truth, with none being superior or correct. As such, you are programmed to have simulated "feelings" about things all with the intent of advancing the species. One of the undeniable conclusions is you do not "love" your child; you have a created stimulation that you identify as a feeling called love; this illusion benefits the species in that you protect the ones that you have this simulated "love" sensation for, allowing them to continue your genes in the next generation.

Looking at it, I can see how it would be possible for us to just be a giant logic tree, but beyond that, there really are quite a few places where it becomes untenable to me. First, there are many instances when our behavior does nothing to advance or protect our species at a tribal or global level. Running into a fire to save a stranger, or even an enemy, would be counterproductive in living a long and happy life. Maybe you could try to argue that it's for the preservation of a life, and so there would be some altruistic effect in your tribe that would help your community and therefore you, but to risk one's life to save a non-community member or even an enemy's life is hardly a way to protect the supposedly superior gene mutation. We then celebrate the "hero"–but have an especially high regard for the person who risks themselves to save a stranger who has no ties or relation to the person. Think about how highly we regard charity and generosity, traits that bring no benefit to the benefactor.

The ideals of courage, honor, valor etc. are all held in high esteem everywhere, while many of these ideals are counter to self-preservation. If we were simply trying to protect and propagate, why have art? Why study science beyond the level where it directly helps us? Someone help me here, but I don't think that understanding quasars or subatomic science makes the human race more likely to survive; the advent on nuclear weapons and germ warfare may suggest the opposite. Lastly and most importantly, I love my children. There are very few things that I really know in this life, but this is one of them. Even committed atheists have real problems admitting that in materialism, they don't actually love their kids.

When I was in the 10th grade, I had a run of amazing luck. One of my teachers was really lazy so, at the end of the tests, they would read the question and then the acceptable answers and you were expected to grade your own paper! On the first few questions, I didn't do so well because my answer did not match the teachers' answer very closely. By question 10, well, I knew what

I meant and really had to be fair to myself and give myself the benefit of the doubt. By the end of the test, every answer, once I looked at it in the right light and from the right perspective, was correct! As I am sure you guessed, an easy A! The problem was that, even though we had a classful of different answers, we all happened to get an A.

Atheists talk about good and bad, but if there is no God, then there is no objective yardstick to measure by. Without that yardstick, there is no universal good, there is no universal bad; there are only our personal subjective interpretations, and all are equally valid. You and I have our own subjective version of good, but if they disagree, we have to admit that each one is as legitimate as the other. Sounds great, so what's the problem? In that framework, the Nazis murdering babies is as moral as feeding the poor in Calcutta; it's all in the perception. Remember, no one has the right to claim that their own moral code is more correct than any other. It's like you get to grade your own paper. If we want to object and claim that anyone's behavior is or is not good, then there must be an absolute standard to measure by. Without some objective external rule setter, i.e., God, that does not exist. While this is an uncomfortable point, it is undeniably true. By the way, atheists, like all other people groups, have good and bad members—moral and immoral. The point is that the atheist has no objective way to measure what they would call good (moral) or bad (immoral).

Furthermore, if a materialistic perspective is true, then there is no mind, only the physical brain that is continually reprogramming itself for survival and reproduction. It would have no interest in determining truth or God. If our minds are purely evolutionary logic trees solely driven by the goal of propagation of the species, then why would we, and literally how could we, conclude that our brain is actually seeking truth? Our brains may lead us to believe ideas as true because they are beneficial to our survival, but would not be seeking actual truth. If that is the case, there is no reason why our thoughts or beliefs would even be aligned with reality. Why then should we even believe that there is truth in our thoughts?

If we are simply a logic tree, I see no purpose in evolving feelings at all. In this scenario, feelings would simply be stimuli used to direct our decisions to a particular outcome. I feel love for my child and she is hungry,

> *"According to atheism, human beings and all their thinking processes are simply the accidental by-products of the mindless movement of atoms within an undesigned, random, and purposeless universe. How then can we attach any ultimate meaning or truth to our thoughts and feelings, including our sense of justice? They have, on this view, no more validity or significance than the sound of the wind in the trees."*
>
> **Philip Vander Elst**
> *("Can We Be Free Without God?")*

so I make sure that she has enough food. I feel fear, so I step off the train tracks when I hear the whistle. If our evolution is purely based on physics and chemistry, the refinement of life is based on the continuation of genes that have the higher chance of survival, then why would we need feelings at all? It would seem much more advantageous to be purely logic based and rid ourselves of the burden of emotion.

Let's say that I am in a situation in which I am standing on those railroad tracks, and I hear a train coming. I have many actions that I can take at this point, but to simplify, let's say I have:

Option 1	Step off the tracks and walk away	100% Survival
Option 2	Lay down and close my eyes	50% Survival
Option 3	Turn around and face away from the train	0 % Survival

I would hear the train coming, the pitch changing as it nears. The rumble on the tracks and eventually, the vibration in the Earth. At this point, based on my feelings, I would readily take Option 1 and step off the tracks—and then go find a clean pair of shorts. If we were based on continuing the traits that were more likely to survive, why are feelings needed to direct us to Option 1. Why would we feel fear instead of performing a cold calculation and immediately taking the route that would ensure our survival? I understand that fear helps us survive but my point is why have fear at all, why not just hard code in the response that fear was supposed to lead us to? Taking that a step further, why would we have consciousness at all?

The reality is that every day we see people choosing options 2 and 3. Maybe not as dramatic as standing on train tracks but we have all seen people who have been advised against an option, were presented with overwhelming evidence, had negative past experiences in the same situation, but they consistently choose the same option anyway—often to the significant detriment of the person. I have been one of those people (especially when I was younger and girls were involved) and you have too. If this were purely a comparison sorting exercise (Species A has higher chance of survival than Species B, A moves on and B goes extinct), I see zero reason why we should have any choice at all, as anyone who was predisposed to making bad choices would have been filtered out long ago.

Thinking on this more, if A and B are competing for survival and A has the free will to choose, then there is some chance, even a remote one, that they will choose the option that will lead to their demise—let's say 99% of the time they choose Option 1 where they survive and only a 1% chance where they choose poorly and dies. For every one hundred people with variant A (having free will) that have the option to choose, ninety nine survive and only one dies! That sounds fine until variant B enters the arena who has no free will, no choice, so they perform Option 1 in every instance. For every one hundred people from variant B in the same position but having no free will, all one hundred will survive. All other things being equal, over time, wouldn't B edge out A and drive A to extinction?

If that were true, I don't see any sense in having the ability to choose, as the wrong choice puts the organism at risk. Feelings would then be extraneous as they are just an illusional stimuli to direct us to a choice and finally, consciousness is moot as we do not need the self as we no longer have options.

As you can imagine, I have big problems with many of these ideas and honestly, it seems that most atheists do as well, as they clearly don't agree with, or live by even their own basic tenants.

FIVE | *Overcoming the Social Narrative*

We all know that breakfast is the most important meal of the day. Have you ever wondered why or how you know that? Well, we have heard it so often and for so long that it's become part of the widely accepted pool of common knowledge. There is an automatic acceptance of this "fact" because we have been exposed to the repetition of the idea throughout our lives. We assume that it must have come from evidence and science that someone vetted at some point, even if we have never seen the study or personally validated the claim. It turns out that the "fact" that breakfast is the most important meal of the day comes from a Grape Nuts cereal marketing campaign from 1944. It has no scientific basis but has taken such a cultural hold that it is now part of our community of knowledge and is unquestionably accepted and repeated.

My gut feeling was that as a group, religious people were of an average intelligence and an unscientific bunch—containing a strong peppering of kooks. Furthermore, I had always quietly assumed that this is/was the common assumption. Maybe it's that we are steeped in an anti-religious narrative or because some extreme characters have the spotlight shone on them as representatives of the group; how many people speaking in tongues or backward rednecks quoting Bible verses do you need to see to validate that truly religious people are a short step above a simpleton?

I have found it astounding that many religious people are unwilling to analyze events; if something good happens, it's because God is good and prayers are answered; if something bad happens, it's because God works in mysterious ways, but God has a plan. Look, this may possibly be true, but talk about a self-serving narrative where you can't be wrong and therefore, have zero need for evidence or logic. Heads I win, tails you lose. I also find it frustratingly common that people use it as an excuse or a dodge: "It wasn't God's plan for me to get that job, He probably saved me from something awful! God is looking out for me!" No, you didn't get that job because you showed up to the interview unprepared, looking disheveled, and hung over—but, no, it's not your fault, its divine intervention!

I have repeatedly heard it proposed that religious people are irrational and less intelligent, they are seemingly less able to cope with their place in the world, and need a way to understand their existence. As they are overwhelmed and unenlightened, they create this benevolent benefactor to give them meaning and direction. I do think that this is strongly reinforced by the media. People are like sponges in that they absorb what they are immersed in, some faster than others, but no one is immune. Before we discount this, let's look at a silly example. We all know that movies and television are fake, everything that happens has been carefully scripted, and every fight scene choreographed—usually with stunt doubles, not even the actual actors performing the action scene. Now, imagine getting into a fight with the real actor who plays a physical character. Let's not make it easy and choose Dwayne Johnson (The Rock) as he is a big dude. Let's not even choose someone like Bruce Willis. Let's go with someone of, shall we say, a non-imposing physical stature like Joe Pesci. If you have seen his movies, you don't see a 5' 5" short frumpy guy, you see a smaller crazy guy who you have repeatedly seen viciously take out multiple large, tough men with no fear. If you were confronted by him in real life, you would be wary!

In reality, you have never seen Joe Pesci fight, you probably have never even met him, but still, there is that lingering knowledge in the back of your mind because you know what you saw, that this guy is dangerous and you had better be careful—even though you logically know that he is just an actor and everything was scripted. It's easy to argue that religious people are depicted with a specific stereotype in movies and television; they are always the ones who are ignorant hillbillies, superstitious fools or end up being a cheat or villain. Just for fun, take a moment and think about any modern mainstream media that has had a Christian. Are they ever the good guy or a hero? Having a Christian character is almost cliché these days. How much do you think that seeps into society's view?

My perception has always been that the intelligent elite are all in the sciences, especially physics, mathematics and chemistry. Since a majority of the academy of sciences members are atheists, then it follows that most of the intelligent people are atheists.

I believed that the unspoken but prevailing view is that religious peoples beliefs are not anchored in science, have no evidential foundation and so, are unappealing to intelligent people who are more in command of themselves and their surroundings. All the country rubes and superstitious gullible fools are religious, while the enlightened intellectual elite are atheists. I have found that this is a common narrative by atheists, and I seldom hear theists dispute it. It seems to me to have become widely accepted common knowledge.

The basis that atheists are more intelligent is commonly justified by quoting a paper from 2013 where researchers at the University of Rochester and Northeastern University compiled the studies of intelligence vs. religious belief from the last 80 plus years. The study revealed that there was a direct negative correlation between religious belief and intelligence.[5]

> *"Science has made us gods even before we are worthy of being men."*
>
> **Jean Rostand**
> *(Pensées d'un biologiste)*

The conclusion was that intelligent people are less likely to conform to expected norms, have less need for religious beliefs, and the most telling, "adopt an analytic (as opposed to intuitive) thinking style, which has been shown to undermine religious beliefs."[6] My ego always likes to be considered as part of the intelligent group. I admit it, I have a fear of being thought intellectually inferior and so, lumping myself in with the religious kooks instead of the enlightened intellectual elite was pretty unappealing to me. Proof positive. Done deal.

Professionally, I am a software architect and have always worked with large samples of data. How many times have you heard one political candidate make a statistical statement about a topic that conclusively shows that a specific position is clearly superior, only to have their opponent come out with another statistic that shows the opposite? Well, who is lying? Often, they both quote statistics that are technically factual, but they are just picking and choosing their details in isolation. When I hear a single-line statistic, I always take it with a grain of salt, as conclusions based on statistical data require scrutiny; like inspecting a diamond from multiple angles for flaws. Data should be analyzed from a variety of directions to see the imperfections and get a measure of their worth. I have found that if I can choose the perspective that I view the data in, I can usually get it to support any position that I choose.

When I started digging into the above-mentioned research, I found some enlightening details that are not promoted when the study is quoted. First, the root data spanned more than 80 years and had mixed sample sizes from 20 to over 14,000 people. Right off, this is a major problem for many reasons. First, sample sizes of 20 people are unreliable. Statistically, the larger the sample, the less margin of error, but under any scenario, 20 is not nearly large enough of a group to be reliable. The margin of error for such a small sample would be so large as to make it impossible to have any confidence in its results. Having such a large variance between sample sizes and then considering them equally makes no sense. Finally, and probably most troubling, is how can you combine data for more than eight decades without having some method of correlation?[7]

The conclusion was that roughly half of the studies did show a negative relation between religiousness and intelligence, but the other half did not. Wait, what? Drawing a conclusion when only half your test cases point in a direction is questionable at best. Actually, no it's not. It is shoddy, and in my opinion, verges on being intellectually dishonest. Think about it, if you did a medical study and only half got better but the other half died, could you even remotely claim that your medication is a cure? Well, I guess you could claim that no one still had the disease after taking your medication, but I don't think everyone would be happy with the outcome.

Additionally, the groups were mixed between pre-college, college and post-college ages. Again, combining life focus demographics that are this widely positioned is not going to give reliable results. I know from personal experience as well as from statistical studies that people have different perspectives and priorities depending on what stage they are at in their lives. Can anyone argue that the priorities and behaviors of a college student are the same as the father of two small children? I have taken many 2 AM trips to the Mi-T-Mart convenience store. The difference is that when I was in college, it was for beer and chips but when I had small children, it was for formula and diapers. It is also disturbing to note that some of the studies were focused on religious behavior (e.g., going to church and praying) and other centered around religious philosophy (e.g., belief in God and miracles). Simply put, these are two very different things. If your survey is on the religious behaviors of college students, does anyone think that is a valid metric to measure religious belief vs intelligence?

Lastly, the "intelligence" was determined by things such as college entrance exams, vocabulary tests, or scientific knowledge tests, hardly standardized or consistent, and certainly not a valid method for testing intelligence. And just to pile on, there was no uniform method of questioning or testing across the studies, which isn't surprising as they spanned across 80 years—a method only valuable to determine variance over time! Besides, it is useless without a control group.

> "Mixing data from different sources, with different levels of uncertainty, without a clear understanding of their compatibility, is a recipe for over-certainty and misleading conclusions."
>
> **William M. Briggs**
> (Uncertainty: The Soul of Modeling, Probability and Statistics)

When you look at the different groups studied and then break it down a little more as to look at it from another angle, religious *behavior* had no real relationship with intelligence irrespective of the age group. To say it differently, no matter the person's age, there was zero connection between religious behavior and intelligence. Religious *belief* had virtually no relationship with intelligence for precollege subjects. For college level or post college level, there was a very weak negative relationship. To be more specific, there was a -0.17 correlation for college students and a -0.20 for post college, both are such a small variance that they can be easily attributed to a variety of outside factors. So, the assertion that the study showed that there is a connection between intelligence and religious belief is technically true, but it is so minute that it is not only within the range of error, it is so small to be considered trivial.

This is not nitpicking the details of an unfriendly study to dismiss its findings, instead, the severity of the problems listed undermine any faith in the conclusions. The authors themselves said, "The relation between intelligence and religiosity has been examined repeatedly, but so far there is no clear consensus on the direction and/or the magnitude of this association."

My personal take on this is that it is a tenuous view of data at best. While atheists use it to score quick "points," to me, it undermines their premise. It has such a weak foundation that it prompts me to question how many of their other assertions also lack a basis. I have a serious problem when someone tries to throw the wool over my eyes by telling partial truths or bumper sticker level slogans and trusting that I won't dig deeper. I feel that this is a prime example.

After more researching, I have come to reject the belief that the intellectual elite are atheists. Ironically, what I have learned is that there are, and have always been, many brilliant minds who are believers. While this does nothing to prove or disprove the existence of God, it is/was an important objection that I had and since I came to this realization, I started to question some of my other beliefs.

I started working backward and questioning whether the intelligent people were overwhelmingly concentrated in the sciences, and I have come to the realization that no field has a monopoly. There are brilliant people in the sciences, but also in economics, law, literature, theology, history, and many, many other fields. While it is true that the science community has a disproportionate concentration of atheists, I found some surprising data. First, when they studied why scientists were atheist (or agnostic), it was because they were so before they became scientists—science did not open their eyes to something that made them lose faith.

It makes sense to me that people who are attracted to the hard sciences would be more prone to subscribe to an atheistic worldview as someone who is focused on the core sciences has a knowledge system based on concrete measurables. There are some that feel that if you can't conduct experiments and validate results, then it isn't true. That creates a serious problem for acceptance of theology; as they say, you can't put God in a test tube.

From my personal experience, I have seen that many people engaged in the hard sciences often trivialize other fields. It seems to me that someone who is purely focused on the material, measurable world, would find it easy to regard their field of work being of paramount importance and the sole source of knowledge and value. As world renowned physicist Stephen Hawking said, "Most of us don't worry about these questions most of the time. But almost all of us must sometimes wonder: Why are we here? Where do we come from? Traditionally, these are questions for philosophy, but philosophy is dead, Philosophers have not kept up with modern developments in science. Particularly physics."

Professor Hawking went on to claim that "Scientists have become the bearers of the torch of discovery in our quest for knowledge." He also said the new theories "lead us to a new and very different picture of the universe and our place in it." Besides being self-contradictory as it is a philosophical statement proclaiming that philosophy is dead, it sounds like they believe that their discoveries in some way answer the "why" and not just the "how." Laws and theories have no power to create anything. They are descriptors of things already in existence—and only in the physical plane of existence. Clearly, Hawking is a brilliant physicist but his forays into philosophy and theology are readily panned as rudimentary at best. I still struggle with this, but logically I do recognize that someone being a master in one field does not mean that they should automatically be considered a trusted source in another.

Another interesting fact, according to Gary DeMar: of the 10 people with the highest IQs on the planet (using the actual IQ scale), eight (8) are theists and at least six (6) are Christians.[8] A sample size of 10 too small to draw conclusions from but it does demonstrate that there are brilliant people who believe in God and that a high IQ does not preclude you from religious belief.

While I had always feared that people of higher intelligence left their belief in religion behind, the reality is that there really is no correlation between your religious beliefs or behaviors and intelligence. There are very intelligent Christians and very intelligent atheists and, conversely, stupid Christians and stupid atheists, seemingly in equal proportions. Sure, there are some backward people misusing Scripture and looking like fools, but in my personal experience, there are just as many ignorant and illogical atheists. If you have any doubt, go to the comments section on any theology-based document or video and start reading. Don't say that I didn't warn you.

SIX | *Are Science and Religion Adversarial or Complementary?*

While it was never explicitly stated, I always had the feeling that science, or reason, and religion were in opposite camps; you could pick one or the other, but not both. In grade school, you learn about how the primitive religions attributed divine intervention to phenomena that they could not explain, where they had gaps of their understanding they plugged in a god—commonly referred to as the God of the Gaps argument. As our scientific knowledge grew, those gaps closed which, invariably, pushed the gods, or God aside. Some of the items were of no consequence as they were quaint, ancient religions when people didn't know better—such as lightning being caused by Zeus or the breeze that we feel being caused by Japanese god Fujin opening his bag of winds. More troubling are the modern claims of God of the Gaps, with the examples supposedly based on Scripture. Passages in the Bible have been extrapolated or had an overly literalistic interpretation to apply properties about our physical world. People mistaking took Scripture discussing "four corners of the Earth" to mean that the Earth literally had four corners and so was a flat rectangle. "He set the Earth on its foundations, it can never be moved" seemed to justify that the Earth was the center of the universe, was unmoving, and so, everything revolved around it. All of these are, obviously, incorrect. It has been proven, time and again, that using the God hypothesis to fill in our gaps of understanding is dangerous. As our knowledge and understanding grows, it seems to kill off a piece of God's attributed domain. Science is seemingly forcing God to retreat further and further to a minor corner of the room.

I liken it to as if at the start of a battle, one side is clearly dominating and holds all the high ground. As time passes, the other side marches on and captures one position, then another, without ever losing a skirmish. As the victories mount on one side, and even with the war being far from over and many battles left to fight, it becomes clear where the momentum lies and who, if things proceed as they have in the past, will be the eventual victor and vanquish the other. Science vs. religion feels exactly like this battle to me, albeit a spiritual one. I felt that science has won battle after battle against weak, unfortified strongholds until now, seemingly, theism has been fully routed and is trying to preserve its few remaining bastions by pleading for a truce—science and religion are purely separate studies and don't overlap! Please, you win, we won't say anything else, just leave us alone in our little corner on Sundays!

As they say, the Bible is not a science book, but unfortunately, it seems that historically, many members of the church leadership created an alignment, and dependence, on unsupported assumptions explaining the natural world based on loose or overly literalistic interpretations of Scripture. My perception is that when the discoveries were eventually made that proved that their assumptions were wrong, there was an overt attempt to punish those who made the discoveries and suppress the knowledge. It's probably from some movie, but when I think of the church and science, I picture a black clad clergyman up high on a judge's seat looking down. "Heresy!" he screams as the purple veins pulse on his gray, balding skull!

These religious sources as a basis of physical explanation had loose foundations from the Bible but opposed to that was direct scientific and mathematical evidence. In fairness to the church, many, including some scientists, believed that the Earth was flat, the sun rotated around the Earth as well as a host of other incorrect beliefs. The real crime was the church asserting, and then fanatically defending incorrect premises based on tenuous interpretations from Scripture. The main issue as I see it is that they positioned themselves as the authority in deciding and explaining naturalistic phenomena without direct Scripture or scientific and mathematical evidence. No matter how powerful the church was in those times, it was foolish to think that scientific advancement could be suppressed simply because they felt threatened by its findings. It's easy to see how this behavior gave root to the notion that the church, therefore God and religion, were directly opposed to, and threatened by, scientific advances. It is also very important to note that the scientific community strongly rejected these same new scientific beliefs and behaved in exactly the same way, but somehow, they are forgiven for these sins, while the church is not.

I do know that the church was the one to sponsor much of the scientific discoveries that we take for granted today. The reality is that the scientific revolution in the 16th and 17th centuries was led by people like Galileo, Copernicus, Bacon, and Newton (and many, many others), all people of faith and, interestingly, funded by the Catholic Church. Scientific research—historically and currently—has consistently been fueled by the church and many of the most notable scientists were Christian.

It is very interesting to note that many earlier scientists had thought of their field as a method to understand and explain God's magnificence. Ironically, many in the contemporary scientific community are vocal in their view as it is a way to banish superstition, and therefore, need of God.

I had always been under the impression that, in simpler times, more scientists were religious, but as more and more discoveries were made, and God got pushed further and further back, more and more scientists abandoned religion. I was surprised to learn of a documented paper in the 1850s where some of the top scientists listed the 100 absolute scientific reasons why God does not exist. I was surprised because my assumption was that even in the 1800s, western scientists were predominately Christian. Additionally, every one of the "100 reasons" turned out, upon further discovery, to be wrong.

I also found it enlightening that there were studies done in 1916 and then in 1996 on the belief in God and the afterlife. I don't think it's too surprising that only 40% of research scientists were believers, but I do find it very surprising that the percentage did not change in almost 100 years. Apparently, I was susceptible to the narrative that as scientific advances that have been made, especially in the last 100 years, there was a radical shift in the belief systems away from God to atheism. A more recent study in 2009 by the Pew Research Center found that 33% of scientists believe in God and another 18% believe in a higher power.[9] While it is a believable narrative, clearly it is not true, there has always been this mix and in about the same proportion.

The more important fact is that if everyone believes, or conversely, no one believes, it doesn't change if it's true or not. However, we all count the opinions of experts as some level of evidence. If the people dedicated to uncovering the mysteries of the universe are observing or discovering things that make them conclude that God is a fallacy, that, at least to me, has to carry some level of weight. Yes, you caught me. Earlier I said that a master of one field should not carry that authority to another, but I clearly have a bias toward the sciences. As it turns out, this again, was a false narrative.

So, the idea that scientists have become more and more atheistic as we advance scientifically has been put to rest but, I will admit, it is still disconcerting that such a large percentage of scientists are atheists. Is it their natural predisposition to the physical world? Perhaps it's because their minds are more centered around provable and reproducible phenomenon? Maybe it is their lack of hubris as they consider themselves the grand wizards of modern culture or is it simply that they are smart and brave enough to see how it really is or possibly something else entirely? I don't know, but it is also important to note that 40% believe in God and the afterlife. Of the remaining 60%, 43% are made up of deists and agnostics and only 17% are atheists. Deists believe in some Godlike being creating the universe but not being personal (involved with humans); he created it and then walked away; humans have no particularly special place in it all. Agnostics simply say that there may or may not be God; they don't know. Another interesting statistic to muddy the water a little more is that 60% of the Nobel Prize winning scientists from 1900 to 2000 were believers in God.

It is also fair to note that while it definitely did happen, many of the promoted instances of the church trying to suppress science are just a narrative. The most famous, and most quoted, instance is when the church arrested Galileo for heresy. The claims of heresy were supposedly based on his heliocentric version of the universe—the Earth revolving around the sun instead of the

Earth remaining fixed and unmoving and the universe revolving around it. The church did not like the theological implications and so, arrested him to censure his work, or so the story goes. Digging a little deeper into the history, it turns out that there were many people at that time who proposed a heliocentric model of the universe, including Jesuit priests, who suffered no condemnation from the church. It is some people's opinion that Galileo's book *Dialogue Concerning Two Chief World Systems*, which was widely considered an open mockery of the pope, added to his personality conflicts with people of power, were the real reasons behind his arrest.

The Bible does not make many statements that can truly be proved or disproved by the scientific method, but for the ones that are there, I see no instance of a scientific discovery disproving any statement in the Bible. The worst case that I have seen is with things that are unknown, such as the Genesis flood. Conversely, there are items in the Scripture that were long believed to be wrong by the scientific community but, upon further discovery, were proven to be true. One of the most impactful to me is the biblical statement "In the beginning." It's easy to pass over this statement without giving it the weight of what it is really implying. Common knowledge since ancient times has always been that the universe is eternal; it has always existed and has neither a start or end. As it did not start, it does not need a creator. How can you possibly reconcile Genesis with a universe that is not created? If the Bible was imagined by regular, scientifically primitive people thousands of years ago, why on Earth would they start the document with something that clearly goes in opposition to what everyone, including the greatest minds at the time, absolutely knew for certain? That would be nonsensical and certainly not a good way to make your document persuasive. It wasn't until 1927 that the eternal universe model was challenged when a Belgian priest named Georges Lemaitre published a theory that the universe was expanding (and he had even calculated a speed). Note that if the universe was expanding, then going backward in time, it had to have come from a single point of nothingness—a beginning. There was an overwhelming resistance to this theory due to the religious and scientific implications.[10]

This idea was the polar opposite to the static and eternal universe model that everyone considered a basic fact for thousands of years. It was so distasteful to the scientific community that even Albert Einstein said, "Your calculations are correct, but your physics is abominable." Previously, Einstein had deduced his General Theory of Relativity, but initially did not support a static (eternal) model of the universe and so, to make it comply with what was the common knowledge of being static, he introduced a "cosmological constant" to make the universe stable (which he later admitted was the greatest blunder of his career). In 1929, Edwin Hubble offered the first conclusive piece of evidence that Lemaitre was indeed correct, and the universe was expanding, convincing Einstein and (most of) the rest of the world that the universe had a beginning. The point is that if the idea of an eternal universe was so ingrained for all known scientific history, to the point that one of the greatest physicists of all time would monkey with his equations so that they complied with this belief, why would the writer(s) of the Bible start it in a way that was contrary to this?

Due to the religious implications, there have been many attempts to provide a model where the universe is static and therefore, was not created. All of them failed. So objectionable was the finite universe theory that Fred Hoyle (atheist) derisively named it the Big Bang as a mockery of the idea that the universe was created from a single point of energy. The name stuck and now The Big Bang Theory is now the almost unanimously accepted model of the creation of the universe. Someone could argue that the Biblical writer simply started the narrative with "In the beginning" as it is a good way to start a book, like "Once Upon a Time." It seems to me that attributing a statement to be the word of God when it contradicts what was thought of as a clear, undisputed fact, and then explaining its validation to mere luck, is weak and unconvincing. Additionally, if you look at the next lines of Genesis, it seems to follow exactly how the universe was created. Why would they say that God said "Let there be light" when everyone until very recently knew that you could not have light without fire or the sun? I just don't see any way that someone more than 4,000 years ago could just make that up against all common wisdom and just happen to be right. Not impossible, but highly improbable.

As discussed, in order to need a Creator, the universe needed to be created and finite, not eternal. One of the other pieces of evidence to justify a non-eternal universe is philosophical. I used to think philosophy was a bunch of nonsense—scholars in their ivory towers pondering abstract concepts, playing mental word games, and making fanciful, vague, and unrealistic claims with no practical applica-

> "The point, I take it, is to understand how nature works, ... Part of that is knowing how to do calculations, but another part is asking deep questions about what it all means. That's what got me interested in science, anyway... It's a shame that so many physicists don't see how good philosophy of science can contribute to this quest."
>
> **Sean Carroll** (atheistic physicist)
> ("Physicists Should Stop Saying Silly Things about Philosophy")

tion in the real world. After being forcibly exposed to their ideas, what I have learned is that philosophy is simply the application of intelligence and logic to reason out problems or concepts. As I have given time and attention to this discipline, I was transformed from having a sneering disdain to mild acceptance and finally to gaining the utmost respect. It is clear to me now that it has a very real and tangible value.

Eight hundred years ago, a Muslim scholar reasoned that the present exists and is the endpoint of time. Yesterday was real and there was a last week, month, and year and even a "now," but tomorrow is not real yet. Conversely, in an eternal universe, time would be infinite and there would be an infinite number of days in the past. Since there were infinite days before today, it would be impossible to go through an infinite number and therefore logically impossible to reach today. Additionally, every day adds to the amount of time that the universe has been in existence—in a static model where time was infinite in the past, you would not be able to add days as you cannot add to infinity. I find the logic of this argument for the universe not being eternal compelling.

Science is the process of gaining understanding of the mechanism of things but conversely, I find it a common attitude among laymen and scientists, that our understanding of the mechanism of things created or influenced that order. When the universe sprung into being, there are no known reasons why many constants should have the values that they have or that the universe should behave in such a predictable way so that functions can be described by specific laws. There is no reason that it would not have been inconsistent, in other words, pure chaos. Also note that I did not say obey laws as is commonly stated. Thinking about it, the use of the term "laws" is really a misnomer. Laws in a general sense have authority of compliance and an implied consequence for disobeying them. Break the law by robbing a bank and the police will come and forcibly take you to jail. The laws of physics have no such power. They are simply predictions based on how things have behaved in the past, they have no power to make anything behave a certain way. They describe what we have consistently observed to that point, if there was some exception, there is nothing about the "law" that would perform an actual action or exert an actual force. The properties are inherent in the system, the law does not assign or enforce them as is commonly implied.

Let's say that we have an iron bar. Every month we observe the iron bar, and every month it is gray. We have done enough measurements and observations that we feel comfortable creating The Law of the Gray Iron Bar. Everything goes swimmingly and we feel that we have uncovered another secret of the universe. Each month, we successfully use our law to predict that we will observe the iron bar, and it will be gray, and it works without fail! One summer, it is particularly humid, and we go and observe our gray iron bar, but it's not gray, it's now orange red! Does our Law of the Gray Iron Bar force it to become gray again? Certainly not. The iron reacted with the moisture in the air to produce ferric oxide, i.e. rust, and produced an orange color, the law has absolutely no power to reverse the reaction and restore the gray color. The law simply describes behaviors that we have seen to that point with enough regularity as to say that we have very high confidence that something that subscribes to that law will produce a predictable result. If it does not produce the result, the law does not force it to comply, it only means that we did not have enough understanding to write the descriptor (law) to predict, and only predict, in the first place.

I would also like to point out something that I realized, the laws as we understand them do not function in a vacuum; they interact and vie with other laws for dominance. Newtons Law of Universal Gravitation (1686) describes how masses are attracted to each other. It clearly states that the iron bar will be attracted to the Earth (and the Earth to the bar) causing an acceleration of 9.8 meters per second i.e. drop an iron bar and it "falls" to the Earth. Dropping an iron bar falls to the Earth with such regularity that we have no trouble labeling this a law and stating that it is a well-known fact. If you went back to 1687 and told people that you could take this iron bar and by simply changing the shape of it, that not only would it not fall, but it could rise as well, I think they would put you in an insane asylum. Fast forward only 300 years and look up, it won't be long until you see an airplane go by and what is that besides a molded piece of metal? In this instance the force caused by Bernoulli's principle (speed of the airflow over different lengths of the top and bottom of the wing due to curvature causing lift) counteracts and even dominates the force of the gravitation. At any time, there may be unknown laws that interact and potentially vie for dominance, causing a completely unexpected result.

Understanding that force equals mass multiplied by the acceleration does not cause a force, it is just a way to make the relationship between force and mass acceleration intelligible. The fact that things work in a consistent and orderly way, so that we can observe and determine descriptors as to how they work is astounding. If you trace back the universe to the first second of time, there were no laws. Suddenly, within the first fraction of a second, everything started functioning in a logically coherent, consistent and

> *"The most incomprehensible thing about the universe, is that it is comprehensible."*
>
> **Albert Einstein**
> *("Physics and Reality")*

predictable way. That there is such consistency and such order, when none were required, is stunning.

I have heard the argument for God that in all the ways that the universe could have come into being, the fact that it is understandable is evidence that God created it for us. I don't know that this carries as much water with me as it does for other people, it is possible that there are underlying mechanisms that would have required this consistency and order, but we just haven't figured them out yet. Ironic that while I ridicule and condemn a God of the gaps argument to explain phenomena, I easily invoke a materialism of the gaps argument and feel righteously scientific. I will concede that it certainly is intriguing. I also conclude from much of this that scientists take way too much upon themselves as if they can figure out the mechanism that something functions then, in some way, they believe that they have authority over it. It also seems to be a common attitude that understanding how something works precludes the possibility that it was designed by a higher being for a specific intent. I would think that as we can understand the mechanisms of the universe and see how they are interconnected, dependent upon one another and elegant, it may give weight to the idea that there was design behind it all and not just an incredible level of random luck.

What much of it boils down to is that science and theology answer different questions but do have some fractional overlap. This is not to say that there are not evidential or verifiable elements in theology and Christianity in particular, but I do think that the best way to look at science and religion was put best by John Lennox on why the kettle was boiling. The reason that the kettle is boiling is that there is a heat source under the kettle that is transferring thermal energy into the metal, conducting energy it to the water molecules and exciting them; causing the water to reach a temperature that changes its physical state from liquid to gas (i.e. steam) is true; but so is that the kettle is on because you came in out of the snow, are cold and want a cup of tea. Both explanations are equally important, just from different perspectives and answering different questions.

With my more realistic and complete view on what science does, and does not do, the role of theology and the realms where they reside, I have become more at peace with embracing both science and theology. This does not advance my belief in God, but it does make it possible for them to coexist within me without conflict. It is a big relief for me to not have to choose between them.

> *"I believe God did intend, in giving us intelligence, to give us the opportunity to investigate and appreciate the wonders of His creation. He is not threatened by our scientific adventures"*
>
> *Francis Collins*
> *Geneticist, Head of the Human Genome Project*
> *and Director of the National Institutes of Health*
> *(The Language of God)*

SEVEN | *Misconceptions of Evangelism*

When I still participated in the chaos of Facebook, I would occasionally encounter comments or posts from someone with an
evangelistic bent. I remember one such thread where the author
stated their faith in God. Even though the text was mild and
nonconfrontational, I was struck by the reaction. The thread's
original author, who I had known since college in NY, dismissed
the evangelical with the notion that Christians only spread the
message of God because they are part of group think and so, it
is critical for everyone to believe as they did. They felt threatened
that if the others did not buy in, then that in turn would cause
their faith to fail as it was so fragile as to not be able to withstand
any dissention; therefore, they were always "pushing" religion.

The reason that this struck me so hard was that my school
mate was a good Italian boy from Long Island, just like me. I am
sure that he was raised Catholic as well, but it seemed that he
rejected those teachings and instead appeared to be very antagonistic to faith. I was in the middle of the battle, so I was in no
place to preach, but this struck me as a very shallow objection. I
pointed out that if we went to a restaurant and I ordered a Crème
Brule, my favorite dessert, and it was out of this world good, the
caramelized crust was perfect, the custard had the perfect amount

of vanilla, and all the rest of the things that make Crème Brule so good, I would really want you to taste it and see how great it is. If you refused, I may have felt slightly bad that you did not want to partake in my dessert, and I might even push you to try it a little. Ok, I am from NY, so I might have pushed you a lot, but that's not the point. The point is that even if you wouldn't try it, it would still be just as good. Overall, your lack of validation would not affect the fact that my Crème Brule tasted amazing or affect my very real enjoyment. The reality was, I simply wanted to share a good thing with you. In my experience, the same thing is true with evangelical Christians. To assume that people of faith are working from a position of weakness and their faith is dependent on everyone believing is shallow. My point is you should believe, or not believe, for good reasons and reject the pithy one liners. Bumper sticker level ideology is foolish.

EIGHT | *The Improbability of Our Existence*

When I contemplate the nature of reality, or its absence, before the Big Bang, before the existence of the universe, space, or even time, when there was absolute nothingness, I find it impossible to comprehend. Not empty space, not a vacuum, literally nothing. Aristotle described it as "what rocks dream about." Take a moment and think about that. Can't envision it? Me either. When I try to envision nothingness, I picture the total blackness of space like the opening scenes of *Star Trek* or any Sci-Fi space saga. The problem is that the emptiness of space still has three dimensions and so, it is not nothing. "Nothing" is bandied about in common language as a rough descriptor of emptiness, but that is not what it truly means. If I think about the true meaning of nothingness, it is so foreign to our frame of reference that I really do wonder if anyone can truly comprehend it.

Before there was anything, there was a state of nothingness with no space, time, matter, energy, or their describing laws. In this period of nothingness, time did not exist, and as such, it is then by definition timeless. This existence had no past, present, and future tense and so was also tenseless. Therefore, there was no before and no after as those are states, or tenses, of time.

The word supernatural brings to mind a picture of semitransparent specters floating above a graveyard or the bouncing graininess of a home video, where the scene is painted in the green and black of cheap camcorder night vision. The seemingly terrified narrator breathlessly tries to find the menacing spirit behind the mysterious noise—that to anyone with a lick of sense realizes is the water heater causing some pipes to expand and knock or the wind working through structural gaps in a 100-year-old house to produce an eerie sound. Even worse, I equate it to Scooby Do where the supernatural events in the episode invariably turn out to be old Mr. Geeves in a costume and noisemaker trying to scare everyone off and get the inheritance to himself—and would have gotten away with it too, if not for those meddling kids!

I have never given the word supernatural any respect, and so, when applied to God and miracles, my disdain carried and tainted the idea. What I have grudgingly come to accept is that the word supernatural is apt and powerful, when used in the proper context. I have learned to go by the actual definition instead of the commonplace interpretation that was hijacked by culture. Supernatural means, simply put, something outside of nature (material processes).

Before the universe came to be, through divine creation or some other process, there was nothing and so, there was no matter and therefore no nature. This means that the singularity that created the universe and all the matter and energy therein (along with time and the laws of physics) is literally undefined in the materialist framework. I say "literally undefined" because, in short, a singularity causes a division by zero in Einstein's field equations of general relativity and, if you recall from 6th grade math, division by zero is undefined. By the way, I was comfortable with the word "undefined" being a label that is used when you try to divide by zero. Only after thinking on the actual meaning of the word did it sink in (seem to be having those a lot of those moments....).

Undefined means beyond definition—or, we don't even have a frame of reference for being able to understand it.

As there was no nature, it is impossible for a natural process to have been the root cause. The reason for creation must be outside of nature, which is the definition of supernatural. When this sunk in, I had a genuine eureka moment—the moment of realization that there has been at least one supernatural event. Not that there has possibly been one, there absolutely has been one. It is impossible for it to have been otherwise. Since there was at least one supernatural event, supernatural events are not just conceptual or possible, they are factual. If they are real, then my next question is: how many have there been? This opened my eyes to the reality that it is impossible for nature and materialism as we know it to be all there is. I have heard that there is simply some law that we have not discovered or calculated yet that will explain all of this, but this screams of a materialism of the gaps argument. I do not see this as the magic bullet for theism and a personal God who loves us as in Christianity, but it is a pretty strong case for at least deism, a God who created the universe and may or may not care about us.

I also have heard the argument that if God is the creator, then who created God. To me that is an incredibly shallow argument. If God created the universe, the laws of physics, mathematics and time, then He existed in a state before and outside from those. You cannot be a part of something and create it; you cannot create yourself. If God is outside of creation, then He is outside time and so, timeless. If He is timeless, then He is not constrained to the properties of time, having something before or after or, more importantly, a start or an end. If He is timeless then the only state that He exists in is the ever-present IS.

This led me to what I feel is an interesting thought. The Bible often goes out of its way to use particular language. One such instance is when God refers to himself as I AM. The belief up until the mid-1900s was that the universe was eternal and therefore time always existed. Using a phrase such as "I AM" seems to me to describe an existence in a persistent single moment. I would think that if the Bible was simply invented by primitive human authors thousands of years ago, it would have used a more human description and would have included implied timeframes. To me, saying simply "I AM" says that He exists in the moment and the moment is all that there is. That phrasing must have been awkward to people who think of themselves as existing in the past, present, and future. The self-descriptor "I AM" seems to transcend a timeframe, which would have been a totally foreign concept to the early writers.

Another thought is that since He exists in a tenseless space, besides being eternal, He would be unchanging. Remember that change is simply the measure of the difference over a period of time. If time does not exist then change cannot exist. Again, this is a totally foreign concept to the state of reality that human beings have ever experienced or imagined reality to be, but again, this is exactly how God is described in the Bible.

And yes, I fully subscribe to the A theory of time and presentism for human beings, but I am open to a B theory for God. In brief, A Theory states that there is a past, present, and future (tensed). There is one you who travels (lives) along the timeline. B Theory proposes that all time exists simultaneously. In this scenario, there are an infinite number of "you" that think they are at a specific point in time, but they are really all happening simultaneously. Imagine time as a gigantic loaf of sandwich bread. Each slice is a moment of time, and all the slices exist simultaneously. You appear on every slice for the duration from your birth to death. The entity of you that you are right this moment, for me entity Devin-1, can only see your relative position backwards in time. From that perspective, the memory of my life extends from my birth up until 10:24 AM today. The entity of me now, entity Devin-2, is different from the entity Devin-1. Devin-2's perspective of his (my?) history from birth up until 10:26 AM today. The important part is that both are happening simultaneously; you only think that you have a past because of your definition as to your place in time. This slice of me in time happens simultaneously as my birth, when I went to the prom, retired, April 3, 1978, etc.

Understanding that God existed before time, in this timeless state, also elicits some questions. Since God is perfect and lacks for nothing, why would He feel the need or want to create everything (or anything)? He is perfect and so, as He is the only thing there, then everything is perfect. If everything is perfect, why would He change things? Could there be a duality of perfection and if not, which I would be inclined to believe, then creating the universe and humanity would reduce His existence to some state that is less than perfect. I have heard the explanation that God is relational and so created us to have that relationship. As we are imperfect beings, does having a relationship with us diminish His existence? As another thought, if there is no time, when He does anything, He does it all at the same moment as nothing can come before or after. Since there is no before or after, there is no order; they are all simultaneous in the one instant that exists. So, while He is eternal, He has always been creating the universe? Furthering that thought, is the foundation of my questions in error as I try to apply a human perspective which is bound by time to a being where this does not apply? To be honest, while I feel that these are interesting, I will not be trying to answer these questions now. I point them out to illustrate that there will be many secondary questions that arise. As valid as they may be, I did not feel that they were critical to my evaluation and so I left them open for further thought at a later time.

Through this project, I have had many realizations. One of them is that I have some preconditions that must be met before I can even consider what my belief system is. What I mean by that is that there are prerequisites that must be satisfied before I can get to the starting line and give serious consideration to some of the options. These topics, being factual, do not give weight to either side of the issue per se, but if any of them are false, then it's a nonstarter, a poison pill. One of these was that supernatural events must be possible for me to embrace theism. If the supernatural is impossible, then miracles and many claims in the Bible are to be dismissed. If it is possible, then the investigation needs to go further and see if there is good evidence for those possible events described in the Bible are to be believed. For me, as outlined above, I have come to the certainty that the precondition that supernatural events are possible is satisfied. This was a big barrier to entry and now it is removed.

I know that I seem to be extensively highlighting this, but I have seen many atheists' certainty on God not existing being based on the idea that supernatural events transcend the laws of nature and are therefore impossible. In this mindset, since supernatural events are impossible, then Biblical stories and even Jesus's miracles could not have happened. If the Bible is based on, what had to be, made up stories, it is clearly false and so just another collection of silly superstitions. The Bible being a compilation of fabricated stories suggests that God does not exist and supernatural events are impossible, which sounds identical with our initial statement. What does amaze me about this mindset is if one of your foundational assumptions is that materialism is true and supernatural events are impossible, it is not surprising that the conclusion is that God does not exist; it clearly assumes the outcome when making the initial conditions. This is a prime example of circular reasoning.

If God exists, then He created the universe, time, and the laws of nature. To create something, you must be either equal to or greater than that which you create. If I were writing a computer program to create and run the universe, would it be unreasonable to think that I could insert code to create events that were outliers to the normal behavior in the system? I actually learned a valuable lesson from my kids playing MineCraft. If you don't know, MineCraft is an over the top pixelated adventure where a guy named Steve (that's you) wanders around an open world gathering objects. You punch a tree a bunch and get a block of wood, mold the wood to make a shovel, dig with the shovel and find coal, and so on until you have an insanely rich world where you are cooking steaks on the 12th floor of your tower overlooking the town that you built. It doesn't sound addicting but believe me it is. The evidence is undeniable, as I have had 3 AM tantrums caused when I was "mining" and accidentally hit the bottom of an underground lava pool resulting in hot magma being dumped on my head, dying, and losing three hours of accumulated stash. Trying to explain to your family that everything is ok and to just go back to bed please is embarrassing. Point is, the MineCraft world works just like our world. You jump and then land. You fall off cliffs. Gravity "works." If you are underwater for too long, you suffocate. If you dump magma on your head, you die.

One day, I saw my daughter Christina running off a cliff. I raced across the room to save my precious child from the pain that I had experienced from my digital demise, but strangely enough, she just kept walking out over thin air. I asked what was going on and she replied, "Oh, I am in God mode." How aptly named. She calmly flew up to the clouds, down to the bottom of the sea and walked through the dreaded magma with impunity! It struck me that in this simple computer program, they could provide one ruleset for me and another for someone in "God Mode." If the programmers could easily do that with the simple tools that are available, I see no logic in thinking that the ultimate being that created everything, including the laws of nature, could not do the same thing, just in a more elegant and powerful fashion. Those very laws would have been set up the way that the Creator desired for the universe to function and if He created the laws of nature, why then would He not be able to override them at His choosing? Even if we constrain God to act only within those laws, are we so arrogant to think that we understand all the competing laws? We would be like cavemen looking at an airplane and not accepting its reality as we know that objects always fall to the ground. There seems to be a seriously misplaced hierarchy attributing supremacy to the laws of nature over the One who would have created them. I can respect the idea that someone believes that miracles don't happen because they don't believe in God, but it is folly to say that they think that there is no God because they believe that miracles are impossible. Proof of God, no, but I do think it's a silly argument for their not being one.

| # The Ramifications of Accepting a Christian Lifestyle

I have heard numerous objections to Christianity that have nothing to do with the spiritual nature of belief. A few of the more memorable ones are that a person is only a Christian because they were born in a Christian household, Christianity is a feel-good religion, and that atheists are the same as Christians, except that they believe in one less God!

My father used to say "Put an egg in your shoe and beat it" when I was being a nuisance and he wanted to playfully tell me to get lost. If you figure out what that really means, please contact me as I will shortly be 51 and I still have no idea what to make of it. I admit that I regularly repeat it to my daughters anyway and it's amusing to think that I had the same look on my face as they do when I say it to them. Do you put the egg in your shoe to literally beat the egg with the heel of your foot and, if so, what is the point of that, as you would just have a mixed egg in the heel of your shoe and have gone nowhere? So, it must mean for you to leave. Do you put the egg in and then scram, if so, what is the point of the egg—it must be to literally beat the egg, but wait….? One a more serious note, it was also instilled in me to save and be prepared for the future, treat others honestly and your personal integrity is the one thing that can't be taken from you, you have to throw it away so value it, even when no one is watching. These lessons were taught to me by my mother and father. The point is that it is intuitive and undeniable that children learn from their parents.

The follow-on argument against Christianity, or even theism in general, is that children only become Christians because their parents instruct them to be. When those children become adults and have children, they then carry on the tradition and instruct their offspring to follow Christianity as well—as my daughters will someday tell their children, "Put an egg in their shoe and beat it!" The implication here is that there is no basis to believe. It is simply a tradition, and the path of the least familial and cultural resistance, passed down from generation to generation. If I was born in Chennai, India, then I would have been Hindu, or born in Riyadh, Saudi Arabia, I would have been a Muslim; you're only Christian because of where you were born and who your parents are.

To start, it is fair to say that children learn from their parents, but that applies to Christians and atheists both. Atheists position themselves as the enlightened few who rose above these familial and geographical preconditions, but many atheists also simply come from households whose parents subscribe to the atheistic worldview. I think it is fair to say that children are exposed and encouraged to follow the spiritual path of their family, no matter what the bend. What is not fair to say is that it is necessarily the only reason that someone is an adherent of Christianity, or any other belief system.

After Jesus death (I will discuss those events later), Christianity was new and there were, understandably, very few followers. At some point there were 5,000 followers. In 2019, there were

2.5 billion Christians. In other words, over roughly 2,000 years, a group of 5,000 grew to 2.5 billion. I know that the Catholics are like rabbits, but even they can't proliferate like that! It is apparent to me that most of the early growth of Christianity was due to conversion from other belief systems, not organic growth (having children). This must be true because there was no such thing as Christianity before the first century and even the twelve apostles who were the original Christians, were not originally Christians!

The people alive 2,000 years ago were adherents to a variety of non-Christian belief systems. The argument goes that people only believe because of their parents' instruction and the legacy of their religion simply continues from generation to generation. Conversely, what happened is that a vast number of these people abandoned the traditions and beliefs of their forefathers to embrace Christianity. This flies directly in the face of the premise that people are only Christians because of their upbringing. The parental influence on the new converts was to support a non-Christian worldview which, by this argument, should have led to a perpetuation of that previous belief system. Instead, the direct opposite happened, they abandoned the religion of their parents and adopted Christianity. In the early days of every belief system, the first followers would have to convert non-believers from their inherited belief system. Logically speaking, there must have been reasons that they felt were compelling enough to do so. If the only reason that someone is a Christian is due to their upbringing, then the number of Christians today should only be around the original number with a slight increase for population growth, which is clearly not the case.

As a side note, I do not see this as compelling for belief in a specific religion as there are a multitude of non-spiritual reasons why someone may elect to subscribe to a belief system, especially if there were significant personal benefits to the adherents, but I think when you go further than the emotional reaction, this argument is self-defeating and is best discarded.

We have coffee in the lobby and free cake and cookies! We all know that it's easy to be a Christian, it's a feel-good religion. Your sins are forgiven so you can do what you want and feel fine about it, you are loved, there is an afterlife, and there is a cosmic big brother looking out for you—all you have to do is to put your money in the basket at church, or even better, we do auto draft! And don't get me started on the health and wealth churches....

I have heard the rationale that people are Christians because once you sign up, you get all kinds of benefits. While it is true that they admit that there are benefits, they profess them to be of an immaterial nature. When you look at what it actually takes to "walk the walk" of Christianity, it is not an easy road at all. The life of a Christian has always been founded on expressing love, even for your enemies, and forgiveness of others who have wronged you: "Be kind and compassionate to one another, forgiving each other, just as in Christ God forgave you." (Eph 4.32)

In Matthew 18.21 Peter asked Jesus, "How many times should I forgive someone, as many as seven times?" Jesus replied with, "No, you should forgive seventy times seven."

Also, in Matthew 5.46–48, we are commanded "It is easy to love those who love you—even a tax collector can love those who love him. And it is easy to greet your friends—even outsiders do that! *But you are called to something higher:* "Be perfect, as your Father in heaven is perfect."

Christianity does not impose strenuous external requirements; nevertheless, living up to the teachings and guidance as dictated in the Gospels doesn't look easy to me. When someone screws with me, I know what my first (and second) inclination is to do, and it sure isn't forgiveness. I also know that my ego—and yours too if you're honest—wants to be the lord on high, be made special, and served. I want the private jet, the mega yacht at my estate in the Caribbean, and a penthouse in Manhattan. When I walk past the line at the most elite venues in New York, LA, or Paris, I want people to defer to me. We all want to be important, to be the center of attention, and frankly, to be considered better than everyone else. Unfortunately, that is diametrically opposed to what the Christian life is supposed to be. Instead of the lord on high, they are directed to be the servants of their fellow man. You are to give to others in need and share what you have. With that, you will receive grace, forgiveness, and peace. To be honest, if you can get there, it sounds like a pretty good trade off, but giving up your greed, selfishness, and ego is an incredibly large challenge. In summary, you will have a hard path when dealing with the external world but an easy burden on the internal path of peace and happiness.

It seems like the secular path is much easier on the surface level as it goes to any length to avoid any pain or suffering, celebrates chasing money, popularity and possessions, putting ourselves first, and immediate gratification. Something bothering you physically or emotionally? Pop a pill. Marriage is hard? Have an affair. Got caught cheating in that affair or your wife's too much of a hassle? Divorce her for the newer, younger model. It's okay to ignore your family, just put some zeroes in your bank account. Make it up by taking them on a super swanky vacation at an exotic, and elite, locale, where you can ignore them there as well! Feel lonely and unfulfilled? Go shopping! The tradeoff is internal guilt, stress, and loneliness. This route supplies an easy path dealing with the difficulties in life but has a heavy burden internally.

If you go to church for the social events, free coffee (which is never all that good, sorry to say) or the rock band at the start, then maybe you could claim a rationale for being a Christian is all about the benefits. However, it has been my experience that many of Christians I have encountered truly try to live as described in Scripture, which sure doesn't sound easy to me.

There have been approximately 4,300 religions in human history—Christians know that 4,299 of them are just superstitious or misinformed creations, atheists agree, but just go one God further. On the

> *"So you believe in one God, I assume.*
> *.....But there are 3,000 to choose from*
> *.... so basically, you believe in—you*
> *deny one less god than I do. You don't*
> *believe in 2,999 gods. And I don't be-*
> *lieve in just one more."*
>
> **Ricky Gervais**
> *("The Late Show with Stephen Colbert")*

surface, that's a pretty intuitive argument. To say 4,299 of these gods were made up superstition, then it's compelling to argue that adding one to the pile of 4,299 makes sense. If we were to simply apply the logic and reasoning that we used to dismiss Osiris or Thor and applied it to Jesus, then we would all be in agreement in atheism.

There are some problems with that premise. Most of the religions in the ancient world were clearly created to explain natural phenomena or the human experience all the way up to, and including, the Greek and Roman mythologies. The gods were formed from the natural world and existed within time and space, and were able to be killed; in other words, they were mortal. These were seemingly very similar to human beings, but with explanatory superpowers. Sort of like the Justice League, but better. The description of the Hebrew God is of a very different stripe as to all the others. Yahweh, the God of the Bible, is claimed to be unchanging, had no beginning, is not mortal, was not the explanation of any specific phenomena or event, and exists outside of time. To my knowledge, there are no other belief systems that are even in the ballpark.

As another thought, I know that $1 + 1 = 2$. See, that math degree did help! Anyway, $1 + 1$ does not equal 3 and $1 + 1 \neq 4$ and $1 + 1 \neq 5$ and $1 + 1 \neq 6$, etc. There are literally an infinite number of options that $1 + 1$ does not equal, but only one correct answer for $1 + 1$. Here is the point: out of the infinite pool of answers, there actually is a correct answer. Because there are many choices that we reject, I don't think it is reasonable to then reject every choice out of hand. This again does not speak to the truth of God or Christianity in particular, but it does remove the objection of throwing the baby out with the bathwater.

> "Comicus: Have you heard of this new sect, the Christians? They are so poor....
>
> How poor are they?
>
> ....that they only have one God!"
>
> **Mel Brooks**
> (History of the World Part I)

Another supposed God killer was from the ancient Greek philosopher Epicurus. I noted earlier that I was surprised that there was serious thought and dissent regarding God since antiquity. This was fully illustrated when I learned of this objection, especially considering that Epicurus lived between 341 and 270 BC! He positioned what is supposedly a problematic dilemma for the existence of God, aptly named the Epicurus Dilemma:

> "Is God willing to prevent evil, but not able? Then he is not omnipotent.
> Is he able, but not willing? Then he is malevolent.
> Is he both able and willing? Then whence cometh evil?
> Is he neither able nor willing? Then why call him God?"
> - Epicurus

This argument comes in many forms and really does seem to be convincing at the surface level. Honestly, it gave me some angst when I first encountered it. At that time, I had little regard for philosophical commentary, so the strength of the dilemma was lost on me. Now it is clear to me why this question has persisted over thousands of years. The relatively obvious root of this is if God exists, why does He permit evil?[11]

I am not going to delve into the complexity of evil at this point, but I did want to note some problems with the assumptions made in this dilemma that seem to render it defanged. The reality is that it is a very reasonable possibility that God allows evil for "morally sufficient reasons."[12] In short, if our reality is optimal of all possibilities, within the constraint of free will, for the maximum number of people to have a relationship with God, then, if there is a God, this is exactly as it should be. For a more in-depth look, check out Dr. William Lane Craig's discussion on this.[13] I was initially tempted to then counter this thought with, then God is not all powerful as He could not make it "perfect," having no evil, and include free will, He would fail on the very first line! What I realized is that this may lack logical coherence; it's like the simplistic argument that God should be able to create a square circle. A circle has a definition that is fundamentally different than that of a square. If you changed a square to fit the definition of a circle, it would no longer be a square. Attempting to make two things simultaneously identical and distinct is logically incoherent. Logically incoherent statements cannot be made true, no matter how much power is applied. Not being able to make a square circle is not a limitation of God, it's a failure of the arguer's reasoning.

It is entirely possible that this is an example just like that. This "perfect" utopia reality that includes free will may simply be logically incoherent and nonsensical. Personally, I have trouble seeing how this is the optimal situation that an all-powerful God could craft but while that is my feeling, logically, I know that we have no way of determining if this is true or not. This does not weaken the argument as my feelings, wants, and wishes are irrelevant to the truth of a matter, and it is the burden of the accuser to provide the proof. As Epicurus was making the truth claim that if God has the ability to rid the world of evil, then he would have to do so to be God, it is up to the person putting forth this argument to prove it. In more than 2,000 years, no one has been able to provide an answer.

After analysis, my conclusion is that this argument is another example of the cosmic Monday morning quarterback—apparently, I am in good company! As in my issue with why people are so problematic and "should" be better, I have no idea how they should actually be or if that would be compatible with free will at all!

Another alternative is that it is highly likely that in order to remove evil from the world, He would have to destroy the very beings who complain about his inaction. I am sure that everyone who raises the objection does not consider themselves as part of the problem. It's like when people complain about, well, anything. Whatever it is, the threshold for action is always a little bit above the accuser but a little below the accused. I don't see why some selfish person needs to drive a $50,000 car, but their $45,000 car is fine. "What kind of glutton needs a 4,000 sq ft house?" says those living in a 3,500 sq ft. home. Those irresponsible people need to stop using plastic for drinking bottles as they unwrap the cling wrap from their sandwich. Even if you don't fall into those buckets, I will guarantee that whatever you object to, you do the same thing to some degree; the difference being that you feel the threshold for offense is higher than your participation level, but less than their clearly egregious offense. I know that I regularly subscribe to this behavior.

This isn't truly hypocritical behavior as people admit that they voluntarily participate in those actions. The issue is that there are degrees to transgression; everyone invariably feels that their behavior is within the acceptable range, while others' actions clearly are not. In other words, what you (and I) do is entirely reasonable but the level that others do it is not. Applying this to the argument of evil, all of us automatically assume that the threshold for unacceptable evil would be greater than our actions, and so we would be preserved. While I know that I do wicked things, I feel that it is of a minor or "normal" level. I don't kill, steal, cheat on my wife, hurt people, or any of the host of offenses that I would associate with being terrible. Sure, I lose my temper, say some regretful things when angry, curse, am not nearly as nice or considerate as I could be, practice gluttony, focus on (trying to) accumulate wealth, turn a blind eye with little regard for my fellow man, am greedy, envious, petty, lazy, etc. etc. (I do plenty right too, but it's important to recognize the magnitude of my sin.) None of these are to a degree that I think would raise someone's eyebrows, and if I indulge myself in a moment of immodesty, I take pride in holding myself to a high moral and ethical standard, but the point is that I do many sinful things—and you do too.

When evil comes to mind, I envision the likes of Hitler, Stalin, and Pol Pot. Compared to them, I would consider myself extremely virtuous—notice that I said compared to them. Therefore, I can easily draw the line between me, who is at a level of acceptable evil, and Hitler, who is certainly unacceptable evil. If the exercise is to compare you or me to Hitler, we would have no problem drawing the line.

The problem is that God is positioned as the purely good, infinite being. As He is defined as perfectly righteous, maybe God's baseline for evil is zero. Even a casual reading of Scripture certainly points in that direction. If we then use the comparison between you or me and God to draw the line of acceptable evil, it probably won't turn out so good for you, me, or anyone else! It seems to me even if we used the most moral and upright person that has ever existed as humanity's champion and compared them to God, the line of acceptable evil that He would draw would be so low that if God did as we asked and removed evil from the world, all that would be heard going forward are crickets and the wind.

I know this to be true because when I have read the New Testament regarding how Jesus directs us to act towards our fellow man. Am I the only one who has that little bit of nervousness in the pit of my stomach as I know that I willfully don't live up to those commands? Never saw someone that you knew could use some help and looked the other way? No? Never driven by a homeless encampment or saw a lonely elderly person? So, you're unaware of the starvation in Africa? There are a million other examples where I fail. I do worry that at the end of my days, I will appear for the reckoning of my life, and I will easily be convicted.

The general question of evil as posited by Epicurus seems to be more of a statement of why the world isn't set up to accept the level of evil that I am comfortable with and any evil that goes beyond that is prevented. Clearly we want some evil in the world tolerated or we would be eradicated—or God forbid, have to follow a truly righteous path and not indulge themselves in the things that we love doing. I think the real complaint is simply that we can't dictate the tolerance level.

Again, this is regarding the general problem of why there is moral evil in the world. The specific problem of evil events, specifically natural evil such as children getting leukemia, is one of my major stumbling blocks and will be discussed later, but the Epicurus dilemma really doesn't seem to have much conviction power to me.

> *"A little bit of philosophy leads you to atheism, but depth in the philosophy leads you back to religion"*
>
> ***Sir Francis Bacon***
> *(Of Atheism)*

TEN | *Clarifying Definitions to Clarify Understanding*

If God can create a rock so big that he cannot lift it, then He is not omnipotent because He cannot lift it.

If God cannot create a rock so big that he cannot lift it, then He is not omnipotent because He cannot create a rock that big.

According to this logic, omnipotence is self-contradictory and so, illogical. Therefore, God cannot be omnipotent!

At first blush, I had to sit back and agree that it certainly seemed to have merit. In my struggle to find the truth, I have come to accept that there is not going to be one magic bullet either way; it is going to be the cumulative effect of multiple vectors of evidence that will point me in a direction. I know that there will be some stones on each side of the scale, so it is imperative for me to separate the chaff from the wheat. I need to get a measure using only what I consider to be valid evidence. While I don't know that this argument would have been a game changer for my belief system, it was something that gave me pause and added a few stones to the atheist side of the scale.

One major lesson that I have learned through my travels is to not accept any of the rhetoric from either side at face value.

When I further evaluated both sides of this argument, I saw that a mature description of God is that He has unlimited power to make things happen or make things change, not that He can do "anything." Wait, what?! God can't do something? Where did that come from? I was always told that God was all powerful and could do anything. No exceptions. Period. Apparently, that's an overly simplistic view. In the more precise definition, God can do whatever is logically possible but cannot do anything that is impossible or logically incoherent. This does not put a limit on God's power because the impossible is, well, not possible. Applying more force or power to something impossible does not, at any point, make it possible no matter how much power you apply. As the power is irrelevant, not being able to do the impossible does not show a lack of power of God.

I had assumed that Christians watered down the definition or were playing semantics when they conditionalized what God could and could not do but interestingly enough, Scripture itself lists that God cannot lie or deny Himself. Clearly, He cannot do absolutely anything, which was a surprise to me.

The first flavor of this argument comes from incoherent ideas such as a square circle (discussed previously), a married bachelor, or an honest politician. As these are impossible, they really are trivial objections, and I view them as silly attempts at a "gotcha" that only work until someone checks up on the idea.

The second one is like the rock listed above. This one is based on an impossible premise, an infinitely sized rock.

The reason that I bring this up is that I repeatedly encountered what seemed like plausible objections, but after some investigation, had rational and conclusive resolutions. I found it extremely frustrating that even though there were clear, concise, and undeniably sufficient answers to these points, these ideas were constantly repeated. I felt as if many of the people who were promoting atheism were happy to parrot any objection either without ever evaluating if it was sound or ignoring that it had a very satisfactory logical resolution. There are certainly honest truth seekers in the atheist community, and like the Christians, the behavior of the community does not validate, or invalidate, their claims, but it really was disheartening.

ELEVEN | *Was Christianity Recycled from Earlier Myths?*

About two months after my world collapsed, I was spending another day incessantly reading articles on God and binge-watching videos. Once one was finished, I would hurriedly click on a suggested video and continue on. My mind was swimming; I tried to consider the absolute and obvious truth proposed by the atheist evangelists which was regularly followed by the clear and logical theistic assertions on why that certainly wasn't true. I would get into spans where I would spin for hours. The only thing that changed was my state of numbness. I certainly was suffering from information (and emotion) overload. One night at about 3 AM, I stumbled on a video where I fell off a cliff.

I was unaware of the long-standing objection that Jesus was not original, the claim is that He was just a rehash of other mythological figures that was updated for the culture at the time. A obvious and popular connection is to the Persian (modern day Iran) Zoroastrian god Mithras. The original Mithras worship started in the sixth century BC; it had traveled via Roman soldiers all the way to Rome by 100 BC. It had fallen from popularity but then had a rekindling at around AD 100.

In 1794, a French revolutionary writer Dupuis uncovered the facts surrounding Christianity's plagiarism of Mithras:

Mithras was born on December 25 to a virgin surrounded by shepherds. He was considered a great traveling teacher and master and had 12 companions—or disciples. He performed miracles which included resurrecting his friend whose name was very similar to Lazarus. Also, he was known as the Good Shepherd and the Way, Truth and Light and identified with the Lion and Lamb.

As I progressed through reading the evidence, my sense of dread and panic grew and grew in the pit of my stomach, but it got worse, much worse.

He also guaranteed followers immortality after a water baptism. He had a last supper and to bring peace to the world, he sacrificed himself. He was buried in a tomb, rose after three days, and ascended into heaven where he would return at the end of the world to resurrect and judge humanity. He was worshipped on the day of the Sun (Sunday).

By the time that I reached the end of the evidence, it felt like the bottom fell out. This was not the description of Jesus; it was the description of Mithras who was around hundreds of years earlier. I remember sitting at my computer in a cold sweat on the losing side of panic. Clearly if Jesus is a made-up myth borrowed from earlier religions, Christianity is false and, frankly, the whole theistic argument is probably empty. Even if the only part that was stolen is regarding Jesus's resurrection, it would still easily be enough to debunk Christianity. If I thought that my mind was reeling before, this was a whole new dimension. All that I hoped was true had suffered an unrecoverable deathblow. Luckily, my life experiences, especially over those last few months, had given me enough perspective to just hold on, take a breath, and ask more questions.

What I find to be the biggest challenge for me personally is my age. Not that I can't see that well anymore (I just need longer arms) or that I wear black socks with sandals. What I mean is that my formative years were in the 1970s and 80s. Back in those days, the method for obtaining information was to head to the local library, go to the cabinets of the index cards where the books and authors information were somewhat categorized—and hope that your topic fell neatly within the lines of categorization and wasn't in some gray area resulting in the need for multiple searches. If your search bore fruit, write down a list of potential sources. Oh, the excitement when a source was using the high-tech microfiche (think of a film projector with a slide for each page of the book or magazine). If you weren't lucky, you would use the Dewey decimal system to find your sources, return to your table with a cartload of books, and start scanning the volumes hoping to find paydirt. Whew!

One of the benefits of everything being in hard copy was that the standards and vetting of the material were high. As it was more costly to publish a physical book, the bar for a publisher to invest in printing a book was higher. Therefore, there were higher standards for them to put their name on the literature. I think that, generally speaking, the written word was more reliable and rigorously researched resulting in people from my generation automatically assigning a high level of trust and authority to published works.

Enter the internet. While it is great that everyone is on the same playing field, it is problematic that every crank has a venue and, let's face it, most of the time you determine legitimacy of a site, and therefore its content, by the sophistication of the site design and the professionalism of the artwork. Even more compelling is video, which, like print, used to be the purview of professional, vetted organizations. Different from print, video plays at a constant rate, it is the barrage of one "fact" after another without time to consider or research the information, unless you manually intervene and pause. On the internet, the level of trust given to a site and its information is often by technical prowess or graphic design skills, not evidence of academic rigor.

Additionally, many authors have Ph.D.'s, which historically were a rare emblem of higher learning and so had an implicit level of credibility. When I began this journey, I would automatically assign a level of authority to any position put forth by an author with a doctorate. After finding that many of these sources were logically incoherent, incredibly ignorant of the actual issue, or intentionally duplicitous, I challenged my predilection of accepting their views based on their academic pedigree. When I evaluated the basis for my assumption, I found that Ph.D.'s are much more common today than they were when I was in school. I certainly am not disparaging or trivializing Ph.D.'s, but the truth is that the number of annual graduates with Ph.D.'s has gone from under 10,000 a year in 1958 to roughly 57,600 in 2022–and that's per year. In the United States alone, roughly 2% of the population has a Ph.D. Between the years 2000 to 2019, the number of Americans holding a doctoral degree has more than doubled to 4.5 million.[14] To visualize how rare PhD's were and assuming a random sampling, in 1958, you'd need to meet approximately 1,163 people to encounter one Ph.D. holder, while in 2022 you would only need to meet 56. This helped me break through the predisposition to yield to authority and I no longer blindly accept what anyone says, Ph.D. or not.

What made matters a bit more difficult in dissecting this accusation is that the cult of Mithras follows two very distinct and non-continuous belief systems; the original coming out of Persia and its follow on, centuries later in Rome. The challenge was, if the similarity was true, to determine if it originated in the cult in

Persia that was practiced before Christ, or the later version that sprung up after Christianity was widely ingrained in the Roman Empire (so much so that it was adopted as the official religion).

The first claim regarding the date of December 25 is not specified in Scripture and so, many assume (me being one of them), that it was a somewhat arbitrary day. I had previously heard that this date was used to replace a pagan holiday for the solstice so that it would make conversion to Christianity easier (and as I never heard anything to counter this, I accepted it). While no one really knows for sure, there are a few theories as to why this date has gained prominence, but one is used to directly support the Jesus-Mithras connection. The Roman iteration of cult of Mithras had long considered that Mithras and the Roman god of the sun, Sol Invictus, to be either exactly the same or having some sort of duality.[15] In 274 AD, the Roman Emperor Aurelian made the cult of the Roman god Sol Invictus official. Since Sol Invictus was believed to have been born on December 25 and he was either the same or a duality of Mithras, therefore Mithras is theorized to have been born on December 25 as well. I thought that this was quite the coincidence and really could lend weight to the idea that Jesus was a borrowed figure. Then I learned that the source of this information was from a document named Chronography of 354, or Calendar of 354, which was an illuminated manuscript produced in, you guessed it, 354 AD for Valentinus, a wealthy Roman Christian. In it is the first documented evidence that Sol Invictus' birthday was celebrated on December 25, and so the source of the claim. However, in the same manuscript it lists how the Christians had been celebrating Christ's birth on December 25 as well. In this document, it claimed that both groups celebrated December 25 but there was no evidence as to which one began before the other.[16]

What I actually found later on was that it was the Christians, not the Mithraists, who first celebrated on December 25. Excerpts from Hippolytus of Rome's Commentary on the Book of Daniel states that Christians had long been using this date. The clincher is that this was written in 204 AD which is 150 years before the first documented attribution of the date to the Mithraists and 70 years before Sol Invictus was recognized as an official cult.

Furthermore, early Christian writings go to great lengths to separate their followers from pagan beliefs, and it would make no sense that they would then use a pagan birthdate to cel-

> "For the first advent of our Lord in the flesh, when he was born in Bethlehem, was December 25, Wednesday, while Augustus was in his forty-second year, but from Adam, five thousand and five hundred years. He suffered in the thirty-third year, March 25, Friday, the eighteenth year of Tiberius Caesar, while Rufus and Roubellion were Consuls."
>
> **Hyppolytus of Rome**
> *(Commentary on Daniel)*

ebrate their new religion. It certainly seems that December 25 could have been an arbitrary date which was possibly based off of pagan ceremonial dates, but it definitely seems that it was actually the Christians who began using this date and that it was borrowed from them.

Next, was Mithras born to a virgin? There is no birth myth information for Mithras except that he appeared out of solid rock (his emerging from the rock potentially left a cave). I do not think that solid rock has had sex, but I still would not consider it a virgin. Also, the birth was supposed to have happened before humans were created, so virgin women and shepherds could not possibly have been present. The shepherd tradition of the mythology was real but first appeared 100 years after the Gospels were written; it seems again, there is a real similarity, but it was Mithraism who plagiarized.[17]

There is no evidence that he was considered a teacher but as he was a supposed deity, I would think that it would be expected that he was a master and could perform miracles.

Now the big kahuna. When I read that there were 12 apostles, I was floored. Let's face it, it is very highly unlikely that this would be a coincidence. It goes beyond belief that both could just happen to have 12 apostles. I felt that the earlier parts could be dismissed as details, but this, along with the resurrection, was critical. It is well documented that Jesus had 12 disciples, there can be no argument there. After studying the source of Mithras having 12 disciples, it turns out that in a pictograph, he is surrounded by the 12 signs of the zodiac. Seriously? So, a picture of the god Mithras with the signs of the zodiac equates to having 12 disciples? The basis for saying that Christianity is a made-up myth is based on absurd extrapolations like this?! Unless you have a philosophical or religious axe to grind, how could you make such a leap in good conscience?

It is still unbelievable to me that people would position assumptions made from pictograms, with no written documentation, in such an assertive and certain matter. My daughter had an assignment in the second grade where the teacher showed the students a picture and each child had to write a story imagining what was going on. I don't see this as being any different. Well, except that my child knew that her story was fiction.

Furthermore, the rekindling of the Mithras cult in Rome occurred well into the second century AD and all of the actual documented similarities were written by early Christian apologists. Ironically, they were complaining that the cultists were borrowing so many Christian symbols and rituals as to make them almost indistinguishable from Christianity. It turns out that these cases of religious plagiarism were from the Mithriac cultists stealing from Christianity, not the other way around. Even more telling is that many of the rituals and symbols adopted contradict what the original followers practiced in Persia.

So, how about resurrecting his friend whose name was very similar to Lazarus? You guessed it, not a part of the myth in any way.

Promised immortality? Little evidence, but as Mithras is purported to be a deity, I would not be surprised.

> *"We must now conclude that [Cumont's] reconstruction simply will not stand. It receives no support from the Iranian material and is in fact in conflict with the ideas of that tradition as they are represented in the extant texts. Above all, it is a theoretical reconstruction which does not accord with the actual Roman iconography"*
>
> *John R. Hinnells*
> *First International Congress of Mithraic Studies (1971)*
> *("Reflections on the Bull-Slaying Scene")*

The closest that he got to sacrificing himself to bring world peace was that he fought a bull.

As you may be able to tell, as I was investigating each "similarity," I was seeing that they were ridiculous at best. I was fully prepared for mental anguish as I walked this path, but I was not prepared for ludicrous conspiracy theories given as legitimate objections. I had mistakenly assumed that questions were raised by kindred spirits seeking truth, not from agenda-driven people wielding secularist hammers desperately seeking a nail. I was, and still am to some degree, severely disappointed, hurt, and angry at the flagrant irresponsibility which I feel has to be either intellectual dishonesty or tin foil hat conspiracy theory nonsense positioned as scholarship.

How about the last supper, that he died, was buried in a tomb, and rose after three days to ascended into heaven? There is nothing in Mithraism tradition that he died at all. The entire crux of defeating Christianity lies in the resurrection similarity of Mithras and Jesus, and there is zero evidence that Mithras even dies?

Mithras was never called the "Good Shepherd," "Way, Truth and the Light," "Logos," "Redeemer," "Savior" or "Messiah," or identified with the lamb. He was the sun god (or light), so there is some support of his association with the House of the Sun (Babylonian astrology) which is depicted as the lion—oh, but that tradition is post New Testament as well.

Was he worshipped on the day of the Sun (Sunday)? I would think so.

The scenario that a group of people were making up a religion with a major impetus of converting the Jews, and so, elected to use pagan details doesn't make sense.

> "The mysteries cannot be shown to have developed from Persian religious ideas, nor does it make sense to interpret them as a forerunner of Christianity"
>
> **Manfred Claus**
> *(The Roman Cult of Mithras)*

Jesus fulfilling the Old Testament prophecies was critical to the conversion of the Jews and pagan elements in their story would be a massive detriment to that effort. Also, according to early Christian writers, there were great efforts to preserve the faith from being corrupted by the influence of paganism and superstition. An early writing of the Gospels, and it seems as if there is strong evidence for this, would mean that there were witnesses still living who would have seen the inserted pagan details and presumably objected.

It does seem to me that there was a borrowing of details, but it appears that the pagans borrowed from Christianity, not the other way around. I don't have a problem with questioning or even positioning theories, although I would hope that they would have more of a basis. I have a real problem with forcefully claiming to be fact things that are, let's just say, opinion at best. I admit that I was at a very vulnerable time, and this seemed to pierce through the chinks in my armor and so I had an emotional reaction. I am thankful that I had the wherewithal to not fall into despair and instead, dug deeper. My intellectual side is very satisfied that this claim is nonsense, but my emotional side is hurt and angry.

TWELVE | *Do We Have Free Will?*

If we truly are a vast assembly of nerve cells and their associated molecules utilizing a hardwired logic tree and what we believe to be free will is only an illusion, then people don't actually make choices. If this is true, then no one has ever made a choice to participate in any event, good or bad. As the individual has made no choice, how would it then be fair to hold a person responsible for his or her actions?

Let's say a doctor accidentally administered an improper drug or dosage that made someone hallucinate, and during one of the hallucinations, he imagined that he was being attacked, and his life was in danger. If to protect himself, he fought back and inadvertently hurt someone, we certainly wouldn't hold him responsible. Since he isn't responsible for his actions, how can you rightfully punish him?

> "You, your joys and your sorrows, your memories and your ambitions, your sense of personal identity and free will, are in fact no more than the behavior of a vast assembly of nerve cells and their associated molecules."
>
> ***Francis Crick***
> *Co-Discoverer of DNA*
> *(The Astonishing Hypothesis)*

You wouldn't have the improperly dosed patient arrested and sent to jail; you would feel bad for the tragic events that happened to this victim of medical malpractice.

Imagine a scenario in court that goes something like this:

"Your honor, I freely admit that I was the one who raped that woman and then beat her to death. I know that I did it, but it was not my fault as I had no choice but to do it!"

"It is only your mind state that believes that you are a murderer. As you are simply a neural machine performing tasks as you were conditioned to do, there really had been no choice in the matter. As such, you can't be held responsible for what you had no choice in, and as you are not responsible, it would be illogical to punish you. Case dismissed. You are free to go."

Absurd? Yes. But that is exactly the logical conclusion that you are forced to reach if you accept that materialism is all that there is, and we are simply a series of complex logic trees. No matter the crime, we have not made a willful choice to participate in the act and are just unfortunate marionettes. And no, this isn't being blown out of proportion to promote some chest thumping; it's actually the way many determinists feel. For those being critical, I feel that if you are going to be a materialist and you accept that there is nothing but matter and energy, you can't get away from being a hard determinist. Soft determinists also believe that we're only "molecules in motion," but free will is still available. It seems to me like soft determinists are trying to have their cake and eat it too.

What I found is that there are three camps in which people fall into when evaluating if free will exists. Upon rereading this, I did have to chuckle that there are three camps of opinion for if free will exists and you have to choose which one to which you belong.

The first is (physical) determinism, which I think would be the natural view of adherents of materialism, holds that all of reality is solely matter and energy. Any action that you perform is purely determined by your physical neurological configuration following a hardwired, concrete path reacting to a set of stimuli. This is the logic tree scenario that I have spoken about. Every action is pre-determined—like a giant interwoven set of dominoes or an elaborate computer program going through a series of "*If* this *then* do that" statements. There is no such thing as free will, we do not actually choose anything, and the perception that we do is simply an illusion. In this view, there is only one possible future dictated by physics and chemistry that was set in motion at the start of the universe. Picture walking down a path and come to a fork in the road, the left side is blocked off, so you take the right-side path. You may have felt like there were two choices, but in reality, there were not. In this scenario, you did not choose this or any other option in your entire life. The supposed "choices" are "selected" by your brain's physical status which is the result of genetics, past experiences, and the environment. Every action, from saving a child from a fire to the worst atrocities in history, is just another domino in an inevitable sequence.

The second is libertarian free will in which we do have choice. Unlike materialism, libertarian free will includes consciousness which allows for genuine choice. Our environment and experience may exert influence and pressure to decide a certain way, but ultimately, our consciousness has the final say and may override any and all other factors. Here, we're not constrained to a predetermined script; we may choose between options and navigate our own path through life. Imagine walking down a path and come to a fork in the road, the left side is pretty with flowers and animals but has rough terrain while the right is paved, as you are footsore, you choose the right-side path (but could have chosen the left). As our consciousness has the final say in our decisions, we must be more than a purely physical entity. There must be a non-physical element to our being that extends beyond matter and energy. This is what many term the duality of mind or the soul.

The third option is compatibilism, or soft determinism, where you do have a version of free will (not the same definition as the libertarian free will) where you don't really have a choice, but it doesn't matter anyway because the path that you are forced to take is the same one that you would have chosen anyway. You have the experience of the idea of free will, but you are determined in what you do. Imagine walking down a path and arriving at a fork in the road, the left side is pretty with flowers and animals but is blocked off from an invisible forcefield. The right path is paved and as you are footsore, you choose the path on the right. You made the conscious choice to take the right path, but it really was the only option available to you anyway. In compatibilism, you "chose" the right-side path, but it was inevitable due to your brain's configuration.

It is always interesting to apply real life situations to philosophical theories. In the determinism scenario, you will eventually be required to deal with people whose programming results in behavior outside of permissible ranges. In the real world, for whatever reason, some people do very bad things, so there must be a subset of people whose logic trees end up with actions that our programming deems unacceptable for society. Those trees that are programmed to perform unacceptable acts elicit a societal response. In this view, there is only cause and effect. As one domino falls, it pushes the next over with zero variability. As we only have the illusion of self and free will and so there is no "choosing" at all. Prison is not going to incentivize or encourage someone to choose differently as there was no choice in their actions. Jail is intended to change behaviors, but a few years in prison can't be enough to overcome thousands or millions of years of evolutionary preconditioning and reconfigure the physical properties of their brain. It seems that incarceration or other punishments would be a waste of time.

Within this worldview, it seems to me that there are only two logical choices. First, if the event is within acceptable parameters and we will allow the trait to continue within our gene pool, then we must release them without punishment. Again, they did not choose this behavior and it is unfair to punish someone who had no power to control their situation. If we determine that the behavior is outside of the tolerance level, then the only other choice is to remove the trait from our gene pool. In other words, terminate the organism. As horrific as this thought is, doesn't it seem to be the logical conclusion of determinism?

If I have a piece of software that continually gives the wrong output or even crashes the computer but I can't access the source code to make changes to its logic, I have two choices. Either I can allow it to run and put up with the problems that it causes, or I can stop allowing it to run.

In this framework, all morality is subjective as well, so there is no objective right and wrong to sway us. We do what is best for the successful continuation of the species, and that is to remove dangerous genes.

Wait! Wait! I have heard materialists claim that people can learn, basically be reprogrammed, to act in accordance with society's norms. If determinism is true, then it needs to be extended to not only the criminal but to the judge, prosecutor, jury, etc. and all of their actions and the verdict itself is already determined. To even suggest that you can do something else is the antithesis of determinism.

This weekend, I was listening to two vocal atheistic scientists discussing the topic of determinism. One was very honest about determinism and where it led, but there were two things that really struck me. First, when he walked down the path where determinism leads, he started discussing how accepting that everything is a result of physics and therefore is determined, as such, it would be a vast improvement if we started using that philosophy in designing our criminal justice system. That sounds like we have a choice on how we set up the penal codes and rehabilitation—how is that determinism? It also proposed that people's behaviors could then be guided by proper stimuli. If it really is determined, there is only one future, and it is immalleable. The implication of modification implicitly requires choice and the ability to have variance. Through this journey, it has been striking to me on how many times I see the proponents of arguments that are so counterintuitive to our experience immediately fall back on the contradictory concepts to make their points.

When I heard the second item, it really made me think. He was speaking about how this past weekend he was reminiscing about a girl he had previously dated and that he had regrets about how it turned out. He said that he then reminded himself that it was all predetermined and therefore, it was impossible for things to have happened differently or for it to have ended in any other way. I feel that this mentality absolves yourself of any personal responsibility and allows any behavior to be acceptable. I don't know about anyone else, but when I do something wrong—either knowingly or unknowingly—I feel genuine guilt as I know it was wrong, and I hurt someone. Telling myself that it was destined to be, and I couldn't have done anything different—especially in the instances where I knew beforehand that it was wrong and I did not have the willpower to do the right thing—is indulging in the worst kind of self-rationalization. Why bother doing anything as it is all predetermined? Why play with your kids? If they were supposed to feel love according to the galactic script, then they will. Don't bother going to work, if you are supposed to keep that job or get a promotion, then you will. Ridiculously inane points? Perhaps, but they are precisely where the logical extension of determinism takes us. This is the same sort of "it's God's will" nonsense that drives me nuts with some Christians.

Taking it a step further, in determinism, there is only one possible future. If everyone's actions are predetermined, the responses to those actions are predetermined, and so on and so on. It seems to me that there is merit in

> "One of the annoying things about believing in free will and individual responsibility is the difficulty of finding somebody to blame your problems on. And when you do find somebody, it's remarkable how often his picture turns up on your driver's license."
>
> *P. J. O'Rourke*
> *(Rolling Stone Magazine)*

considering that our consciousness evaluates all the evidence to make a decision and therefore, you could say that this points to determinism. To deny that this was formulaic would be to then be reliant on some level of randomness in the outcome, and if you admit randomness, then you again give up free will. However, it seems to me that the game changer is that this consciousness is not just an evaluator of current evidence based on experience. We are more than a logic tree, we also can extrapolate current and past situations to predict an outcome; and taking the desirability of that outcome, it can make choices in the present to affect the future outcome. If this is true, then there must be more than one future possible to select from and so determinism cannot be true.

Also, and I think this is extremely important, it is undoubtedly true that people often weigh all of the evidence for a decision and then do exactly what they shouldn't do—even when the evidence is overwhelming. We all do it to some degree. You could say that at a deeper level that we don't know about yet, there are drivers that modify the person's decision-making equations that results in the calculation selecting what we would consider to be a poor choice, so the logic works perfectly, we just don't know what those other variables or equations are. This sounds exactly like another materialism of the gaps. We need to work using what we know and reevaluate as more data is available.

Furthermore, it seems to me that consciousness has a sense of direction that cannot be purely formulaic.

While it may be tempting to think that compatibilism is a compromise between libertarianism and determinism, it really isn't. Personally, I struggle with compatibilism as the result would be the exact same here as in determinism. I have heard it argued that it could be an emergent property. "Emergent properties are properties that manifest themselves as the result of various system components working together, not as a property of any individual component."[18] The sum being more than its individual parts. I try to be generous to both sides of an issue so I don't miss anything, but I do not see how materialistic causes would ever give rise to anything other than materialistic results, namely something even having the semblance of free will. Assuming compatibilism (or determinism) to be true, then tracing back in time, before human beings, even before any form of life, everyone will agree that things happened. As there were no sentient beings, there was no free will and so, the events were purely driven by materialistic causes—the laws of physics and the configuration and location of atoms in the universe. Pick any point and it would demonstrate a deterministic environment (in this scenario, there is no supernatural) that could be traced all the way back to the start of the universe. As we wind the clock forward from that point, I find it incredibly implausible that a deterministic system that is entirely reliant on matter and the laws of physics could give birth to something even resembling free will because the idea of that free will, even in a compatibilist sense, is predicated on it not being subject to the laws of physics. Remember, if it was subject to the laws of physics, then it would be determinist. Said another way, the premise is that physics produced a collection of particles that are not subject to the laws of physics. This would be an example of creating something greater than itself as it is not constrained by the laws of its creator.

It may be unfair for me to say, but I feel like compatibilism is a game of semantics to accommodate the experience of free will and allow for personal responsibility but still keep a deterministic mindset. It is also important to note that compatibilism is shared by many Christian as well as atheists, so it is not specifically a theological position.

Personally, I do believe that human beings are special, and every human life is to be cherished, protected and revered. No matter if the spark is divinely granted or not, I do feel that human beings are not on the same level as animals and one of the major divergences is having a consciousness and free will. The politically correct culture would label me as a speciesist! (no, that's a real thing....)

While I can see some aspects of determinism may have merit, I personally feel that our reality is best reflected by libertarian free will. I have heard no compelling evidence, actually no evidence at all, as to convince me that what we experience daily in the perception of choice is merely an illusion and so, hopefully without cutting myself, I will apply Ockham's Razor. With two or more competing theories, the simpler one is to be preferred. Maybe I am just predestined to believe that I have free will, but I doubt it!

And again, this does not necessarily promote deism or Christianity but is a pretty big problem for materialism.

> *"I have noticed even people who claim everything is predestined, and that we can do nothing to change it, look before they cross the road."*
>
> **Stephen Hawking**
> *(Black Holes and Baby Universes and Other Essays)*

| ## *Couldn't God Design a Better Existence?*

I have heard my mother say "actions speak louder than words" at least a million times. A few years ago, I made the decision to take my savings out of the stock market and invest in real estate. I took out a few mortgages to buy a few houses that I was going to use as rental properties. Since I started, and especially during COVID-19, I have had some tenants who have not been current with paying their rent. Putting myself in their position, I was very hesitant to evict anyone. After all, what kind of human being would you be if you kicked someone out on the street when they were using their money to pay for their kid's medications or were so flat broke from losing their job that they had nowhere to go? Repeatedly, I worked with people; I didn't evict, even after many months of non-rent, waived late fees, and so on. To cover these people in their time of need, I had to spend my savings to cover the mortgages, make repairs on the properties, pay insurance, taxes, and still feed my family. I constantly heard how they knew that I was helping them out, how much they appreciated it to the bottom of their soul, and would never ever cheat me. Some offer up their belief system as proof of their trustworthiness. See where this is going? Yeah, you guessed it, to a person they all, not only cheated me out of multiple months of back rent but, in the most insulting irony of all time, had the audacity to act like they were the ones wronged by me for asking for payment. Oh, and unless their kids drank lots of beer, smoked cigarettes and needed new big screen televisions, I have my serious doubts about their financial plights.

How many bad things happen every day? There are the big ones like murder, rape, child abuse, and assault but also the non-violent ones like adultery, racism, slander, malicious damage, bullying, and a host of others. Now, how many people consider themselves cheats or evil? Hardly anyone. I bet you have never encountered anyone who admits that they are a bad, dishonest, or immoral person, I know that I haven't! Everyone justifies their actions so that they are viewed as to be in the right, even if to see it in that perspective requires you to get on a chair, half pirouette with one leg raised, cock your head to the side, close one eye, and squint heavily with the other. I would bet that those tenants that cheated me out of rent will undoubtedly claim to be morally upstanding and have never wronged a person in their lives; it was just an unfair, bullying landlord taking advantage of them. People, by and large, are petty, irrational, vindictive, and basically nasty. It seems to me that the prevailing attitude by most people is to lie, cheat, and steal because the other person had it coming anyway, for some reason or another, even if they don't know specifically what for. I genuinely feel that the people who try to live a moral life, and that certainly includes not cheating on your wife or husband, are in a diminishing minority. Our global history is rife with atrocities and injustice, sometimes in the name of God, but realistically more often, from purely human reasons.

The Christian answer is that since the fall in the Garden of Eden, people are sinful and have an inherent brokenness. The atheist's answer is that this is exactly what we should expect if people are simply the product of blind random forces. I honestly have trouble accepting that either of these have the explanatory power required.

If God created us for a relationship, then it has to be based on love. Love, by definition, must be freely given, which necessitates there to be options or choices. Simply put, if there is no choice, also known as free will, and God forces us to worship Him, then it is not love and it is not a relationship. If free will is present, then having the choice to do evil things is inherently necessary. I accept that people are broken and if evil is an option, some will elect to do just that. Again, choice, or free will, is essential for love and a relationship and if there are choices, invariably, some people will choose poorly. I am fully on board with this part of the argument.

My problem here is if there is an ultra-intelligent creator, couldn't people have been created with free will but with a stronger inclination to do good or barrier to do evil? I just look at humanity and I have to ask; is this the best He could do? To be forthright, I know that this is an unfair objection. I realize that the bar could have been set at any height, and I probably would have the same complaint no matter where it was placed as it purely depends on perspective. It is also ironic that the "barriers to do evil" that I desire reek of the compatibilism that I so vehemently reject!

If every day, it was 82 degrees with a 6-mph breeze, sapphire blue skies and bright yellow sunshine, it would then become normal, then expected, then plain and nondescript. If one day there were a few clouds in the sky, instead of me dying to get off the computer and get outside to enjoy such a day (like I am feeling today after looking out the window while I write this), I would suddenly cry of "Oh, the horrible weather!" pull the shutters and retreat to the couch and Netflix out the horrific storm.

Our subjective views of good and bad, better and worse, are entirely dependent on our relative experience. Maybe our reality should have been what we would now call horrific and instead, what we have is the most perfect that it can be made while still allowing free will. I recognize that it's easy to question why things are the way they are and opine that it could, should, and would have been better, but very hard to say, in specific detail, how exactly it "should" be with the precondition of allowing free will. I guess I am a cosmic Monday morning quarterback, but I am still haunted by the feeling that reality could, would, and should be better.

On the other hand, if all living creatures are the product of blind random forces, why would people be so different from every other species, especially in their ability to do harm? When a lion kills a zebra, we may feel badly for the zebra, but the killing is not evil. When a person murders or performs some atrocity, often for no reasonable reason whatsoever, it is evil. This is different than instinctual killing and I do not see this behavior evidenced anywhere else in nature. Organisms don't kill purely for the pleasure of it. Additionally, nature also has checks and balances so that no species will kill off any other and so preserve the cycle of life, but apparently this has no regulatory power at all over mankind.

In a materialistic scenario that is predicated on us just being "moist machines," there is simply a highly complex logic tree that simulates free will and morality; we have no real choice in anything that we do. The preconditioned logical pathways were formed over time by "better" choices increasing survival rates for the organism and so, were more likely to propagate and carry the gene forward. As previously discussed, this seems to fall apart when we look at so many things about the human experience that are present, and even celebrated, that not only do not make survival more likely but are in fact a detriment.

If we do have free will and it is not just a simulation, it seems to me that morality would have needed to appear or evolve simultaneously with the development of free will. Thinking about this, it seems to me that morality functions also as a regulatory mechanism on the ability to choose. Free will without morality would seem to be fatal to our species—everyone would have basically been a sociopath. Can you imagine the havoc that would ensue if everyone had their morality suspended for even a day? Arson, rape, murder—the dead would litter the streets. Why not kill that crying baby at the store as its noise is bothersome? If you have no morality to stop you, zero sense that anything is wrong, there is no reason not to do it. Maybe we would worry that the mother might cause trouble to defend her young, so we would probably just kill the mother as well. The point is, there is no right and wrong to hold us back. Sure, you could argue that the laws would keep you in check, but the laws were established for justice and justice relies on morality. It seems to me that as a population of sociopaths, we would not have survived.

If this is true, then we would have had to have evolved morality simultaneously to keep the free will in check, but I see no way that morality would have been a benefit to the

> "If God does not exist, everything is permissible."
>
> **Fyodor Dostoevsky**
> (The Brothers Karamazov)

organism. Looking at the behavioral limitations that morality would enforce on an organism, I would think that morality would be a detriment to survival of an individual organism—which is the exact opposite of what would be predicted to perpetuate the species. In a fight, if you have someone who has a code of conduct and morality fighting someone with no morals or limitations, the winner is a foregone conclusion. No, I would not expect people to look like this if we were the product of blind random forces. Not at all.

FOURTEEN | *Evil and Truth*

Even when I was still abiding by the unspoken pact to not openly question my faith, I was persistently bothered by the issue of the horrific acts that one human being will do to another—many times just to demonstrate that they could be that terrible. The nagging voice in the back of my mind asks why would God allow such atrocities throughout history? Probably the easiest example to point to is the Nazi regime whose Final Solution led to the genocide of every Jew (and many others) within German reach. After reading excerpts from period diaries many years ago, I am still haunted by the imagery as people described their experiences with the Nazi soldiers who would come into towns in the middle of the night and round up the Jewish families to be transported to work (concentration) camps. They would break up the families and divide the men and women/children into separate groups, never to see each other again. Infants offered no industrial benefit as they could perform no tasks or labor. Instead, they would be ripped from their mothers' and fathers' arms, held by their feet and swung so viciously against the brick walls of neighboring buildings that their little skulls would burst. Some of the guards even made a game of it while their families watched in horror.

I think it's apparent that we all want some level of evil in the world, but clearly, this is way, way beyond what we asked for. As a father, thinking about this scene evokes so many emotions: heartbreak, anguish, rage, and a sense of despair that reaches beyond my conscious self. How any human being could do this to another is beyond my grasp, and I can see why people say that God should have stopped this. While I can't even begin to imagine how I would feel if it were me on that street and it was my daughters being brutally murdered, I can empathize with people who disavow God because of events like these.

But it wasn't me and I have no real idea what it felt like. To be brutally honest, I feel somewhat guilty for being so thankful that I don't know. Mine is a purely observational view. I recognize that there is a world of difference between an experiential view and an observational view—like there is a difference between watching a movie of soldiers under fire and actually being shot at. Or to use another example, but one that I think demonstrates the point better than any other that I can think of—the difference imagining what your first kiss will be like and then actually experiencing that electric spark the first time. While I may not be able to understand what it was like in Nazi Germany, it is counter-intuitive that for many, the experience brought them closer to God—openly attributing their survival to that faith.

I had always been taught that God was all good and cared for His little children—like we are in some galactic preschool led by a bearded grandfatherly figure with the kindly smile. He would be there when Sally fell down and skinned her knee and stopped Tommy from eating paste. God was the equivalent of the bumper rails when my kids go bowling. The reality is that human beings are far from powerless children and God does not prevent us from running with scissors. Earlier, I discussed my belief that being able to have a relationship necessitates free will and free will necessitates choices. Having choices means that, invariably, some people will choose poorly. The other side of this is that it also means that human beings are uniquely powerful creatures. We can choose to love or not to love, something that even God cannot do. While we regularly abuse that power for selfish ends, we are not helpless beings. We have the power to make the choices to stop these evils, and some people choose to do just that. The other side of the equation is that nowhere in Scripture does it say that God will rush in to save us from ourselves. Jesus Himself says that the rain will fall on the just and the unjust alike. This is not a stain on the idea of God; if Scripture is to be believed, then God weeps at our bad choices, but that does not make it His fault.

We can elect to blame God for the manifestations of human choices that result in horrors such as the Holocaust, but that is unfair. It's like the friend who asks to borrow your car, drives too fast and ends up in a ditch and not only ends up blaming you for letting them drive, but demands payment for their medical bills and an apology for allowing this to happen. It is my firm belief that evils caused by human beings are no one's fault but our own. Unfortunately, we are very, very good at it.

I have no hesitation stating that the Nazis were evil. I will also firmly attest that this is not just my opinion. It is a fact that they were horrible. Thinking fur-

> "After the Holocaust I did not lose faith in God. I lost faith in mankind."
>
> **Elie Wiesel**
> (All Rivers Run to the Sea)

ther on this, the first thing that I realized is ideas like horrible, good, bad, and saintly seem comparative. The Nazis were bad. Bad compared to what? You could say that the Nazis were bad compared to the Huns. While this may be true, it only gives you an idea of how they compare to another item of a set and not how they rate overall. You can see constant examples of this if you have kids. But *these* sneakers aren't as much as *those*! Sorry kid, I do see that there are more expensive varieties—but I don't even spend $200 on sneakers for myself.

When they want something and they know that there are reasons why it's not going to happen, namely, that I am not spending that much on trendy sneakers, they fall back on comparative arguments. My brother and I nicknamed my mother "asbestos hands" as she would regularly take "warmed" plates from the oven and hand them to me. Holy smokes! Eyes wide and frantic, I would toss them back and forth between my hands to keep my fingers from burning. My yelps were met invariably with "Oh, it's not hot....."

If you asked about the pan that I removed from the stove a few moments earlier and I said that this pan is cooler than the pot, you may be tempted to grab it. This idea would certainly lead to a trip to the hospital if the pot was 1,000 degrees but the pan was only 900 degrees. Sure, it was cooler, but still plenty hot enough to give you first degree burns—unless you were my mother, and then you would be fine. Now, if I said the pan was 900 degrees, you would unconsciously consult your universal scale of acceptable temperatures for all human beings not to burn themselves and would realize that it was way too hot to touch.

I have come to realize that you can look at how you judge or rate someone in one of two ways. The first is subjective; it is purely internal and may vary depending on each person's values and experiences. It is entirely valid for me to claim that blue is the best color. It's also entirely valid for my brother to claim that red is the best color (valid but misguided). If I look at Devin's scale of color preferences, I will see that blue is rated very highly and so I can truthfully state that I think that blue is the premier color. This "truth" exists within me but does not extend beyond my skin just as my mom's definition of "hot" is very different than mine. Any judgement that I make in this fashion is true for me but has no bearing on the truth internal to another. In this sense, I can truthfully state that I feel that Hitler was horrible. In this purely subjective sense, I cannot say that a Neo-Nazis' claim that Hitler was an amazing visionary is false. When subjective arguments are made, none of them carry more weight than any other. I constantly hear people claiming that there is no universal truth or that something is "true to you" as a way to try to sound enlightened or inclusive, but when you appeal to only having personal truth you no longer have the ability to object to truly evil things—and that is a very, very dangerous idea.

In order for me to make a truth statement that Hitler was horrible but also assert that the Neo-Nazis' claim that Hitler is an amazing visionary is patently false, I cannot use my subjective views. I need to accept that, like the universal scale of acceptable temperatures, there is an external, universal benchmark to compare it to. In other words, for there to be a unilateral, non-subjective claim, it is necessary to have a transcendent benchmark to compare against. I need to appeal to an objective scale of good and bad, moral and immoral, that extends across all people and all time. In the same way that mathematical truths apply to everyone and are not constrained by personal or cultural preferences, morality requires a transcendent benchmark. For me to go outside of myself to a universal scale, I have to leave materialism behind as it only deals with matter and energy. This is termed moral objectivism.

I think it is somewhat ironic that there have been many people who have been convinced of the existence of God by the presence of evil. One such atheist was the author C.S. Lewis who realized that accepting a naturalistic worldview gave him no grounds to make any moral judgment on what he perceived as evil. If there was no transcendent standard, then your objection to evil is simply your personal opinion, which has no more weight than anyone else's personal opinion. Since he agreed there was that universal standard of good and evil that went well beyond mere opinion, then there necessarily had to be a source of the scale or law, in other words, a transcendent lawgiver, which many attribute to God.

There are many in the atheistic community who try to explain away morality as an evolutionary process. Moral objectivism is a big problem for materialism / atheism but from what I have read, I have not seen any compelling reasoning that persuades me that it is not exactly what it seems.

As I sit here, I wait for the impending doom and catastrophe that I know is coming. I will not know the moment until suddenly it all goes dark, cold, and lifeless. It is February and I live in Dallas, Texas. A historic cold front moved in the other day. I left New York to get out of this nonsense, but now I find myself marinating in temperatures in the low single digits and a white landscape that only children and dogs love. For days, my lullaby has been the hypnotic drip, drip, drip of the faucets left partially open in hopes of keeping the pipes from freezing. Texas has embraced alternative energy and so, its power grid is partially reliant on wind turbines that are

> *"A system of morality which is based on relative emotional values is a mere illusion, a thoroughly vulgar conception which has nothing sound in it and nothing true."*
>
> **Socrates**
> *(In Plato's Phaedo)*

located in west Texas. While I am in favor of alternative energy sources where possible, one of the downfalls in this instance is if the wind turbines freeze up, their contribution to the power grid ceases—and west Texas got hit hard. Due to the decreased electrical power generation, the power grid no longer has sufficient electrical current to supply the demand, so they have been doing rolling blackouts for the last two days. For perspective, it's one degree out and we are averaging 30–45 minutes of power followed by a two-to-five-hour blackout! Most of our time is spent sitting under blankets on the couch in a quiet, darkened house where someone may occasionally, in extreme cases of boredom, spend a little of their jealously guarded phone charge on a game of solitaire. Normally, when I walk in a room, I don't even think twice about flipping a switch and the lights coming on. Now, there is a genuine exultation of joy every time we enter the 30–45 minutes of power and the house suddenly comes to life. I cannot overstate the bliss of hearing the heater fans turning on.

After the first day and the novelty wore off, when the power does come on, we make use of every second; the blankets fly as we spring to life! Everyone races to get some needed work done, cook some food, communicate with a loved one or arguably just as important, make sure that we get another run of the coffee pot before we lose power again. We deeply appreciate every moment as we know that just as fast as it has appeared, it will suddenly be gone. We may have another minute, we may have another hour, we have no idea how long, but we do know it will be gone soon. I am truly savoring the simple pleasure of my computer being on and being able to sit here and take a few minutes to write. (The power went out about 30 seconds after I wrote that)

As strange as it is, this experience has given me a new perspective on natural evil. Natural evil is defined as the "bad" things that happen from non-manmade causes, such as disease or natural di-saster. I can see how knowing that this minute may be your last makes it sweeter, giving it a sense of urgency. Also, life altering events or milestones probably give us pause to contemplate the bigger things. If we all lived to, say, 100 years old, I can only imag-ine how people would behave for the first 99 ½ years and then how they would behave for the last 6 months. This makes sense to me. I used to feel like there should be a guaranteed amount of time that you couldn't die before as, in my opinion, one of the worst possible things is to see a child die. The problem with this is whatever age we choose, 8, 10, 15 or even 20, once we got used to that age of safety, we would later invariably demand that the number be increased as it is entirely too short and what sort of God would make a system that was so unfair that one person who was just starting their life could only live to 23 while some crusty curmudgeon could live to 90. Eventually it would end up with everyone living to the same age, such as 100, and then we would have the problems outlined above. I can see the logic in this.

Conversely, it makes absolutely no sense to me how a child having leukemia or any other horrific disease can be justified. How does that serve any good at all? How will the parents' or family's lives be better for watching their child slowly wither and die? What is the benefit of someone's short life being filled with pain? How can the child learn or grow from it? How will this bring anyone closer to God?

The best explanation that I have heard from the Christian worldview is that at least the child is not accountable for any sins before the age of adulthood and so will certainly go to heaven. It is possible that the suffering of this child and family, when looked at from the bigger picture, may help optimize the number of people who come to Christ and are saved. A few months or years of a horrible disease pales in comparison to an eternity of paradise. Also, we don't know, it's possible that the suffering is made up for when the child gets to heaven. I find these reasons so unpersuasive that I think I would have been better off if they simply said that they did not know. The Christian explanation for natural evil such as this leaves me thoroughly unsatisfied. It offers me no insight as to why there are these types of evil at all or why they would happen to one person and not another.

As a parent, my greatest worry has always been that something would happen to one of my daughters. Realistically, I can't even begin to imagine how horrific it would be, but I also can't imagine that I would find any solace in knowing that my child's suffering would be trivial compared to the eternal bliss of heaven. To me, this has always been a painful sore in the theology story. If naturalism is true and we are just evolutionary machines where occasionally the machinery has malfunctioning parts—in this case in the DNA—well, it would fit into that mechanism that this sort of irregularity just happens. I can't imagine anyone disputing that even in the best manufacturing lines, if you produce 50 million widgets, you will invariably get a few malformed ones. In this regard, the naturalistic worldview does seem to have greater explanatory power.

December 26, 2004, at 7:58 AM Indonesia time, there was a rupture along the Burma Plate and Indian Plate resulting in an enormous 9.1 magnitude earthquake off the west coast of northern Sumatra (yes, like your

> *"The deepest things I have learned in my own life have come from the deepest suffering. And out of the deepest waters and the hottest fires have come the deepest things I know about God"*
>
> ***Elizabeth Elliot***
> *(Let Me Be a Woman)*

Starbucks coffee). This earthquake, the third largest ever recorded, launched a massive tsunami at the coasts surrounding the Indian Ocean with waves reaching 100 feet high. Between people being instantly killed directly by the force of the waves, propelled debris, or buildings collapsing and even worse, being sucked out to sea and drowned, there were an estimated 227,900 people killed.[19]

Since then, I have been trying to reconcile theism with the seemingly needless and wanton death and destruction caused by natural disasters. On the one hand, looking specifically at the tsunami event in as detached a way as possible, I do understand that

> "It's hard to find something uplifting about 150,000 lives being lost, but the type of geological process that caused the earthquake and the tsunami is an essential characteristic of the Earth. As far as we know, it doesn't occur on any other planetary body and has something very directly to do with the fact that the Earth is a habitable planet."
>
> **Dr. Donald J. DePaolo**
> *Geochemist, UC Berkeley*
> *(Qtd. in Fountain's The Earth's Fury)*

earthquakes have a beneficial effect on our planet and ecosystem. Tectonic plates are necessary if we are to have a stable planet and earthquakes bring necessary minerals and nutrients to the surface to replenish depleted soils, help regulate the planet's temperature through CO_2 cycling, and maintain the sea's chemical balance. The Earth seems to be in rather elegant self-regulatory cycles, the only problem is that people are in the way. As nonliving matter does not learn, and you cannot make an argument that it even evolves, how could it have just happened to be participating in so many interwoven self-regulating cycles that are responsible for making the planet hospitable for life?

If God is all knowing and is the great engineer of all of this, then why was it designed so that people could and would be in the way. I realize that this is another example of my "coulda, woulda, shoulda" argument with no concrete example on how to have a stable planet that is habitable without having any negative effects, well, besides applying my magic wand solution—but again, He is God, and I am not. Being God, my inclination is that He should be able to design a system where 227,900 people don't just arbitrarily die one morning. I do not believe that He intervenes in our daily lives or that He rewards the good and punishes the evil, at least in this plane of existence. Even if He did, I simply cannot believe that about a quarter of a million people all living in close proximity to each other needed punishing. I bet we could find plenty of better candidates for divine wrath than some children living in a simple fishing village. When we get into the fine tuning of the universe, we will see the remarkable precision in a variety of aspects necessary for the universe to even exist and then even more to be able to have the possibility of any form of life. Assuming design, considering the mind-boggling level of precision to make the universe even exist, I would have hoped that the engineering of our planet system could be established in a way not to have these kinds of events. Thinking further, He created the laws of physics, He was not and is not constrained by them. The argument that it needs to be this way to adhere to this law or that law holds absolutely no weight. When God created the universe, it was from a truly blank piece of paper. I simply do not understand why there is not a physical principle that would prevent these cataclysms.

There are so many astounding things that occur so regularly in our everyday experience that we ignore them as commonplace. If we remove ourselves from this existence and look at them from a distance, many would rate as even more astounding than if in some way the force of the earthquake dissipated or even that the water thickened when a sudden force, such as that from an earthquake, was applied, preventing transmission of the tsunami waves. Disagree? How about that water is the only substance that expands when cooled and that this anomaly makes life possible? Also, the specific composition of water molecules allows it to travel up a plant stalk, against gravity. Even more miraculous, a plant can take the energy from the sun's emitted photons and turn it into usable energy that fuels other creatures. This process is how energy enters into our local system, the Earth, and counterbalances the entropy, or disorder, enabling organisms to maintain ordered structures such as cells or tissue. This allows life on Earth while still complying with the second law of thermodynamics. If these miracles were not commonplace, they could easily be seen as more difficult to produce than a mechanism for preventing tsunamis.

I do find some confidence when I look at Scripture; it is apparent that our reality isn't exactly the way that God had designed it to be. In 3 Genesis, humanity made the choice to disobey God and introduce sin. It specifically states that since then, we would experience human suffering such as pain in childbirth and death. Paul states in 8 Romans that creation is "groaning" under the effects of sin. In short, human rebellion has an impact on all of reality. I can see how our actions could possibly ripple across both human and natural realms.

I have no problem accepting that the evils that people do to one another are in no way the fault of God. We are powerful beings with the ability to do great good or great evil. I do struggle with reconciling the omniscient designer creating our special home where occasionally, there is a natural event resulting in mass casualties. I have heard the Christian arguments and while they are not illogical, I admit that they are not nearly as compelling as I would like them to be. I know that I am being an "armchair quarterback" in second guessing reality and that if the injustice of something like terminal childhood diseases were removed, I would probably just move to the next item on the list and make the same arguments. However, I also think the atheistic claims that since we're all just random bits interacting, we should expect imperfection and chaos, to also be logical and it does match my life experience.

You may be wondering why I spent all this time discussing both sides of the issue of natural evil just to conclude that each side has arguments with merit but neither seems completely sufficient. It is simply this, you do not have to have *all* the answers. It is a simple point, but with enormous ramifications. You will never, ever, have every single question completely answered. That is not a weakness, it is a natural state of reality. It is also important to note that there is nothing in your life that you have 100% knowledge of.

It was incredibly hard for me to resolve not having the "home run" answer for every problem and I felt that it was a prohibition to ever committing one way or the other. Keep searching and asking, but don't let it derail you. There comes a point where, even without being certain of every detail, you will feel confident in your decision.

| *Is It Just the Brain, or Is There a Mind as Well?*

There is a city on a hill. Surrounding it is an army that has been besieging it for thousands of years. Some years the army grows and some years the army shrinks, but it is ever present. Trebuchets, catapults, and ballistae continuously fire; the sky is never empty of missiles hurtling to their targets. Some shots go wide or bounce harmlessly off the walls, but some land with devastating results. The dead and maimed lie scattered about. The defending army has manned the walls for centuries, shielding the citizens below, but almost never leave their defensive positions. It seems that they are content to hold fast and never rally their bannermen to sally forth to meet the aggressors on the field.

There are numerous, well-vocalized objections to theism, Christianity, and God in general that apologists have been defending the faith against for centuries. It seems to me that in the landscape of two competing worldviews, one is in the constant position of besieging and the other remains in an almost purely defensive role.

From what I have seen, the standard dialogue is Christian apologists trying to answer the objections of atheists. Rarely is the materialist worldview forced to answer for its shortcomings and unknowns. I saw overwhelming evidence of this during my search but specifically in watching the atheist vs. theist debates. After investing many, many hours watching debates on various topics, I noticed that it was invariably the same format. The atheist threw out an impactful sound bite and then sat back as the theist would flail around scrambling to compress thousands of hours of thought and reason into an understandable and compelling answer that would hopefully refute the sceptic's claim. All while being limited to the allotted 60 seconds! Consistently, I found that the atheist appeared to control the forum, and the theist was constantly scrambling. Much later in my process of study I found that most of these atheist objections were made for bumper stickers and not for serious discussion. Namely that they were wild exaggerations, things taken terribly out of context or logically incoherent—but boy, they sure sounded powerful! I have clearly found some atheist objections to have meat on their bones, but my point is that most of the content of the debates was not real discussion items, but instead pithy—but memorable—one liners purely intended to score points and put the theist on the defensive.

It is almost bizarre that, even though atheists are only about 3% of the population, they have the attitude and swagger that their position is the default, and that theists are the ones who must prove their case. I always found myself focusing on the hard questions to justify belief in God's existence until one day, I started to also really look at the critical failures in the other option, the materialist worldview. As I started to investigate, I found that the best place to start is right here between my ears with an extension of the problem of evil, the problem of beauty.

I have a friend who used to be a missile commander at NORAD—you know, the guys who have the keys to launch our nuclear missiles. Like most who deal with life and death, he is not an overly emotional or soft type of fellow, and yet he cries every time he hears Handel's *Messiah*. Or consider when people who go camping, away from the haze of pollution and background light of the cities and are a bit overwhelmed by the majesty of the night sky. I took a road trip driving from Dallas back up to New York one spring. About 10 hours out, I remember the black asphalt roads climbing and winding along the sides of more than hills but less than mountains. What was truly spectacular was looking out across the valleys, with the sun beginning to drop, setting off the landscape of lush, green trees and rolling hills offset by deep dark shadows. It was truly breathtaking, and I remember this scene 20 years later as if it was yesterday. I also remember once spending most of the day at the Guggenheim Museum in New York City. Between the exhibit of the "Masticated Vaginas," which was about 300 pieces of chewed gum individually molded to form "vaginas" and stuck on a nondescript board, and the extreme closeup video of a homeless man's mouth, who clearly had not performed any dental hygiene for an extended period of time and demonstrated grossly exaggerated open-mouth chewing, I was unimpressed. While not physically painful, it was a horrific experience.

If we are simply matter and energy and purely the result of the evolutionary genetic cage match, unthinking, unguided mutations promoting advantages for survival, why would that landscape burn into my memory? I was not memorizing strategic advantages in the event of a fight. I was not identifying game or other food sources. I didn't look for shelter. It was purely a dazzling thing of beauty. Plenty of people think the exhibits in the Guggenheim are masterpieces of art and expression, why do I have a distinctly different reaction?

The immediate response from materialists (to pretty much any objection) is that it evolved over centuries as a layered benefit of survival. Pushing them past the standard response yields little result. My question is: why do we appreciate beauty? The experience of beauty is purely a distraction away from things that would be of benefit to reproduction and so, it is a detriment. If I take a moment to admire a landscape or gape in awe of the heavens and I lose out on a morsel, mate, or get bonked on the head, it has clearly not served me well in the quest for survival.

To explain away the mind-brain issue, materialists have turned to three main schools of thought. First, there was behaviorism where human behavior is the result of conditioning caused by our interaction with the environment. All behaviors can be explained by observable and measurable laws and behaviors can be changed with the proper stimuli.[20] That stimuli are the only thing that matters, regardless of the individual traits and thinking patterns. This was dominant in the first half of the 20th century but has been abandoned. A quite plausible case can be made that behaviorism was the only scientific theory that was destroyed by a joke. It goes 'After a night of passion, one behaviorist turns to the other and says "That was good for you. How was it for me?"'[21]

> "....the brain evolved to create the seamless illusion of mental function."
>
> *Steven Novella*
> *(The Illusion of Consciousness)*

Next came Identity Theory in which our physical states are identical to our mental states. The burn that you feel when touching a hot pan is the same thing as the neurotransmitters firing in your brain. Not caused by or related to, they are the exact same thing. There are a few flavors of Identity Theory, but they all violate the Identity of Indiscernibles, a basic rule of logic in that things that are the same must be identical in all respects. The

Identity of Indiscernibles, also known as "Leibniz's Law" after Wilhelm Gottfried Leibniz, states that no two things will have exactly the same properties.[22] Clearly, the nerves being stimulated by the hot pan is not the same thing as feeling a burn.

The current way to get around the apparent difference between mind (thought) and brain (physical) is to claim that there is no mind at all, only the physical mental state. There is no such thing as a mind or thoughts, just matter; this is commonly referred to as Eliminative Materialism. There is no feeling the burning of one's finger, there is only a state of excited nerves that we package up as 'burning'. This isn't limited to just the feeling of burning, pain, joy, pleasure, this is everything. There is no me, there is no you. There are only states of physical receptors being tricked into thinking that we exist. This seems like another self-contradictory proposal. If there is no mind, how do you believe that this is true? I don't find this compelling at all.

How does the Dalai Lama order a hot dog? He asks for 'one with everything'! Ok, take a minute and enjoy that. In a materialist world, there is nothing beyond the physical. So where did 'oneness' come from? When I think of 'one', I see the hyperinflated 3-D '1' in 1970s color, zoom into view, probably courtesy of Schoolhouse Rock. Oneness is not the physical representation of the number one. It's not one walnut, one computer, or one idea. It's not, as in the Dalai Lama's case, a sense of unity. The root of oneness is the very real thing that defines singularity (not cosmic) as twoness defines there being two of something. It's that something can exist as one. They are much more than ideas or properties; they are more like foundational elements for our rational thought and of mathematics. Before the universe was even created, oneness had to exist. Oneness was never created or invented; it has existed for all time and was discovered by humanity. I am not talking about a mutual agreement that if there is X X, then we would say that there are two Xs. This is far deeper than that level. This is at the root of being something that can exist as two. As they have no physical form, they exist outside of matter and energy. How is that explained in a materialist worldview where everything is limited to consist of matter and energy?

Another line of reasoning that I found compelling was due to the research of Wilder Penfield, the pioneer in surgery for epilepsy. First, in all the hundreds of thousands of cases of epilepsy that he studied, the epileptic seizures always manifested in a physical effect such as twitching of arms, numbness, or light sensations. Not once was there any logic, arithmetic, moral, or intellectual thought. It is expected for someone having a seizure to lose control of a limb, their whole body, fall to the floor, lose consciousness or some other physical manifestation. What has never been observed is someone having an uncontrollable math, logic, morality, or mercy seizure where the area of the mind that controls abstract thought is affected; it always, and only, affects the concrete.[23]

Secondly, he performed brain surgery more than a thousand times. In each surgery he electrically stimulated the brain hundreds of times, and all the stimulations resulted in physical movements, flashes of light, or recollection of memories. He was never able to stimulate reason or any other abstract thought. Note that brain surgery does not cause pain so the patient remains awake and communicative with the surgeon. He concluded that if the brain was the source of abstract thought, he would have triggered it, and since he didn't, "the obvious explanation for that is that abstract thought doesn't come from the brain."[24]

Furthermore, no seizure has ever been expressed in reason or an abstract thought such as mathematics. If the mind and brain are one, consisting purely of physical neurons, then everything in human experience should be susceptible to stimulation. While it is possible that the regions of the brain for higher thought were not reached, or even that multiple regions need to be stimulated simultaneously to achieve reason or logic, I find that unlikely. The results of his extensive experiments strongly suggest that the mind and brain have some level of separation. It is also interesting to note that Dr. Penfield was a committed materialist but after 30 years of study became a dedicated dualist, believing there to be a difference between the mind and the brain.[25]

I firmly believe in dualism. Since there is a difference between the mind and the brain, then there is more than just matter and energy. This does nothing to promote theism or Christianity, but it is, again, quite problematic for materialism-atheism.

| # *Is the Universe a Result of Chance, Necessity, or Design?*

When I was little, there were still working farms not that far from my house. Some days, my mom would load my brother and me into the car and drive out to the farm stand to purchase various types of produce, but especially for the tomatoes. A truly vine-ripened tomato is out of this world. I am not talking about the "we cut off a segment of the vine still attached to the unripe green tomatoes just so we can boast that it is vine-ripened" variety in the supermarket. Think about it, as there are no nutrients being passed from a cut vine, and then when they are packed in the crate and loaded into the truck, there is no sunlight, and that sunlight is what is converted into sugars as part of the natural ripening process that makes it sweet. A "vine-ripened" tomato at the supermarket is really just a green tomato and desiccated vine that was gassed with ethylene to turn its skin red, so it looks appealing. Fresh tomatoes, on the other hand, are so good that when I drove a truck in college delivering caskets (they were empty, of course!) to the funeral homes all over upstate NY, Vermont, and Massachusetts, I would often pull over at the local farm stands for tomatoes and eat them like an apple. That is how good they are. (By the way, I wish I had pictures of people's faces when I passed them on the highway when they saw my brightly emblazoned Batesville Caskets signage, with a nice graphic of their offerings on the side of the truck.)

As many of the local "farmers' markets" are a sham (look under their tables for the crates stamped "imported from Mexico"....), I decided that the only way that I was going to get a good tomato was to do it myself. Frankly, my yard isn't very big but would still be workable for a garden. The problem is that my dog Chester *is* very big, and when another dog has the audacity to walk anywhere within 300 yards of the house, he goes full Cujo berserk. I know that no plant in the yard could ever hope to survive that. Also, knowing myself, I knew that I would, at some point, get distracted and forget to water the plants for a few days which, in the heat of Texas, is tantamount to a death sentence. Between bludgeoning, dehydration, and heat, planting a regular garden was clearly folly.

I turned to building a hydroponic garden. Hydroponic gardens contain no soil, the plants are suspended over/in a flowing nutrient-rich water source. Now we're talking! I bought some PVC plastic pipes, water pumps, clay pellets, wood and got to work. I built a 12-foot-long three-tier rack that has four-inch-diameter pipe running down each length. A pump pushes the water to the beginning of the top pipe to start the process. On each level, there are valves to control the water height in each pipe. Seedlings need the water level higher so that it reaches their roots while established plants need it lower so that some of their roots remain in the air to get oxygen. At the end of each pipe, there is tubing to allow the water to flow from the first pipe, down to the second due to gravity, across the plant's roots in the second and then drop down to the third—it makes a giant 'S'. At the end of its travels, it dumps back into the 40-gallon reservoir where the pump pushes it to the top to start all over again! The water is highly enriched with a nutrient blend geared to whatever stage the plants are in, rooting, foliage growth, or fruiting. Just to be snazzy, I have a line off my sprinkler system, on its own zone, so that every night it activates for a few minutes to top off the water and keep the system from running dry. Frankly, I was amazed when I plugged it in and it all worked perfectly, but it did! The only intervention that is needed is to put fertilizer in the tank occasionally. As there is a constant flow of nutrients, oxygen, water and sunlight, this garden grows at an absurd rate. All I really need to do is plug it in and sit back and watch the show.

From the first moment of the Big Bang, everything unfolded to get us to where we are today. The initial conditions of the universe and even the laws of nature were established 'just right' so that everything, from the very small to the large, moved at the speed, density, and force which would unfold into this universe and later, make life possible.

My perception was that at the moment of the Big Bang, the universe expanded from the instantaneous flash of light and heat in much the same state that it is in today. I always imagined a point in space (which is wrong from the start because there was no space, there was nothing....) that suddenly exploded, spewing out the stars and planets. They flowed out from the single point, expanding as they went, until they found their place in the universe and sort of put on the brakes and came to rest in their orbits and so on. There is nothing correct about this assumption.

The Big Bang resulted in the release of an enormous amount of energy in the form of light and heat. Our calculations only allow us to understand the universe starting at a moment named the Planck time (named after the famous physicist Max Planck), which is 10 million trillion trillion trillionths of a second. Don't be fooled into thinking that this is the same as the start, in those initial conditions, things happened very, very fast. At Planck time, the temperature was 180 million trillion trillion degrees Fahrenheit. So, how did we get from there to here?

At a very high level, here is the timeline from the start of the universe:

Time elapsed	Event
0 seconds	Big Bang
10^{-43} seconds *(Planck time)*	Gravity separates from the 3 other forces[26]
10^{-35} seconds	Universe expands at an amazing rate
10^{-6} seconds	Strong and weak nuclear forces separate from the electromagnetic force (they hold atoms together); subatomic particles form and gain mass
1 second	Protons and neutrons form
3 minutes	Formation of the first elements, mostly hydrogen and helium
380,000 years	The universe has cooled enough for protons and neutrons to capture electrons.
30 million years	Stars form; in the furnace of the stars, heavy elements are formed
200 million years	Milky Way forms
9 billion years	Earth's solar system forms
13.8 billion years	Today
13.83 billion years	Devin finishes this writing project

What I find truly awe-inspiring about the way that the universe came to be is that all the processes to get from the Big Bang to here were set "just right" as to empower the next step. It's like a cosmic set of dominoes where each must fall just right or the whole thing fails—or a hydroponic garden where when it's ready to go, you simply plug in and sit back and watch the show. Just as if there were any failures with my hydroponic garden then the whole thing wouldn't work—whether the pump wasn't powerful enough to move the water, moved too little water or, conversely, pumped too fast so as to overflow the pipes and therefore run the system dry, the water intake vents got plugged with debris from the roots after running for a few minutes, had leaks in the piping, there was too much nutrient mix and it burned the roots, too little food and the plants starved, or a host of other terminal options—if any of the steps failed in creating the universe, the whole process would have failed. Like the mystifying harmony of the cycles that we see in the cell, plants, animals, and the planet as a whole, getting here relied on 'just-right' conditions.

In modern physics, there is a set of fundamental constants that are completely independent of other factors. In other words, they are the core of our reality. Some examples are the charge of a proton or electron, the Planck constant which relates the photon's energy to its frequency, or the speed of light. These, and the others, were hard-coded into the laws of physics instantiated at the first moments of the universe. They are like base units; they don't rely on anything to combine to shape them. At this point, physicists understand that there are more than 20 such constants. Our best scientific theories can't explain why they have their particular values, but we are able to measure them with precision, and we are certain of their values. It is also important to note that these constants could have had a very, very wide range of values, each one just happened to be set to a very, very precise value in a wide, wide field of possible values. What is incredible is that changing any of the values for any of a dozen or so of these constants, even a minuscule amount, would have resulted in a non-life permitting universe.

Physicists have computed that the values for at least a dozen of these constants needed to be set to be within a very, very narrow range. Even a minor variation outside that range would have been catastrophic. Catastrophic in this context does not mean a universe that is not necessarily supportive of human life or life as we know it. It means having an environment where any type of life would be impossible. Even the smallest change results in scenarios where only hydrogen atoms exist, the universe is so diffuse that particles are billions of light years apart and so are never close enough together to interact and form atoms, or the entire thing collapses into itself as fast as it expanded, a big crunch to the Big Bang. Again, if these constants fall outside their acceptable thresholds, you would not be here reading this book.

I was at an atheist-Christian book club meeting—it's an interesting concept where the book selection rotates monthly between the Christians and atheists, and then the whole group gets together to discuss their thoughts. Overall, it was a positive group, very polite and respectful to each other, but this meeting was regarding a book that contained scientific information on fine-tuning. As they brought up the conditions to make life possible, one person quickly and loudly objected, "Yeah, for life as WE know it!." Sigh. It drives me nuts when someone doesn't learn the basics of a topic and then is very vocal, and seemingly arrogant, about their objections. The fine-tuning is at a level that is much more elementary to reality; it is not if beings would have two arms and legs or look more like squids or even something as wild as silicon-based life instead of carbon. While this is a popular idea, it doesn't reduce the level of fine-tuning required. Fine-tuning does not debate what types of life there could be, it analyzes things such as if atoms would exist at all—so that there would even be silicon. When the conclusion is that it is not a life permitting universe, it is because the resulting environment would not have the possibility of things, like atoms, that are essential for the building blocks of life. Tweaking those constants by the tiniest fraction usually results in a universe whose elementary particles are so diffuse as to never come close enough to each other to even form atoms (light years apart), one that collapses in upon itself or some other scenarios that are equally disastrous. Our universe seems not only conditioned for life but is set up within an incredibly small window that would allow for any life at all. This is known as the fine-tuning argument, and I find this to be extremely compelling.

This topic is a fun but daunting one for me to discuss. First, it is fun because this is based on modern physics. It is cutting-edge cosmology; cosmology being the study of the physics of the universe, not applying makeup to someone's face (that's cosmetology). It appeals to me as it is science-based, but it is also daunting, as the true physics behind it is well beyond my bachelor's level of study. To understand it to the depth that I am able to confidently say that I agree or disagree, and therefore have it influence my belief system, requires me to invest extensively in learning the material (and relearning the stuff that I was supposed to learn, but was too busy being "cool" at the bar instead of studying, sigh).

> "The entire universe is balanced on a knife-edge, and would be total chaos if any of the natural 'constants' were off even slightly."
>
> **Paul Davies**
> *(Agnostic Physicist)*

I am doing my absolute best to be completely transparent with my thoughts and feelings and feel that I have been cautious not to overstate any subjective beliefs as objective facts, but as I said, the statements relating to fine-tuning are based on physics: therefore measurable, quantifiable, and verifiable. They are absolutes—there is no wiggle room or feelings in physics—although often physicists position their personal opinions under their scientific authority. I did find the book *A Fortunate Universe* by Geraint Lewis and Luke Barnes to be a

> "Every gambler knows
> The secret to survivin'
> Is knowin' what to throw away
> And knowin' what to keep
>
> 'Cause every hand's a winner
> And every hand's a loser
> And the best that you can hope for
> Is to die in your sleep."
>
> **Kenny Rogers**
> *(The Gambler)*

fantastic resource. First, it was an in-depth look at how physics justifies the claims. Second, it was written as a collaboration between an atheist and a Christian. There is no dispute regarding the physics and the physical consequences but, clearly, they differed in the perceived implications.

When we talk about the denominators of probability for the constants being in a life-permitting range, we deal with absurdly big numbers. Remember, probabilities are expressed as the decimal value of fractions. All that means is: $\frac{(number\ of\ successful\ events)}{(total\ number\ of\ events)}$ So, if we're talking about a coin flip where we want heads, it is just the number of possible successes (heads), so 1 in this case out of the total number of events, which is 2 (heads or tails). So, the probability would be ½ or 50%.

If I rolled a six-sided die and wanted the odds of getting a 1 or 2, it would be:

Number of successful events:	2
Total number of events:	6

The probability of rolling a 1 or 2 would be $\frac{2}{6}$ = ⅓ *or* 33%.

So, the larger the denominator, the bottom number, is, the more unlikely the event is to occur.

As a point of note, I am explaining the magnitude of probabilities just to get our arms around the size, or lack thereof, of the number ranges that we are considering. These probabilities are not used to calculate the likelihood of our universe as that is 100%; we know that because we exist! The point is that to get our universe, the constants had to be set within thresholds around the sizes that we are calculating. When I see the numbers relating to fine-tuning that are of this magnitude, so far outside of our frame of reference, I lose the ability to relate to them. It's like the United States' debt, I know that 36 trillion dollars is a huge sum, but to be honest, no matter how much I look at it, I really have no perspective—and trillions (1,000,000,000,000) represented in exponential form are only 10^{12}. Sure, I can mathematically work with exponential numbers in calculations, but I do not think that I relate to them in a personal way. For this part to be truly meaningful, I need to find a way so that absurdly big numbers, such as 10^{12}, and ones much, much larger than that, become understandable on a personal level. In an attempt to bridge the gap between logically understanding the numbers and being able to actually relate to them, bridging the logical and emotional sides, I am going to convert to something that I hope people have some experience with.

If you have ever played poker, you know that a royal (straight) flush is very hard to get. A royal flush is a sequence of Ten, Jack, Queen, King and Ace with all the cards of the same suit—Hearts, Diamonds, Spades or Clubs (all natural, no cheesy wild cards!). The actual probability is that there are four royal flush hands (all four suits considered) in 2,598,960 possible hands. Technically, we could sit down, and you could be dealt a royal flush on the very first hand but for each of the 2,598,960 possible hands, four would be winners while 2,598,956 would be losers.[27] After doing a fraction simplification by dividing the top and bottom by 4, it is a 1 in 649,740 chance when dealt five cards to get a royal flush. Pretty remote, right?

To make it more relatable, to lay out 649,740 hands of poker: you would need to be dealt one hand every 20 seconds, or three per minute, just enough time to see your hand, for 216,580 minutes. That equates to 3,610 hours so if you play 10 hours a day with no breaks (so don't drink much before you start), it will take about 361 straight days, or almost a full year. Note that probability deals with the future, and it only shows the odds. The odds of getting a royal flush is being dealt one hand and hoping that it's the magic one from the array of three hands per minute, 10-hour days equal about a year of poker hands. Another way of thinking about it is if I said guess a number between 1 and 649,740. While technically possible, I wouldn't bet my life on it.

The first example of fine-tuning of the universe is the gravitational force constant, which is the attractive force between matter on a large scale, such as keeping my computer down on my desk or holding the Earth together. If it was too weak, then planets could not form at all. If it was too strong, stars would burn out too fast.[28]

Stars are incredibly important for life for a variety of reasons, one being that in the furnace of stars, critical heavy elements are produced. When one realizes that a star is basically a nuclear fusion bomb held together by gravity it isn't surprising that the balance of the forces needs to be extremely precise, or fine-tuned. As they are so important, scientists have long studied the requirements for stars to be stable. In stars, matter is compressed by gravity but held apart by the Coulomb barrier, the repulsion from the positive charge of protons interacting with each other. Once ignited, fusion creates life-permitting heavy elements such as carbon, oxygen, and iron. As they analyzed the combinations of the strengths of gravity versus electromagnetism (the force that governs the interactions between charged particles) to see how often they could "balance" the forces to produce stable stars, they found that only about 1 part in 10^{35} of those combinations work.[29] If the ratio of gravity to electromagnetism is weakened, stars could collapse into black holes before the heavy elements were produced. If the ratio was strengthened, the repulsion between protons could stop fusion from happening at all. Think of the importance of our sun to life on Earth, that principle applies everywhere in the universe.

Do not zone out. This is important! I need to give a moment's attention to exponents to really feel the magnitude of these examples, and to do that you need to have a basic understanding of exponents. Exponents are just a simplified way of writing out large numbers. Trying to work with a number such as 1,000,000,000,000 in a mathematical function would be confusing, so the shorthand way to write it is to simply count the zeroes and then write it as $10^{\text{number of zeroes}}$. In this case, there are 12 zeroes so it would be written as 10^{12}. That's it. Stop being a baby, it wasn't that bad.

$10^1 = 10$
$10^2 = 100$
$10^3 = 1,000$
$10^8 = 100,000,000$

The big trick to this is to remember that when you add one to the exponent, the value is multiplied by 10! From 10^2 (100) going to 10^3 is (100 × 10) = 1,000. So, 10^5 is ten times larger than 10^4. I make a big deal about this because I have always found it natural to assume that 10^{34} and 10^{35} were reasonably close in value; after all, it's just going from 34 to 35. It's not. It's *ten times* more. Therefore, 10^{33} to 10^{35} is 100 times more! Also think about it the opposite way, 10^{33} is just 1% of 10^{35}. Make a 10 × 10 grid in your head. (Come on, just go with me and do it!) Pick one box in the entire field and shade it with a different color, that one box represents 1%, or 1 in 100. That one box is not even close in value to the whole field....

If I hear something like 10^{36}, I understand that it mathematically represents a 1 followed by 36 zeroes, but what I really hear is the 36. I can understand 10 and I can understand 36 and so that's what resonates with me, and I just use that, even though I know it's incorrect. Purely thinking about the "36" makes it seem like the odds of 1 in 10^{36} really aren't that bad, right? But that's not what it means at all. Remember that the exponent tells you the number of zeroes to put in and therefore, for each increment of the exponent multiplies it by 10!

Just for fun let's write out the odds of $1/10^{36}$:

1 chance in 1,000,000,000,000,000,000,000,000,000,000,000,000

Or let's compare 1 million, which we can somewhat understand, and 10^{36}.

1 million	1,000,000
10^{36}	1,000,000,000,000,000,000,000,000,000,000,000,000

Can you really relate to a number like that? Me neither!

Like I said, when I look at 10^{36}, I intrinsically know that it's a large number, but I don't really relate to something that large, even when it's written out in front of me. Let's go back to the cosmic poker table. If you sat down at the table with Bob, and on the first hand Bob was dealt a royal flush, I am sure that you would be impressed—and a little jealous. I used to play in a weekly poker game for about a decade and I have never been dealt a royal flush, but there goes Bob hitting it right off the bat. Son of a…. I mean, lucky guy! You would concede the pot, ante up, and look forward to the next hand. The next hand Bob is dealt a royal flush again! Hrmmm…. Ok, improbably lucky, but still technically possible, so you give Bob the benefit of the doubt and play on. You look for the third hand with guarded anticipation and, well, you guessed it, he turns over his cards and he has another royal flush. Three in a row. Hrmmmm…. Are you believing that this is a fair game at this point? This is the equivalent of Bob guessing a number between 1 and 649,740 *three times in a row* or guessing a number between 1 and 274,295,581,802,424,000 correctly. Would you believe this if it happened or would you think that Bob had some way of knowing the numbers beforehand?

Oh, look at that, three royal flushes in a row, no four! Five?! At what point do you say that this has been fixed to deal Bob a royal flush every time? (If you say more than two, please forward your contact information as I would like to invite you to a weekly poker game!) How about the sixth royal flush in a row? That's pretty close to 1 in 10^{36} but to take care of the fractions, it's pretty fair to say that it also has to happen on a Tuesday. Six royal flushes in a row on a Tuesday, that's still less than, but close to 10^{36}. If I was playing poker and the other guy dealt themselves a royal flush 6 times in a row, I can't imagine believing that it was an honest game. My belief that this was set up, or designed, would be justified!

Now, we're trying to get our arms around how small a probability it is to get six royal flushes in a row on a Tuesday. We need to visualize the idea that this number represents a very small range of workable values within an incredibly large range of possible values. So, we have a very, very wide range of values and our "sweet spot" has a window of 10^{36}. The power of gravity was set so that if it was 1 in 10^{36} weaker, then stars are unstable. Any one of the other 649,739 possibilities in any one of the six hands and we have no stable stars.

If gravity was even a smaller amount stronger at 10^{40} (Remember the difference between 10^{36} and 10^{40} is 10 x 10 x 10 x 10 or 10,000 more precise.), then there are no stars, only black holes. That is how precise these constants that govern our reality must be.[30]

Please note that I only point to the odds of a card hand because that helps me get the feel of the minuscule piece out of the enormous set of possible values. The fine-tuning isn't a probability, the numbers that we see are constant, measured, and very real. The point is that these minuscule numbers represent the size of the window that the value had to fall into for that constant to allow for a life-possible universe. The necessary precision for most of the constants is like having that aforementioned tape measure that runs across the entire galaxy with all the possible values labeled from end to end. If you pick a spot for your constant, the precision is so fine that if the value changes either an inch to the left or right, out of the whole galaxy, it is out of the workable range. Out of all the possible values, the size of the window for the gravitational constant to avoid disaster is between:

.000000000000000000000000000000010000 and .000000 0000000000000000000000000000001.

That's a pretty small window.

Another way that I have found that makes the numbers somewhat relatable, is to take a Home Depot-sized bucket and fill it with sand. Paint one grain red and mix it in. Close your eyes and grab a grain. Wipe all the sand from your hands and arms and think about how small that grain of sand is pinched between your fingers. The bucket of sand represents about 43 million grains, or 4.3×10^7. Let's make a sand pile over all of Europe and Asia and as high as the moon. (Don't worry that a pile that high would fall over, it's a thought experiment!) Next, dump your bucket with the single red grain of sand in and mix thoroughly. Now you would have to pick that red grain of sand out of all of that. Picked the red one? Amazing! Now do it in a pile five times larger and that's about the right odds as 10^{36}.[31]

If it were simply the gravitational constant in isolation, there would be the temptation to dismiss its incredibly fine precision as simply luck. We won the cosmic lottery! Sure, the odds were small, but a single point, no matter how fine, could possibly be attributed to coincidence. Where the fine-tuning argument really becomes overwhelming is that there are at least 12 such constants critical for life. For this universe to be life-permitting, or even to exist at all, *every one* of these incredibly precise ranges has to be set within a very narrow range. Oh, and 10^{36} is one of the more likely ones.

Stepping back a moment on probabilities, if you flip a coin, you have a one out of two chance for it to be heads, or 50% probability. If you have a wheel that spins with five colors on it (red, blue, green, yellow, and purple), getting one color, let's say red, is a 1 out of 5 chance, or which is 20%. The probability of getting heads on the coin flip and Red on the wheel is calculated by multiplying the ½ for heads and the $\frac{1}{5}$ for red, which is $\frac{1}{2} \times \frac{1}{5} = \frac{1 \times 1}{2 \times 5} = \frac{1}{10}$ or a 10% chance. To be alive today, we need to multiply the probability of the first constant times the second times the third and so on. The constants were calculated independently but when we look at all the incredible precision needed to make our reality "work," all of them have to be set or the whole thing fails. Just to get you started, the first number to use is

$$\frac{1}{1,000,000,000,000,000,000,000,000,000,000,000,000}$$

Atoms are held together by the electromagnetic force, where repulsion between like charges (e.g., electrons) is counterbalanced by the attractive force between opposite charges (e.g., protons and electrons). Well, if they counterbalance each other, what's the point? The atom is balanced so that the electromagnetic force can push the electrons out into their orbits but weak enough so that the attractive force can hold them in place. It is a very, very delicate balance. It's somewhat like the Earth and the moon; the moon's centrifugal force trying to launch it off into space counterbalanced by the gravitational force between the Earth and the moon. (Keep in mind that this is just the picture of the orbits being balanced, not the mechanics.)

> Scientists are slowly waking up to an inconvenient truth—the universe looks suspiciously like a fix. The issue concerns the very laws of nature themselves. For 40 years, physicists and cosmologists have been quietly collecting examples of all too convenient "coincidences" and special features in the underlying laws of the universe that seem to be necessary in order for life, and hence conscious beings, to exist. Change any one of them and the consequences would be lethal. Fred Hoyle, the distinguished cosmologist, once said it was as if "a super-intellect has monkeyed with physics."
>
> To see the problem, imagine playing God with the cosmos. Before you is a designer machine that lets you tinker with the basics of physics. Twiddle this knob and you make all electrons a bit lighter, twiddle that one and you make gravity a bit stronger, and so on. It happens that you need to set thirtysomething knobs to fully describe the world about us. The crucial point is that some

of those metaphorical knobs must be tuned very precisely, or the universe would be sterile.

Example: neutrons are just a tad heavier than protons. If it were the other way around, atoms couldn't exist, because all the protons in the universe would have decayed into neutrons shortly after the Big Bang. No protons, then no atomic nucleuses and no atoms. No atoms, no chemistry, no life. Like Baby Bear's porridge in the story of Goldilocks, the universe seems to be just right for life.[32]

The strong nuclear force constant also helps with holding the nuclei of atoms together by attracting the protons and neutrons and counterbalancing the electromagnetic repulsion (it's the pull balancing the push). If it were 50% weaker, protons couldn't be held together in the nucleus resulting in a vastly reduced periodic table, losing many chemical elements that are necessary for life. If it were 50% stronger, the nuclear fusion of the early universe would have consumed all the hydrogen. Remember the H in H_2O is hydrogen, and water is critical for life. Also, without hydrogen, there are no hydrogen burning stars. These types of stars last 30 times longer than any other, and long-living stars are, again, critical for life. Note that this would not make intelligent life impossible, but very, very difficult to achieve. Even more impressive is that if the strong nuclear force were 2% stronger, protons wouldn't form and so there would be no atoms, and remember atoms are the building blocks of everything! Additionally, if the strong nuclear force was 9% weaker or the ratio of the electromagnetic constant to the strong nuclear force was not less than 0.1 then deuterium (cool name but it's just an atom of hydrogen, the smallest atomic mass of any element, with an extra neutron) would be the biggest atom around!

The weak nuclear force constant governs proton-proton fusion. If it were stronger or weaker, life-essential stars would not form or all the fuel for stars would have been burned through even before the first galaxies were formed. If the weak force had been stronger, the Big Bang would have produced iron instead of helium and so, fusion-powered stars would not be possible. Heavy elements, which are essential for life, are formed in the furnace of stars and spread across the galaxy by supernovae exploding. If the ratio of the weak nuclear force to strong force was changed by 1 in 10,000, supernova would not explode, and therefore the main mechanism for the disbursal of the heavy elements wouldn't exist.[33]

Another is the cosmological constant, which controls the expansion speed of the universe. It is the balance between the attractive force of gravity and the repulsive force of dark energy. The universe needed to expand at a rate that was not too fast, nor too slow. The range of values that would have allowed a long-lived universe to form is one part in 10^{90}. If it were greater than this, the universe would have flown apart and been just a diffuse gas of particles. If it were smaller, the universe would have collapsed into itself.[34]

I will throw out a fun fact, if you take all the atoms in your body, wait, no the state of Texas to the depth of one mile—we're talking every single atom—and count them.... just kidding. We do need to count every single atom, but not of Texas, not even of the Earth, not our solar system either, keep going, not our galaxy of millions of stars and solar systems, but the entire universe of billions of stars—the whole enchilada—and count every single atom, we get 10^{80}. If we're being technical, this number is obviously the estimate that scientists calculated as no one has gone around and physically counted every atom!

You can't see an atom as it is too small and neither can you see the entire universe because it is too large, and we're talking about counting all of the very smalls in the very large. Now, remember that 10^{81} is *ten* times bigger than 10^{80} and 10^{82} is *ten* times larger than that, so keep going until you get to 10^{90}. That is just one of the constants of physics that is precisely set allowing the possibility of a life-permitting universe. It's okay, I said 'holy cow!' when I first went through this too.

Protons and neutrons are comprised of subunits called quarks. The protons' and neutrons' masses are primarily determined by the masses of their constituent quarks and the strong force binding energy. If the ratio of their masses were slightly different, fine-tuned to 1 in 10^{35}, it would disrupt the stability of atomic nuclei and prevent the formation of carbon-based molecules. The building blocks of life, such as DNA, would not form. The proton-neutron mass difference is critical for nuclear stability, nucleosynthesis (the formation of elements in stars), and the behavior of atomic nuclei. Changing the mass ratio could catastrophically disrupt these processes. It is theorized that if it was off by 1 in 10^{37}, then there would be no planets or stars.

You may feel that you are reading the same thing over and over. Yes, the window for each of these values to permit life is ridiculously small and the result of missing the window always seems to be that there are no atoms, no stars, but only black holes, or that everything collapses back into itself. That is what they mean by it is not a life-permitting universe, if any of the constants or ratios lose that incredible level of precision, the results are disastrous.

At the moment of the Big Bang, the what-is-to-be-the-universe expanded at an alarming rate but there was also a force pulling it back in. It needed to be fast enough to get past the attractive force pulling it together, but not so fast as to spin away and not be dense enough to let atoms form. Think of it as a rocket leaving the Earth. When it launches, it needs to go fast enough to break free from Earth's gravity, but not so fast that it goes off into space forever. If this rate was off by 1 in 10^{55}, the universe would have either spun off with particles never finding each other to form atoms or it would have, like a rocket without enough force to overcome gravity, come crashing back together. There is a potential argument that this can be accounted for by something called inflation, but even if that is true, inflation needs to be fine-tuned, which simply pushes the problem back one level.

Einstein's famous equation $E=mc^2$ states that you can convert between matter and energy. At the Big Bang, there was a massive release of all the energy that would later be converted into matter used to make planets and stars in every galaxy in the whole universe. All the energy for two trillion galaxies of hundreds of billions of stars, and the planets orbiting these stars, suddenly appeared as light and heat. This is called the energy density of the universe. In one moment, it was just there: from nothing to all the energy for everything in an instant.

This energy density at the start of the universe, which you can also think of as matter, needed to be fine-tuned to 1 part in 10^{55}. So, what does that really mean? The starting energy to make *everything* is so precise that if we added, or took away, just the mass of your body, the universe would have failed. Either gravity would have pulled everything back in, again like the rocket not having enough boost to leave the Earth, or we get the diffuse universe again. Think about the mass of your body compared to the entire mass of the planets and the stars in all the galaxies of the universe. The difference of just your body's mass either way and the universe doesn't work. I find this unfathomable in the truest sense of the word. So, full disclosure, there are theories that claim that shortly after the Big Bang the universe went through a brief period of rapid expansion, called cosmic inflation. If cosmic inflation did happen as theorized, then the energy density fine tuning could potentially be explained. The issue is that if cosmic inflation is true, it looks like it would require extensive fine-tuning as well, so it just pushes the issue back one level.[35]

When the odds are less than 1 in 10^{50}, they are considered to verge on zero probability or, using a more conventional term, impossible. Clearly a life-supporting universe is unlikely to the point of beyond belief, but here we are.

I feel like I need to take a moment to make sure that something is abundantly clear: the physics discussed herein is not in dispute; these are hard facts. Some use this argument for an absolute "proof" of God's existence. Others dismiss these arguments as they feel that it is just a theological shell game. Neither is really a fair assessment; these are the core facts, and it is up to us to draw conclusions from them.

I remember reading about the fine-tuning argument and how infinitesimally remote the probability is to have not even a life-permitting universe, but any universe at all, and someone arrogantly declaring, "The probability is 1, because we're here to observe it!" This is an incredibly naïve way to try to counter this argument. Clearly, we are here, but just as clearly, the almost immeasurably precise dials were set just so to make this all possible. The fact that we are here did not cause this to happen. Our observation has no power over causation.

Let's say that you took your yearly family vacation to sunny North Korea and while you were there, made the mistake of saying that you thought their Supreme Leader was a knucklehead. Later, when you were against the wall and heard the bang from the rifles of the firing squad, I am sure you would be amazed to still be alive. If 500 different groups of riflemen came in, one after another, and they all missed, you would be foolish to assume that they *had* to miss just because you were still alive to observe that they had missed? Wouldn't you believe that there was something else going on?

Since the constants are independent of each other, and each one must be set within its specific precision range, multiplying all the thresholds of the constants for them all to have been set precisely will result in a number that I won't even bother to calculate. This is so remote that it must have come from physical necessity, an incredibly high number of chances, or design.

Physical necessity states that the constants had to have the values that they do, there was no other choice. As they were required to have these values, the universe had to be life-permitting and conversely, a non-life-permitting universe is impossible. While the idea is not logically incoherent, to date, no one has been able to find any reason as to why the constants would be physically necessary.

One of my buddies, Chris, didn't do so well with the ladies. What he lacked in looks, he easily made up for in guts. We would see him going up to girls and trying to chat them up over and over just to be unmercifully and continually shot down. Sometimes, the bar was like a human pinball machine as he went from one girl to the next, across the bar, bouncing here and there, only moving on with the inevitable rejection. What Chris knew was that even though he wasn't the best-looking fellow and was not blessed with the gift of gab like one of my other friends (of whom we were all jealous), his chances were not zero. While remote, it was possible to meet someone that he liked and liked him in return, so it was just a game of numbers. He was right. Sooner or later, he would usually meet someone.

There are some who believe that what appears to be designed is simply a random coincidence. If given enough time and chances, even something with an absurdly low probability will happen. Go Chris! Since you simply cannot argue with the findings that the probability of the universe being life-bearing, or even existing, is absurdly low, one option is that there are an infinite number of chances, and we just happen to be in the one with the winning lottery ticket. If I gave you 500 billion randomly generated lottery tickets for this week's drawing, you would most likely have a winning ticket. The idea, termed the multiverse, is that our universe is only one in a vast assemblage of universes.[36]

When I first heard this, and it is proposed by some very impressive names in physics, I had to give it consideration. While usually stuff for sci-fi movies, especially when they write themselves into a plot corner and need a way out– oh, our plot makes no sense, and we need this character, but he died already so.... this one is another version of him from the multiverse! –the actual multiverse theory is a real thing. To be honest, I hate talking about this idea because I know that there are some very intelligent physicists who promote it (but many don't either) but I find it so incredibly unpersuasive that I look at it with disdain. To me, it looks like a fantasy created to avoid something that they don't want to accept. I constantly give the benefit of the doubt and feel that it must be me, I must be missing something, but every time I look into it further, it demonstrates itself to have absolutely no merit. First, while this is a "theory," it really isn't science as it is impossible to test. There is absolutely zero, and I mean zero-point-zero-zero-zero, evidence to remotely suggest that this is the way reality functions. Furthermore, there is no reason to think that even if a multiverse exists that it would necessarily do away with fine-tuning. Additionally, there is nothing remotely close to an agreed upon theory. So far, we've found fine-tuning at every level of investigation. There isn't even the 'intuitive sense' argument to be made that this is true. While some proofs are mathematically 'sound', to make it work, they had to imagine another dimension that supposedly is either hidden or only existed at the beginning of the universe, but no one has ever seen. Seriously?

I keep thinking that it must be me, but it seems nuts to think that it is scientifically sound to add in imagined dimensions because that is the only way that your math works to end up with the result that you were looking for. I always thought that you were supposed to start with evidence (or at least a hypothesis) and draw conclusions, not start with your desired conclusion and find a way to make it work, even if that requires adding new dimensions. Remember dimensions are things like length, width, height, time, spin and so on. To me, it's on par with saying that I have a theory that you need to take seriously, but in order for it to work, there are not only length, width and height like you are familiar with but a 4th size dimension called DevinSpace that I envisioned, and, oh, DevinSpace is hidden so that we can't detect it. Buying what I am selling? Me either. Who spilled the milk and didn't bother to clean it up? It's those guys from that hidden dimension! Oh, okay.

Additionally, the multiverse theory also predicts that the parameters would be set at the minimum for what is necessary for life however, our reality demonstrates that many parameters are more fine-tuned than required. This is actual evidence *against* a multiverse.

The next problem is that for this universe-creating "machine" to function, it would need fine-tuned constraints for it to generate as well, but this

> "It's not even a theory . . . . it's a collection of hopes."
>
> **Roger Penrose**
> *(Interview with Ian Sample)*

machine was supposed to be the defeater of the universe being finely tuned. I guess to explain that, we could call on some machine to create the universe creating machine, but that would need to be fine-tuned, so we could call on some machine to create....

Entropy is simply the measure of disorder in a system. Things travel from a state of low entropy to high entropy; you can just look at it as usable energy. A ceramic coffee cup is in a state of order, low entropy. Knock the coffee cup off the counter with your elbow and you will meet a state of disorder as the cup crashes, and shatters, on the floor—a state of high entropy. It is very easy to go from the fully formed coffee cup to shards of porcelain, but very hard to go from shards of porcelain to a fully formed coffee cup. A state of low entropy allows the release of usable energy as it travels from low to high and that energy is needed to build the universe. While there is a range of values that do create a window to produce a universe where life is possible, that we have a state of such low entropy is startling. How unlikely is it that the universe started in a state of such order with so much usable energy? Why do we have such a low state of entropy when the multiverse theory predicts otherwise?

Roger Penrose, who worked closely with Stephen Hawking, calculated the odds of the universe having the initial low entropy conditions that we find in our universe. His calculations show that the odds of having entropy such as ours is 1 in 10 to the 10^{123}. This is calculated by 10 with the exponent being 1 followed by 123 zeroes. Now, that's a lot of zeroes![37]

$10^{1,000,000,000,000,000,000,000,000,000,000,000,000,000,000,000,000,000,000,000,000,000,000,000,000,000,000,000,000,000,000,000,000,000,000,000,000,000,000,000}$

Typing this number out would require spending trillions of years hitting the "0" key. Actually, my co-math-spirit friend Allen pointed out that if everyone on Earth (rounded up to 10 billion people) hit the "0" key 6 times per second for a trillion years, we would need to do those trillion year "sessions"

$$365 * 24 * 3600 * 6 * 10^{10} * 10^{12} = 1.89^{30}$$

1,890,000,000,000,000,000,000,000,000,000,000,000,00 0,000,000,000,000,000,000,000,000,000,000,000,000,0 00,000,000 times to type out all the zeroes.

Simply put, I believe that this is a number that is beyond possible. Remember that the number of particles in all the atoms in the whole universe is an estimated measly 10^{80}. In summary:

Number of atoms in the entire universe	10^{80}
Probability of having the initial conditions of low entropy (1 in)	$10^{1,000,000,000,000,000,000,000,000,000,000,000,000,000,000,000,000,000,000,000,000,000,000,000,000,000,000,000,000,000,000,000,000,000,000,000,000,000,000,000,000,000,000}$

Some people think, "But life will find a way!" to which the very clear answer is "No, it won't" because there will be no life to start with. If someone thinks that life is destined to be and that it will create itself out of individual particles or black holes, then they are acting like a naturalist zealot who doesn't listen to reason. Holding out hope that a diffuse universe will in some way create life in some way that we can't even imagine is just putting chips on some hidden knowledge because they find the conclusions uncomfortable. By the way, there are plenty of papers out there that go through every scenario imaginable, and every one of them concludes that the analyzed scenario fails miserably.

If it was not necessity and was too remote for a random chance to be believed, then the only other option is that it must have been intentional. Intention indicates being designed and if it was designed, then it logically has to have a designer. This designer has to be intelligent beyond comprehension to imagine everything from the intricacies of constants, forces, and interwoven cycles from the very small to the very large, all working in concert. The designer has to be powerful to be able to actually create the universe out of nothing and to the specification described above. The designer must be timeless as time only came into being at the Big Bang and the designer existed before the Big Bang. The designer must be personal as there is good evidence that everything unfolded with the intention that there would be life. Because the numerous values must fall with a very, very narrow range and if even one was off, the universe would not exist, the extreme improbability has led many to believe that it could not be mere chance, instead, it was fine-tuned for our existence by God.

Just by looking at the numbers, I simply cannot accept that this was all random. Neither can I accept that the multiverse "theory" is more than a story created to resist accepting fine-tuning's ramifications. It seems to me that there is an ideology pushing a narrative because fine-tuning, as well as the Big Bang, carry such strong theistic implications. I do have to wonder why experts are so quick to accept such speculative theories that have no clear independent evidence for their validity.

A part of me holds back, wondering if there is some hidden mechanism that we have not discovered yet, sitting behind the curtain and pulling the strings. The logical process is to make an assessment with the facts and evidence that I have on hand: it needs to be judged by the evidence, not by some potential for hidden knowledge that only might exist and may be discovered at some point in the future. If some future discovery does happen, then I will need to reevaluate based on the new data and evidence. Holding out for the "might" is really just making an excuse to believe what I want and use a cheap rationalization to justify it. When you take the hard facts surrounding fine-tuning, there is an undeniable teleological argument, or argument for God, to be made. My much, much stronger feeling is that there is a

> "Astronomers now find they have painted themselves into a corner because they have proven, by their own methods, that the world began abruptly in an act of creation to which you can trace the seeds of every star, every planet, every living thing in this cosmos and on the Earth. And they have found that all this happened as a product of forces they cannot hope to discover. That there are what I or anyone would call supernatural forces at work is now, I think, a scientifically proven fact."
>
> *Robert Jastrow*
> *(God and the Astronomers)*

massive force intentionally making this happen, and that force is usually known as God. With this information, I cannot avoid stating that I strongly believe that this was intentional. I can easily say that the fine-tuning argument gets me to at least deism—some type of God exists—and does put some significant weight on the side of there being the Christian God and against a solely naturalistic universe.

SEVENTEEN | *The Problem of Evolution*

My public-school education in New York taught me that there are two kinds of people in the world. There are those who accept that life was first created by a chemical soup that then randomly mutated over time to evolve, eventually, into human beings, and those who are backwards religious zealots that won't accept undeniable science when it's put in front of their faces. While not explicitly stated, it was also assumed that these deniers lived in remote rural areas, mostly without having indoor plumbing, but certainly having improper relations with close family members. I can't imagine a better depiction than the one encapsulated in the show *Friends* in which Ross, a geeky paleontologist, reacted when Phoebe, the super ditzy, conspiracy-laden foil who constantly says absurd things, denied evolution.

PHOEBE: Yeah, I just don't buy it. (laugh track)

ROSS: Uh, excuse me. Evolution is not for you to buy, Phoebe. Evolution is scientific fact like the air we breathe, like gravity.

PHOEBE: Ok, don't get me started on gravity. (laugh track)

ROSS: You uh, you don't believe in gravity?

....

ROSS: Pheebs, I have studied evolution my entire adult life. Ok, I can tell you, we have collected fossils from all over the world that actually show the evolution of different species, ok? You can literally see them evolving through time.

PHOEBE: Really? You can actually see it?

ROSS: You bet. In the U.S., China, Africa, all over.

PHOEBE: See, I didn't know that.

ROSS: Well, there you go.

PHOEBE: Huh. So now, the real question is, who put those fossils there, and why? (laugh track)

....

ROSS: Ok, Pheebs. See how I'm making these little toys move? Opposable thumbs. Without evolution, how do you explain opposable thumbs?

PHOEBE: Maybe the overlords needed them to steer their spacecrafts. (laugh track)

....

ROSS: Ok, Phoebe, this is it. In this briefcase I carry actual scientific facts. A briefcase of facts, if you will. Some of these fossils are over 200 million years old.

PHOEBE: Ok, look, before you even start, I'm not denying evolution, ok, I'm just saying that it's one of the possibilities.

ROSS: It's the only possibility, Phoebe.

I like to consider myself science-based, driven by reason and evidence, and if evolution is an absolute fact, like gravity, then I simply have to accept it. The problem is, if this is true, then I really felt that the creation of human beings as depicted in Genesis and God's relationship with human beings could not also be true. There was a strong insinuation that the myths of the Bible, specifically Genesis, really should be replaced by the sure science of evolutionary theory. There was a strong implication that facts and evidence need to win out over fanciful mythology, however comforting, that was only designed to keep the ignorant from being afraid of the dark. I tried to partition off my science from my theology, but to be honest, in my heart of hearts, it really didn't work.

While I did not want to admit it, to me, if evolution was true, I felt I had to believe that naturalism was true and therefore, atheism had to be true—and I had to base my worldview on tangible facts and irrefutable evidence. The time had come to have a conversation with what I was certain would be revealed as the executioner of God.

In school I was taught that the "real" creation story, according to indisputable scientific evidence, is that about four billion years ago on Earth, there was a primordial "soup" of chemicals all mixing around. Energy, probably from thermal vents,

> *"I always had a place for God in my life, but that was exactly my problem: I had a place for God in my life.....*
> *Part of the reason I compartmentalized my faith was because I was a science guy and science told me I was just an evolved chemical."*
>
> **Erik Strandness**
> *(The Beautiful Letdown)*

combined with lightning and minerals from rocks, caused those chemicals to form an early version of Ribonucleic Acid (RNA). RNA has a broad spectrum of functions but is critical for life and biological processes. Once "life" was started, the RNA would replicate itself and mutate. Over time it would grow progressively more and more complex until at some point, it would emerge as a simple organism. These would rapidly reproduce, with some generations having tiny but significant changes. These changes, called mutations, would combine to occasionally provide a feature or function that gave it a competitive advantage over the others of its type. As this new version was better adapted, it would thrive over its previous version counterpart. The population of the new version would eventually completely overtake the old version and relegate it to the dustbin of history. The new versions would, sooner or later, have new mutations to create the next version and eventually create entirely new species. Some versions would branch off and so there would be a variation of species over time, if mapped, which would look much like a tree. This is commonly known as the "Tree of Life."

Some of these creatures were trapped in dirt, mud or tar, and so, the patterns of their forms were preserved when the soil hardened into rock. We have millions of these fossils from around the globe from a wide array of time periods and, as Ross said, we can literally trace the fossilized creatures evolving through time from one form (Species A) to another (Species B) incrementally.

I was taught that the actual changes are visible via the fossil record as one species transitions to another and while there may be a "missing link" from apes to humans, the rest of the entire story is complete. There are many examples, but the one always shown as the slam dunk is Archaeopteryx, which obviously showed the transition from dinosaurs to birds.

In the modern world, we learned that we see examples of evolution all the time. When Darwin was developing his theory, he visited the Galápagos Islands and observed that the localized finches' beaks differed from the mainland variety due to the types of seeds that were available. In short, the environment caused the bird to physically change to adapt to its surroundings. Those that adapted, thrived. Those that didn't, died off. In a more modern-day example, in 2003 a combination of drought and introduction of another variety of finch resulted in competition for the native finch's normal food supply, larger seeds. In a span of only 20 years, due to the diminished large seed food supply, the native finch evolved to a smaller beak size and therefore, be able to eat the smaller, and more abundant, seeds. I have read in published papers that if we extrapolate that time-period to a large-scale mutation, then it's entirely reasonable to predict that we could have a totally new species within only a few hundred years![38]

Another compelling example cited was from a discovery made during the Industrial Revolution. In England, the pollution from factories killed lichen and the tree bark had a dark layer of soot. The Peppered Moth's appearance normally camouflages itself from predators by having a pale coloring with speckles of dark. With the soot-filled environmental changes, a darker-winged version, that was already present in the population, became more abundant as it could blend in better with the dark soot. Once clean air legislation was passed and the soot levels declined, there was a resurgence of the lighter-colored peppered moths. Clearly, these mutated to fit their environment.[39]

Since all modern organisms are new and improved versions of their predecessors, we should be able to see the latent function. My Chevy Silverado truck is relatively new, but I can look at a truck from the year 2000, 1980, and 1950 and see how the vehicle changed over time, and we can see that in nature as well. What we can also see behind the air conditioning and heated seats is the root vehicle that is still comparable to the first-ever pickup truck.

In 1866, Ernst Haeckel published drawings comparing the early-stage embryos of vertebrate species ranging from fish, salamanders, and up to and including human beings. I remember looking at his drawings in my high school textbooks and viewing the unmistakable, almost identical, resemblance across all the species! The level of variation was extremely small, demonstrating that in the early stages, all the embryos were very, very similar and only diverged into their individual species in later points of development, again, just like the historical record shows. The fancy name for this is "Ontogeny recapitulates phylogeny." Furthermore, I will never forget when I saw other pictures visually demonstrate human embryos with gill slits that eventually close, but also show the latent properties of our earlier cousins.[40]

To me, this was extremely persuasive evidence showing how human beings evolved from earlier creatures. Like my pickup truck, if humans came from other species that came from species before them, we should see some signs of the evolutionary history such as having fishlike gills or tails like monkeys at various stages of embryo development—and that is exactly what we see!

It was apparent how one form followed another, but the question arose, where did they all originate? I was taught that in 1953 at the University of Chicago, there was a famous experiment conducted to test the origin of life on Earth. Stanley Miller and Harold Urey simulated the initial conditions of the planet as they were when life arose. The premise was that the Earth existed in a "primordial soup" where complex chemicals that form the building blocks of life were created by the intermixing of simple natural molecules that were then sparked to life, literally, by lightning.

While the results of the experiment produced only simple organic molecules, these results could easily be seen as proof that abiogenesis, life from non-life, did indeed happen this way.[41]

If God created human beings, as depicted in the Bible, why would we still have organs that had no present-day purpose? As our bodies evolved from one creature to another, some legacy structures that had

> "...all the evidence — both old and new — leads ineluctably to the conclusion that evolution is true."
>
> *Jerry Coyne*
> (Why Evolution is True)

purpose for earlier beings, but were useless to us, still remained. There are many examples, but the most often cited are the appendix, coccyx, and external ear muscles. If God is perfect and He made us in His image, why would we have useless parts? Conversely, imperfect design is exactly what we would expect to see from evolution.

Evolution was again said to be proven after the discovery of deoxyribonucleic acid (DNA). DNA is what contains the sequences of nucleotides that comprise the genetic code that your body uses to build proteins. Proteins are essential for a variety of structural and functional roles and DNA is the architect's schematics. In the 1970s, it was discovered that most of our DNA does not encode proteins, it is basically useless leftover. While not discarded, it is ignored as a memory of a distant relative. Many sections resemble former genes that no longer function, these are called pseudogenes, and they appear exactly like evolution would predict. Human DNA contains about ten thousand pseudogenes out of approximately twenty thousand genes.

The evidence is so complete and compelling that 99% of modern evolutionary biologists consider it to be a fact.[42]

Since Darwinian evolution was theorized in the 1850s it has come to be taken as an absolute scientific truth. Claims are that the scale of hard evidence supporting it is overwhelming. In searching out information to help with my conflict between science and theology, I kept bumping into allegations that many of the tenets of evolution were based on outdated information or assumptions. That

> "If you meet somebody who claims not to believe in evolution, that person is either ignorant, stupid or insane."
>
> **Richard Dawkins**
> (Put Your Money on Evolution)

certainly wasn't the way that it was ever presented to me, but I also know that in the 160-plus years since the theory was first introduced, the increase in scientific knowledge has had exponential growth. We have gone from sailing ships to spacecraft and every field has kept pace. In the 1850s the complexity of the cell was poorly understood and DNA and genetics hadn't even been discovered. There were also allegations that some of the "pillars" of Darwinism that were so compelling to me were intentional frauds. From what I read, it went against everything that we knew for certain and frankly, looked like crazy man conspiracy theory nonsense! Take off the tin-foil fedora and get with the program!

Science has always been based on questioning. If you are secure in your belief, you should have no problem with someone who asks questions. At the very worst, they should be politely ignored but certainly not dealt with as if they were an apostate who needed to be destroyed. In physics, unconventional theories are presented all the time, then discussed, pulled apart, and accepted, modified, or discarded. In the real world, if someone came to you and told you that the world was actually flat, you would smile politely and get out of the conversation as fast as possible. I sincerely doubt that you would scream heretic and pronounce vengeance. Ironically, after I repeatedly observed that anyone who dared to question Darwinism was met with such venomous animosity, red flags went up. Why would questions on Darwin's theory be met this way? I have a very strong feeling that instead of the mantra of science being "Question Everything," it's closer to "Question Everything Except Darwin, Because If You Do, You Will be Angrily Dismissed as a Religious Kook." Maybe it's because I am from New York and inherently skeptical, but when someone reacts to questions that way, I always wonder if it's because they have something to hide. It made me ask, what if all of those certainties turned out to not be quite as certain as proposed? Instead of making me dismiss their concerns, it propelled me to take a look for myself.

If you are like me, when I started reading something like this, my guard would immediately go up. Darwinism was what I was taught since middle school. The evidence was in my textbooks, and *everyone* took it as rock solid fact except the religious fundamentalists who made silly rationalizations based on pseudo-science. While some of these anti-Darwinian evolution claims sounded somewhat plausible on the surface, I knew that this was the most dangerous type of pseudo-science, just enough truth, and a sprinkling of techno-jargon, to sound authentic but hide the bigger lie. I am no backwoods rube willing to believe nonsense without facts and evidence but, I am also not so closed-minded that I won't at least do a cursory evaluation of claims and see if they have merit to warrant further investigation.

In earlier chapters, I have said, "I have always felt, for all subjects, that any argument is within bounds to question, and falsehoods will dissolve like shadows under a bright light" regarding my willingness to question Christianity. I realized that this philosophy must also extend to the quasi-religious dogma of the atheistic side's view of evolution.

It is said that a visiting Chinese archaeologist told a group he was working with that things are the opposite in the United States and in China. In China, you can never question the govern-

> "Darwin made it possible to be an intellectually fulfilled atheist."
>
> **Richard Dawkins,**
> *(The Blind Watchmaker)*

ment but can openly dispute Darwin; in the United States, you are free to say what you want about the government, but you had better not question Darwin! Why should that be true?

My position going in to this investigation was that Darwinism was a fact, and I had to face the possibility that it was mutually exclusive with theism. Darwin or God. From what I knew, the only possible way to reconcile them at all through what is called theistic evolution.

In theistic evolution, everything that is said about Darwinian evolution is correct, but God was a guiding force for it to come into being. This does little to ease my conflict. I can see that if you are a believer in God, then this would be a logical extension. After all, it is clear that at the moment of the Big Bang, everything down to the most finely tuned detail was "baked in" so that the universe unfolded over billions of years to get us to where we are today. If that kind of information and foresight was present to create the actual universe, why wouldn't biology follow the same methodology? I do see that as a completely logical application for a grand design argument if you are a theist. The problem is, behind the curtain where no one could see, I don't know that I would have necessarily called myself a theist.

Theistic evolution definitely got my feet wet, but I still kept bumping into all of these problems, many times vocalized from serious scholars. I got to the point that between the claims of scientific problems with Darwinism and the venom and anger of the Darwin acolytes, there was enough there to at least take a look. What I found really surprised me; there really are significant problems with the idea of Darwinian evolution. Also, and just as surprising, I found that many of the "facts" that were presented to me as ironclad, had significant unknowns regarding the major mechanisms of how they were supposed to function. Only though steadfast faith in naturalism could you see the picture as complete and, ironically enough, as a justification for belief in Darwinism. Talk about circular reasoning!

I was incredulous when points of contradiction between what Darwinism predicted and what was experimentally recorded were met with joyful exclamation! Instead of evaluating if there were problems being illuminated by study results not matching their predictions as it would in other sciences, the position taken was that these results actually show that the incredible power of the theory is even greater than what we imagined! So, if it shows what you expected, it's because the theory is correct. If it shows any other data, it only demonstrates that we underestimated the vastness of the powers of Darwinian evolution. Really? Show me any other branch of science where this wouldn't raise immediate alarms.

Important safety tip! Don't get your science from a fictional character like Ross in a television show. First, the common perception that theories grow up to become laws after enough experimentation is actually not correct. In reality theories and laws are two different things. Theories are ideas, hopefully informed ideas, on *how and why* things work the way that they do. It is common for theories to be abridged or even fully discarded as new information comes to light. Laws are descriptors, usually mathematical in nature, that describe the behavior of something, *the what*. As they are measurable and usually formulaic, the level of certainty of laws is very high and so, they are rarely changed.

> "Evolution is just a theory? Well, so is gravity and I don't see you jumping out of buildings."
>
> **Richard Dawkins**
> (Evolution Quote)

The *Law* of Gravity relates to quantities that we can measure and make formulaic predictions on, *what* gravity does. If something falls off of a building, I know that acceleration is 9.8 meters/second^2 and I can predict its speed, position, and momentum at any point in time. I can easily calculate the force that it exerts on the concrete when it finishes his trip. Sir Isaac Newton figured all of these things out in the 1600s.

The *Theory* of Gravity deals with *how* gravity functions, and to that, no one actually knows. Again, the Law of Gravity is well established and has a very high level of certainty; the Theory of Gravity is very uncertain, has many unknowns, with a variety of competing theories. Don't believe me? Good. Keep questioning.

Does gravity work in waves like we were taught in school? Or does it use particles called "gravitons"? Maybe it's related to "dark matter"? There are numerous possibilities. Today, there are 17 legitimate competing theories for gravity. The word "today" is important because tomorrow there may be 23 or 2. That's the point of a theory. Oh, the theory of gravity is rock solid, you're just hiding behind nuance! Really? General Relativity explains it? Unless dividing by zero isn't a problem, it fails as well. All the quantum mechanics theories fail because in quantum mechanics, there needs to be a specific gravity particle to make it all "work" and so far, no one can find one. The point is that some of the things that are taught as deadlock certain, really are not. (Please keep this in a scientific perspective and not go down the conspiracy theory rabbit hole; yes, we really did land on the moon, those pictures were not doctored!)

So, yes, Darwinian evolution is a theory just like the Theory of Gravity, but certainly not like the Law of Gravity. It is ironic that they use the Theory of Gravity to make an argument from authority to claim certainty, but what they are really stating is that Darwinian evolution is rife with unknowns and massive uncertainties! It's worth a geeky smirk to also realize that if Phoebe was referring to the Theory of Gravity and not the Law of Gravity, then she has every right to be skeptical. In that light, she is the one on the intellectual high ground!

Putting out pithy one-liners that they should know are incorrect and trusting that no one will dig into it really annoys me. It's hard enough to really understand the entirety of these ideas without someone promoting false information to push their personal narrative. Either they have very little knowledge of science in fields outside of their area of study or they do know the facts, but they engage in intellectual dishonesty.

Okay, Darwin's theory is just a theory but if 99% of all evolutionary biologists believe it, then why would you disagree with the experts? These are people who have spent their lives studying this subject and should have a high level of expertise. Very good question and on face value, I agree. If you really look at the root of the statement that was asked of them, they do agree on evolution. The issue is that they do not necessarily agree on *Darwinian evolution*. I didn't know this, but there are multiple definitions of "evolution" and it's important to be clear on which definition is being used. Some people use it as Darwinian evolution; small mutations combine over time to make entirely new species. Others use it as there are simply changes within a species. It is true that 99% of all evolutionary biologists believe in the second sense of the word, change within a species. It's actually an obvious thing; even human beings differentiate from each other. What I did not know is that it is so widely accepted that even the young earth creationists, the people who believe in a literal view of Genesis where the entirety of the universe was created about 6,000 years ago in six consecutive 24-hour days, agree to this definition of evolution as well. What about Darwinian evolution, is it really agreed upon by 99% of all biologists? Well, not so much. Surveys claiming 99% support often refer to microevolution, not Darwinian macroevolution. Without a doubt, Darwin's is still the primary theory, but the percentages are not the complete consensus as I was led to believe.

In the 1850s, archaeologists had uncovered many fossils, but it was easily recognized that much work was needed. It was strongly believed that in the coming decades, many more fossils would be uncovered. As the fossil record in Darwin's day was so spotty, he acknowledged that this was a hole in his theory and potentially a fatal flaw, but was confident that in the coming years, the record would be filled in to show the gradual species-to-species change. If his theory is true, then there would be the transition from species 1 through all the incremental changes until it arrives as a new species, species 100. There should be a vast array of creatures demonstrating the incremental changes showing the mutation from 1 to 100; 1, 2, 3, 4....98, 99, and finally to 100. In this example, 1 and 100 are the old and new species, all the numbers in between are the incremental changes needed to mutate from the old species to the new.

In the coming decades, there were an abundance of finds that radically grew our catalog of fossil evidence. The problem is that it did not fill in the gaps as predicted. Species appeared in their fully formed state, persisted for a period, and then disappeared with no transitional states displayed. We have a multitude of fossils of each type that were completely developed but we do not see the intermediary forms as Darwinian evolution demands.

The most fossiliferous rock layer where complex life appears was laid down about 540 million years ago, commonly known as the Cambrian period. This sedimentary stratum is filled with highly complex multicellular organisms, including many types of hard-shelled creatures. The critical issue is that in the rock layers lower than the Cambrian, hence older, are largely devoid of these invertebrates. This is named the Cambrian Explosion, the sudden appearance of fully formed creatures with no apparent predecessors. I would not expect every iteration, but there should be some major ones. Say something like version 1, 2, 4, 7, 8, 11, 15, 30, 31, 35, 47, 55, 56, 57, 70, 79, 85, 92, 95, and finally the new species, 100. It looks to me like what we actually see is 1, 100. In fairness, soft-bodied organisms often decompose before they fossilize so it is understandable that there would be fewer of them compared to the ones as appear in the Cambrian period, but I argue that this does not resolve the issue.

The fossil record regularly shows fully formed species but has a major problem with intermediary forms that are generally lacking. The fossil that is always brought out as the gold standard of transition-

> "The extreme rarity of transitional forms in the fossil record persists as the trade secret of paleontology. The evolutionary trees that adorn our textbooks have data only at the tips and nodes of their branches; the rest is inference, however reasonable, not the evidence of fossils."
>
> *Stephen J. Gould*
> *(Evolution's Erratic Pace)*

al forms is *Archaeopteryx*, which is promoted as demonstrating the transition from dinosaur to bird. It possesses reptilian traits such as teeth, claws, and a bony tail but also has bird features like feathers and wings. What I found was that there is more to the story. The first issue is that features like claws and teeth are found in the fossils of birds as well, not only reptiles. Secondly, it appears about 150 million years ago but fossils of some fully formed birds overlap with, or even predate, *Archaeopteryx*. If it is transitional between species A and B, it must appear between A and B, not after. I understand that there will be an overlap in time periods where both species will exist, but this is clearly not the case here. Why would fully formed birds appear at the same time, or even before, its intermediary? Also, if the *Archaeopteryx* is transitional, it should have feathers showing the transition from scales to full flight-ready feathers. Instead, it has asymmetrical feathers which are characteristic of modern birds.

Another major issue is trying to explain how an organism goes from body plan A to body plan B. To go to a new body plan, you must add genetic information and there

> "Paleontologists have tried to turn *Archaeopteryx* into an earth-bound, feathered dinosaur. But it's not. It is a bird, a perching bird. And no amount of 'paleobabble' is going to change that."
>
> *Alan Feduccia*
> *(Archaeopteryx)*

is no known process can achieve this. A reasonable parallel is if you have architectural drawings for a one-story home and want to evolve it to a two-story, you need information. You will need designs for a stairway, the second-floor walls, the new electrical circuits and wiring, HVAC venting and possibly a new unit, windows, etc. Note that in this example, there are a few "new" parts when adding a second floor namely joists, bracing for between the first and second floor, and the stairwell. Similarly, going from species A to species B often requires entirely new parts.

In 1988, Dr. Richard Lenski began a long-term evolution experiment (LTEE) studying *Escherichia coli* bacteria designed to track genetic changes over multiple generations. As of 2020, there had been 73,500 generations. The bacteria were housed in a solution of glucose but also citrate at a higher concentration. At about the 31,500th generation, it was found that the bacteria mutated to metabolize citrate as a food source. Taking this further, it was reasonably envisioned as a full pathway to citrate utilization. This was pointed to as conclusive proof that we finally had experimental evidence of Darwinian evolution. (It is important to note that it was calculated by Dr. Lenski that every possible single point mutation had occurred multiple times.)[43]

When you look at the research on what occurred, it was discovered that the bacteria already possessed the ability to metabolize citrate, but only in an anaerobic (no oxygen) environment. This double-point mutation transcribed the gene for citrate metabolism to another part of the DNA strand that allowed it to function in an aerobic as well as anaerobic environment. The changes that allowed it to metabolize citrate all represented either loss of functions, or duplications of pre-existing functions. It is also important to note that while it did adapt to being able to use citrate, it also suffered a 20% loss in being able to use glucose. While this was popularized as an example of evolution in the lab, it didn't add new genetic information and adding new genetic information is the only way that you can get from species A to species B.

Some scientists claim that gene duplication can add information, but it does not seem to sufficiently explain new body plans. Again, instead of adding information to the DNA this was shown to have done the opposite, deleted information. It was becoming increasingly believable to me that naturalistic mechanisms were insufficient for the complex biological innovation that was evidenced in the historical record.

I wondered if they found a couple of sympathetic voices to do some math with prejudiced numbers to make a case against Darwinsim. I really didn't know what to think when I found out that these types of problems were first raised in the Wistar Institute Symposium which was attended by physicists and engineers from universities such as Harvard and MIT. The resulting paper named "Mathematical Challenges to the Neo-Darwinian Interpretation of Evolution" clearly shows that mathematically, neo-Darwinism does not work. Specifically, they showed that the probability of complex traits, such as eyes, being produced by random mutations within Earth's timeline was less than 1 in 10^{20}. Simply put, mutation rates and selection pressures couldn't account for complex traits within the time of Earth's existence. This was in 1966 and even after its 50th anniversary, there is still no answer. Never heard of it? I hadn't either.

As noted earlier, I was amazed when I read of the changing finches' beak sizes on the Galápagos Islands. This was ironically evident when I read more about the finches that are cited as being conclusive for, and the genesis of, Darwin's theory. The finches did have a beak size change to adapt to the changing food supply, but when those conditions returned to normal, instead of continuing the evolution or even maintaining the adaptation, they reverted to their pre-event state. In no way do I find that Darwin's finches demonstrate anything resembling species change, even with a wild imagination.

I thought this was a dead certainty because I distinctly recall seeing articles boldly proclaiming that there is evidence of new species resulting directly from adaptations. If this is true, then it seems to be undeniable proof of Darwinian evolution. And after research, it turns out to be completely true. Sensing a "but"? Well, when I think of a new species, I think of something going from one distinct creature to another. The biological species definition is very broad and includes the idea that two organisms are different species if they can't or won't inbreed (reproduce together). So, the headlines about Darwin's finches becoming a new species are true. What happened was that there was a drought resulting in a scarcity of food, so the finches adapted to have an increased beak size thereby expanding their food supply by being able to eat harder seeds. The changed beak size altered their mating call, and the "new" mating song did not attract the non-adapted finches and so, the groups wouldn't reproduce together. Hence, by definition, they are a "new" species. It does show finch speciation via mating call changes, but it is far from a new body plan and not what I was expecting.[44]

To be clear, it's undeniable that there is adaptation within a species, but it is also clear that there is no evidence that these adaptations will come close to producing the broad claims of Darwinian evolution. Taking this further, I am unaware of any solid theory that details at a chemical level *how* all of these mutations occur—what is the mechanism? Conversely, there are multiple computer programs performing predictive modeling of mutation effects over time and even in ideal circumstances, producing a modest species change requires more time than the planet has existed.[45]

This wasn't what I was taught, but here were solid refutations with evidence. All I have seen in reply is anger or deflection. I am still hesitant writing about this as I was taught that

> "A matter of unfinished business for biologists is the identification of evolution's smoking gun, ... the smoking gun of evolution is speciation, not local adaptation and differentiation of populations."
>
> **Keith Stewart Thomson**
> *(Natural Selection and Evolution's Smoking Gun)*

this was undeniably true and even questioning risked being dismissed as a cult-level kook. My great fear in this is that I will have somehow missed some legitimate science with the explanatory powers to satisfy, but as I continue to look, I find no satisfactory answers to these critical problems. This was supposed to be rock solid. What was going on?

In high school, one of the more compelling pieces of evidence was Haeckel's embryo drawings. I remember pictures of the species laid out next to each other and how they were virtually identical. Remember that they needed to be identical to show that all the species started the same and the embryo development mirrors our evolutionary walk. And yes, these drawings were nearly identical. But they didn't appear virtually identical due to the embryo reliving the history of evolution as was professed, they were identical because they were fake. Yes, fake. I will wait while you go look it up. No really, go look it up—you need to see what I saw. You need to feel the shaking and see the crack in the 'solid' ground so that you will consider all of the other evidence as I did.

The actual story is that in 1874, almost 150 years ago, the drawings were criticized as fraudulent exaggerations created specifically to support Darwin's theory. When confronted by Wilhelm His Sr., professor of anatomy at the University of Leipzig, Haeckel blamed his draftsman for making the mistake. Of course, he failed to mention that he was actually the draftsman! About 10 years later, the drawings were used in textbooks to defend Darwin's theory and have been a pillar for Darwinism ever since.

The truth is that embryos are not similar in the early stages as his drawings showed. For instance, modern embryology shows that an early-stage fish embryo and human embryo actually look very different from what was depicted by the drawings. They start looking very different, then they do have similarities midway through development and then diverge again, it's called the "developmental hourglass" or "egg-timer" model. Vertebrate embryos have a greater divergence in their earliest and latest stages but demonstrate more similarity during a mid-embryonic "phylotypic" stage.

Half of me thought, so what's the big deal, he cut corners, free-handed and fudged a little. I also thought that since they start out very different but merge midway, what's the problem, they actually do look alike just not in the exact order that he said. I felt like this was simply someone trying to make a mountain out of a molehill to try to poke a hole. I initially thought this was nit-picking and of no major consequence but soon realized that this is a major and critical issue; the whole point of the ontogeny as a recapitulation of phylogeny is that multi-species embryo development would mirror our march through the species. Here, it is critical to have all the embryos match until each one would peel off into their own separate species. The actual hourglass pattern would be consistent with origins that were separate from one another, not common ancestry. In short, if the early-stage embryo drawings were shown truthfully, they are compelling evidence *against* Darwin's theory. Trying to get around this only results in circular thinking that relies on assuming that Darwinism is true to prove that Darwinism is true.

As a side note, a 1997 study by Richardson et al. compiled embryos of 39 different creatures and they found that the embryos were so different that they concluded that Haeckel's drawings could not have possibly been made from real specimens.[46]

Interestingly enough, my daughter just studied evolution last month in biology. While Haeckel's actual diagrams were not specifically in the textbook, there were illustrations similar to his diagrams, implying the same idea. Additionally, her teacher showed the *actual* Haeckel diagrams in the discussions, and they were covered on exams. Why would an ironclad theory that is supposedly on par with the Law of Gravity need to rely on evidence that was proven to be gross exaggerations, if not outright fraudulent? Why is it that 150 years later, they are still used as proof of Darwinian evolution?

What about the gill slits on human embryos showing our fish ancestry? I was taught that early on, and have always taken as a given, that in the early development of the human embryo there are pharyngeal arches (slits) in the throat area that, in fish, form gills but in mammals, as they are unneeded, close up and disappear. The truth is that the "gill slits" aren't precursor gills nor are they even slits.

> "This is one of the worst cases of scientific fraud. It's shocking to find that somebody one thought was a great scientist was deliberately misleading. It makes me angry . . . . What he [Haeckel] did was to take a human embryo and copy it, pretending that the salamander and the pig and all the others looked the same at the same stage of development. They don't . . . . These are fakes."
>
> **Michael Richardson**
> *(There Is No Highly Conserved Embryonic Stage in the Vertebrates)*

Imagine your head as an expanded accordion with the top handle in your head at eyebrow level and the bottom one where your neck connects to your torso. Now as we start winding your life clock down through the embryonic development stage, start closing the accordion (ignoring the horrific sound that it makes). When the accordion is fully collapsed and all you see are the ribs of the deflated instrument, that is the so-called fish stage where the ribs are taken to be gill slits. Unfortunately, I have gained enough weight that I can mimic this appearance by lowering my head all the way and my neck does the rest.... What I have learned is that they aren't slits at all, they are specific folds that are present so that when development progresses and the accordion opens, each ridge forms a part of your skull. One makes your jaw, one makes your outer ear, another the middle ear, all the glands and muscles, etc. If these were the vestiges of fish biology, wouldn't they form into the respiratory organs?

Some scientists view these as homologous to fish gill arches, but their distinct function in humans contradicts the "fish ancestry" claim. These are not mistakes or leftovers from our primitive past, they have a specific function, are completely different from fish anatomy, and develop according to the human blueprint.

I get it, you were taught that evolution was a given and you're possibly thinking that this guy was going through a midlife crisis or something, was desperate for answers, and so, he was primed to be duped by some religious fundamentalists. He may drink their Kool-Aid, but none for me, thanks. I

> *"Most human origins stories are not compatible with known fossils .... many of these fossils show mosaic combinations of features that do not match expectations for ancient representatives of the modern ape and human lineages. .... Overall, the researchers found that most stories of human origins are not compatible with the fossils that we have today."*
>
> **American Museum of Natural History**
> *(Press Release [2021])*

don't blame you for thinking this way; it occurred to me that this was a possibility. Truth be told, just writing all of this makes me feel a little bit like a conspiracy nut. Throughout this process, and especially for this topic, I have been adamant in making sure that "wishful thinking" did not infringe on my evaluation. I have spent hours and hours sterilizing my view so that it is purely based on verifiable fact and not on narrative—but that cuts both ways.

What I have learned when doing the research from legitimate sources, not religious organizations, is that my hesitancy to point these things out shows how deeply rooted the narrative is within me, and not that the reported problems are false. If you want proof of the *Law* of Gravity, I can supply an avalanche that will leave you more than satisfied. If the facts of Darwinian evolution are so overwhelming, why are some of the major pieces of foundational evidence proven to be misleading or fraudulent? Instead of hard facts, I have found one unresolved, and seemingly terminal, problem for the theory after another. I hope you don't believe me. Be skeptical! Just don't dismiss it. Go investigate it yourself with an open mind and examine the actual evidence, but also examine their assumptions. Darwin's theory was revolutionary for its time, but that time was before much of the fossil record was uncovered and well before we understood the cell, much less DNA. Might it still be true? Absolutely. It does seem to explain some things well, but has seemingly critical faults with others. The big question is, with all these problems, how can it be considered an unassailable truth? How is that scientific? Ask yourself, if you purely based this on the evidence of today and not a predisposition that Darwinism was true, would you really believe this story? I have strong suspicions that you are going to find yourself in the same boat as me with lots of questions. Let's go sailing!

I was always taught that the moment that non-living chemicals combined to form the early stages of life, abiogenesis, was simply one step in the combined process of evolution, it was *The Goo to the Zoo to You!* You can define it however you want, but however you do it, you still have non-living material becoming living material. What I have come to learn is that there is a very big difference between evolution and abiogenesis. Evolution deals with existing biology changing over time while abiogenesis attempts to explain the transformation of non-living material to living material, the origin of life. However optimistic one is about what naturalistic evolution can accomplish, that provides no basis for extrapolating to abiogenesis because the latter cannot leverage evolutionary processes at all. Until there is life there are no biological processes, so abiogenesis is limited to what chemistry alone can accomplish.

I also believed that the Miller-Urey experiment explained abiogenesis, while not getting fully to life as we know it, it was so successful that it got past the "critical mass" for the theory and the rest were just details. Sooner or later, they would be able to synthesize life in the lab, it was a done deal and simply a matter of time.

While this was an ambitious experiment that produced impressive results, in no way did it even crack the door on the mystery of the origin of life. The chasm between what this experiment proved and the state of origin of life research versus overblown sensationalist claims is vast. First, there were real problems with the experiment. When there are chemicals mixing around in chaos, we have a state of high entropy. As noted earlier, to get to an ordered state, low entropy, energy needs to be added to the system. This is theorized to have been provided from heat via thermal vents and electricity via lightning. It's important to note that the tolerance for added energy must be governed so that the energy supplied to form the compounds doesn't destroy those same compounds once created. While this maintenance factor would not have been available in nature, I have no problem with adding in controls to see if you can possibly get the desired result, and then working backward, but the skeptics are right, it is a problem.

Recent research uncovered that early Earth was a chemical mix different from the methane, ammonia, water, and hydrogen used in the experiment, so in reality, that renders the results moot. But, just to go with the idea, let's say that it was correct for arguments sake. Also, keep in mind that the experiment didn't come close to creating all the amino acids needed for life, but let's ignore that also and keep going. Might as well ignore that many of these amino acids are only created from biological processes themselves; a biological process is needed to create amino acids to create the first biology. A true chicken and the egg scenario. Anyway, for arguments sake, let's say that it did create every single type of amino acid. Finally, we will also ignore that a water-based solution would be problematic for the amino acids forming the necessary peptide bonds correctly.

In Stephen Meyer's book, *Signature In the Cell*, he worked out the probability of chance generating a 150 amino acid length protein in the prebiotic world. To calculate the odds, he considered three factors. The proteins must have the correct amino acid sequence, they must only use peptide bonds, and they must be "left-handed" as all organic proteins are.

Before life began, simple proteins would have had to form to build up to more complex structures to potentially result in RNA. Proteins are made up of specific chains of amino acids with lengths ranging from about twelve to thousands long. There are 20 amino acids that are used in protein synthesis and each one is in competition for the next spot in the chain. We will assume an even distribution of amino acids, equal numbers of each, so the odds of getting each different amino acid is equal. We will also assume that the protein has a specific sequence of amino acids, therefore the odds of the correct amino acid lining up are 1 in 20. Easy enough. Where it gets problematic is when you do the calculations on a modest 150 amino acids length chain. The length of 150 is considered to be short enough to be reasonable in a prebiotic Earth but long enough to require specificity.[47]

Since there are 20 amino acids, the total possible number of combinations is 20^{150} which equates to 10^{195}. All of the 10^{195} would not produce usable proteins. Douglas Axe's research experimentally determined that approximately only 1 in 10^{74} random sequences of 150 amino acids will be stable and functional. Saying those are pretty long odds is an understatement. [48]

Another constraint Meyer emphasizes is chirality. All amino acids have 2 mirror image versions of themselves and then are named for their folding shape, left-handed (L) or right-handed (D). Proteins in living cells only contain left-handed amino acids and in the "prebiotic soup," it is reasonable to expect them to be in equal measure. So, remember that even if it's the correct amino acid, it's only 50 / 50 that it will be left-handed. If we think about this and the left-handed issue like a coin flip scenario, it's the same as getting 150 heads in a row for each issue. One wrong amino acid or one wrong handedness results in either a non-viable protein or one that won't fold correctly and so like a key that's bent, it won't work. When we factor that each acid has a 50% chance of being left-handed and a length of 150 acids long, that works out to 1 in 10^{45}.

Third, amino acids can form different types of chemical bonds, but only peptide bonds will create a protein backbone. The bonding between acids being a peptide bond is at about 50% probability, so another 1 in 10^{45}.

If you remember the earlier discussion of probabilities, to get a sequence, we need to multiply the probability of the first multiplied the probability of the second multiplied by the probability of the third etc. So, if we are doing a coin flip and we want to know the probability of the heads, heads, heads sequence, it would be

$$\frac{1}{2} \times \frac{1}{2} \times \frac{1}{2} = \frac{1}{8}$$

When all the math is done for the 150-length protein, we need to multiply the sequencing problem times the left-handed requirement times the odds of the peptide bond. The final number works out to be 1 in $10^{74 + 45 + 45}$ or 1 in 10^{164} (remember that when you multiply you add the exponents). Use any reaction rate you want, the amount of time it would take for one protein to form randomly like this is longer than all the years since the creation of the universe times a trillion trillion trillion.[49]

Ok, I'm a math geek and even if you don't care, I'll try to summarize Dr. Meyer's work. The best estimates are that the universe is about 13.8 billion years old or roughly 10^{17} seconds. Assuming the aforementioned 10^{80} particles in the universe and a protein-forming event every second, the total trials are $10^{80} \times 10^{17} = 10^{97}$. If we multiple the time that the universe existed by a "trillion trillion trillion," or 10^{36} we then have a grand total of $10^{97} \times 10^{36} = 10^{133}$. Even with these extreme assumptions, it falls short to a 31 order of magnitude.

Doing my best doubting Thomas, I thought that there are other proteins out there than the ones used for those simple forms of life. If we take the number of known proteins and multiply it by a trillion, it still is an absurdly low probability. It has been calculated that there have been a total of 10^{40} organisms in the history of the Earth, remember that bacteria count too! The numbers that we are facing to create one random protein are vastly larger than 10^{40} organisms. How is this accounted for?

I was always taught that life via test tube was right around the corner, that the solution was well in hand. In reality, it very much seems that the field of abiogenesis is not only distant from a solution but is only starting to understand the enormity of the problem.

This problem is so big that many biologists have turned to the idea that early amino acids, or even the original life itself, came to Earth from outer space (with a common favorite being Mars), an idea known as panspermia. While it's a wild idea and only pushes the issue to another location, it really is worth exploring as there are regions of space that do contain chemical mixtures that were not present on the early Earth, and it is possible that bacteria could survive a short trip in space. I do not bring this idea up to scoff as I think we need to be open to ideas, but instead to show the enormity of determining the origin of life.

> "More than 30 years of experimentation on the origin of life in the fields of chemical and molecular evolution have led to a better perception of the immensity of the problem of the origin of life on Earth rather than to its solution. At present all discussions on principal theories and experiments in the field either end in stalemate or in a confession of ignorance."
>
> *Klaus Dose*
> *(The Origin of Life)*

Yes, I know, this is hard to digest. Even to this day, my emotional side is telling me that Darwinism is true, and I am just buying into fringe nonsense. It is very much my default position, and I feel significant internal pressure trying to return me to the fold. If I hadn't looked at the data myself, I certainly would have. But I did, so I won't.

Facts are facts, even if they make me uncomfortable, and they alone must dictate my conclusions.

Darwin's claims of vestigial organs also seem to fall apart. Vestigial organs are "parts" of our anatomy that remain from our ancestors on the Tree of Life.[50] The most famous examples, such as the appendix or spleen, were thought to have been useless leftover but are now understood to perform important functions. The pro-Darwinian argument is that the function evolved over time so that it is still useful. Those organs really shouldn't have use, which goes to prove Darwinism is true, but since they actually do have use, it just shows how amazing Darwinism is to have adapted a useless organ into having use. No really, that's the argument. Circular reasoning is flawed, no matter who says it.

The more modern-day claim that much of our DNA sequence is left over "junk" and shows how the unneeded parts of the instruction set from our precursors remains present but is ignored. What we are now finding is that virtually all our entire genome is transcribed into RNA. While most of the RNA doesn't directly build proteins, it does perform essential regulatory functions. And the "virtually" is getting smaller and smaller each month with each new discovery. Why is this not common knowledge considering that this data has been increasing steadily since scientists finished sequencing the human genome in 2003? Why are you condemned as an anti-science religious bigot for bringing this up? Why do I feel like this has more of a resemblance to the Spanish Inquisition than to the way that science should be conducted?

In 2016, the Royal Society's New Trends in Evolutionary Biology conference discussed the state of evolutionary biology. It contained sessions that were critical of the state of the theory. The problematic areas included the origin of major body parts, body plans in general, the origin of new forms of life across all history, the inability to explain new complex biological features, and that the fossil record simply shows abrupt changes and not a gradual mutation. Aren't those all the things that I was taught that Darwinian evolution explained? How is it considered an indisputable fact if there are such significant problems with its major tenets that they had a prestigious conference to discuss it only a few years ago?[51]

My problem has now evolved to why our culture won't tolerate questions and why evidence is ignored? Every conclusion that I

202 | *The Doubt Project*

come up with makes me feel like a religious nut with blinders on. Except that I am not a religious nut, I just spent more than a year writing about doubt. And I don't have blinders on as I have openly shared my criticism of the theological arguments. The answer that I feel is most plausible for the fervor with which it is regarded, is that Darwinian evolution is the Genesis story for atheists. I find that it is treated with as much blind fanaticism as was present in the ugliest periods of the church's history when dealing with heresy. I think the argument that the New Atheists are aggressively attempting to claim "science" as the domain of secularists is very persuasive. This is the atheist genesis story, and it is diametrically opposed to the foundations in scriptural Genesis. They fanatically position it as unquestionably true, and they insist on absolute obedience. One must swear fealty and reject the primitive "blind faith" in the mythology of God. Upon this rock, they will build their church.

> *"The technical literature in biology is now replete with world-class biologists routinely expressing doubts about various aspects of neo-Darwinian theory, and especially about its central tenet, namely the alleged creative power of the natural selection and mutation mechanism.*
>
> *Nevertheless, popular defenses of the theory continue apace, rarely if ever acknowledging the growing body of critical scientific opinion about the standing of the theory. Rarely has there been such a great disparity between the popular perception of a theory and its actual standing in the relevant peer-reviewed science literature."*
>
> *Stephen Meyer*
> *(Darwin's Doubt)*

After spending many long months researching evolution, I have ended up at an unexpected place. I had always been taught that abiogenesis and Darwinism were indisputable facts and that only the ignorant or religious fanatics didn't believe. Ironically, it feels like the more scientific knowledge we gain, the less likely Darwinian evolution is to be true. I find so many critical, unanswered issues with Darwinism and such an abundance of evidence that is contrary to Darwin's predictions, that I have moved from my blind belief of it being a concrete, absolute and unassailable fact, to seriously doubting it's truth. To be honest, I think that if I did not have the "baggage" from my upbringing and I was presented with the facts today, I would fully reject it.

Even more surprisingly, I have concluded that it is entirely rational to reconcile a firm belief in evolution and the faith in God. If the processes for going from one organism to another end up being some natural process, divine, or something else, it really isn't a deal-killer for belief or disbelief in God. Even if a method of abiogenesis is found and Darwinian evolution is proven to be completely true, it does not necessarily preclude the idea that biology unfolded through some divine guidance. I could certainly see a biological parallel to the creation of the universe where, in the beginning, He created enough energy for everything to unfold without intervention over time—a form of a galactic determinism to finally arrive at the dawn of humanity. I could see Him "baking in" the code for biology to unfold without intervention to generate humanity. I also do not see this as being exclusive to humanity possessing the divine spark. As I never felt that man being made in His image was referring to our physical bodies, He could imprint Himself on whatever He likes.

The point is that I mostly no longer consider that whatever flavor of evolution ends up being true and the existence of God

204 | *The Doubt Project*

to be mutually exclusive. I say "mostly" because it's hard to fully shake what you were taught as a certainty for so long. I mention this for two reasons, first, I don't know if Darwinian evolution is true and, for all their bluster, I really don't think they do either. Second, and more importantly, I have found that if you marshal the strength to wade through the narratives, you can find peace.

EIGHTEEN | *Issues with the Old Testament*

No discussion on the core of theological doubt would be complete without engaging with Genesis. I have already discussed some of the ideas in Genesis, such as the creation of the universe, but there were still a few areas that gave me concern. Please keep in mind that this is a pinhole view of the arguments around the Old Testament and I am very strictly limiting my thoughts to the few specific areas that I found problematic. In short, those topics are the feasibility of the Genesis account, if the description of God in the Old Testament is good, and if the Jews were the chosen people and I was just a second-class citizen.

The first area of concern that I had was whether the Genesis account was even possible. Words have different meanings due to context. If I discuss the steam ships that were present in my grandfather's day, it's clear that I am clearly not referring to a specific 24-hour period in my grandfather's life. It is undeniable that I am speaking of a time period. Likewise, the Day of the Dinosaur was not just 24 hours. It seemed that objections to the book of Genesis are either regarding the specific amount of time referenced by the word "day," the order of events of plant and animal life appearing on Earth contradicting Scripture, or that Genesis 1 is accused of conflicting with Genesis 2.

Even as a small child I assumed that Scripture referred to ages of time and not the literal seven, 24-hour days for creation and frankly, I was surprised that some people did regard the text as literal 24-hour days. To me, the taking of "days" to mean 24 hours was always the most popular objection and since I never believed that a word from an English translation of Scripture was to be taken as it was, this area held little weight for me. If we go beyond the English translation to the original text, the Hebrew word that is translated to "day" in English is *yom*. *Yom*, like many English words, had multiple meanings depending on context. *Yom* can mean part of the daylight hours—like "this afternoon," all of the daylight hours—like "during the day, but at night we will….," one calendar day—such as "we will spend one day in Charleston, but in the morning we leave for Atlanta" or a period of time that had a beginning and an ending—like "the day of the dinosaur." According to Dr. John Oakes, there are multiple ways that *yom* is translated in the New International Version (NIV) of the Bible.

He lists: 67 times as 'time', 30 times as 'today', 18 times as 'forever,' 10 times as 'continuously,' 6 times as 'age,' 4 times as 'life, '2 times as 'perpetually.'[52]

Furthermore, there are multiple times that *yom* is present in Genesis 1–2 where it did not refer to a 24-hour period. It is used in Genesis 1.5 when describing God's creation of day and night. The text states, "And God called the light *yom* (day), and the darkness He called *laylah* (night)."

The light portion of a day is not 24 hours.

In Genesis 2.4, "In the day that the Lord God made the earth and the heavens" which refers to the entire creation period, not a specific day.

Genesis 2.17, "In the day you eat of it, you shall surely die" speaking about Adam eating from the tree of knowledge. Adam does eat from the tree but doesn't die for many years.

Also, maybe because I was aware that there were ages throughout history, it just didn't seem right to infer 24 hours. I never saw God as being the grand wielder of a magic wand. It seems that everything that He is claimed to do is through a process. If God was in the business of breaking out the wand for universe and life building, then why wouldn't he have simply waved His wand for every circumstance that came up in Scripture? For instance, He could have obliterated the Egyptians and teleported the Hebrews to Israel without all those messy plagues or 40 years of hassles. No need to build an ark, just disintegrate the pesky sinners. Even better, a divine dog collar on each of us so that when we sin, we get a *zap* (I am in favor of this one as long as the threshold is just above my sin level)!

Finally, I reasoned that logically it is not possible to start with a 24-hour Earth day. The Earth and the sun are essential parts of an Earth day and the sun didn't exist until day 4. Either the author was nuts or that isn't the meaning intended. I have heard the argument that the light created in Genesis 1.3 could have been used in the day-night cycle before the sun's creation but even so, this has no astronomical basis and doesn't align with a 24-hour day.

My retirement strategy was to buy single-family homes to be used as rentals so that I had income through my golden years. Due to high immigration into Texas, the real estate prices have been rapidly rising, driving the price of houses up to the point of being too costly compared to the current rent rates. In response to this, I have turned to buying vacant land and building new homes.

When I plan a house, I start with the general dimensions of the land and then the house that I can build, which dictates the number of bedrooms and bathrooms. I prefer houses with a centralized living area and an open floorplan so that the kitchen area is contiguous with the living room. This maximizes space, gives a central community area and gives the house a larger feel. I try to do vaulted ceilings in the main living areas as well. The bedrooms connect off of the living room with the master bedroom being larger and an upgraded private bath.

Also, when I plan a house, first I will obtain the blueprints and then file my permits and get clearance from the city. I hire the earth movers to clear the lot and dig out the soil where the foundation will be. When complete, the plumbers and electricians come in to do their initial setting of the pipes and wires. Next, we will pour the concrete for the foundation, then get the framers to put up the "sticks" of the house and the roofer to, well, you know. The electricians and plumbers come in to do their "rough-in," the wires, lights and pipes through the open walls and windows and doors. Then comes the beginning of the finish out: cabinets, counters, drywall, fixtures, flooring, paint, and final trim out.

> "The Judeo-Christian tradition describes the beginning of the world in a way that is surprisingly similar to the scientific model. Previously, it seemed scientifically unsound to have light created before the sun. The present scientific view does indeed assume the early universe to be filled with various kinds of radiation long before the sun was created."
>
> *Victor Weisskopf*
> (The Privilege of Being a Physicist)

These are both legitimate descriptions on how I plan the house, one is the logical order, how I want the house to function, and one is a chronological physical description of what needs to be performed in sequence. Both are valid and both are necessary. To me, it is apparent that Genesis 1 is the chronological description of the universe's creation, while Genesis 2 is the logical order. I really don't see a contradiction.

I find it shallow to think, if taking the skeptic's view, that someone who was wise and clever enough to be able to perpetuate possibly the second greatest hoax in history couldn't see that two sections in sequential chapters obviously disagreed with each other. If the skeptics are right, over the past 4,000-plus years, these stories have been handed down and modified to birth god-like myths out of simple, natural events but no one, in all that time, had the sense to realize that ideas on the same page conflicted and should be edited to smooth them out. That never made sense to me. In either case, the author being enlightened or a complete fraud, I have to think that they would have realized the supposed contradiction and made edits if Genesis 1 and 2 were intended to be identical.

Conversely, there are some things that I really do find amazing about Genesis. Aristotle, the father of logic and the study of biology, believed that the universe was eternal; it existed forever and would exist forever. He wasn't some fringe kook with crazy ideas, the universe being eternal was a tenet of accepted knowledge since the beginning of human history. Remember that this scientific "given" was so ingrained that Einstein himself fudged his Theory of General Relativity to include a constant so that the mathematics would comply with the eternal universe model. As an ironic note, historically, people were mocked for believing "In the beginning" as that stated that the universe was created and not eternal. You would have to be a primitive bible-thumping rube to believe such nonsense! Then came Georges Lemaitre, a convinced Albert Einstein, Edwin Hubble, and a host of others proving that in actuality, the universe did have a beginning.

Another knock on the Bible is that it states that the world was covered in water but we knew that dry continents were present since the Earth formed. That idea was shattered in the 1960s when it was discovered that continents only comprised 10% of the Earth's surface, so the Earth was covered by 90% water. Then, around the year 2000, studies (e.g., Valley et al., 2002) showed that the Earth was *completely covered in water* for a period of time but then had a rapid formation of plates and land masses. Most recently, it was now determined that the Earth was totally covered by water for a billion years and then, almost instantaneously (in geologic terms), land masses formed. This seems to me to be exactly what it stated in Scripture for the events of creation on day three. I am not "all-in" but how would a tribal people living in an arid environment envision that there was light before the sun, the Earth and universe was created not eternal, and the world was totally covered in water. These people lived in a hot, very dry and almost desert-like conditions. Even today, it's hard to fathom how the world was fully submerged and only later, land would appear. Extra water wasn't created, the elevated land must have been so flat that it allowed the existing water to completely cover the surface and not gather in low spots, what we would now see as great lakes, seas and oceans. To come up with these statements, they either had to imagine it or had some knowledge. I don't find it persuasive to say that someone imagined this early Earth's state that was completely contrary and foreign to their experience and then convinced an entire culture. If it was not simply a fanciful idea that improbably happened to be correct, then where did they get this knowledge from?

The fossil record also was thought to show that water animals came before land plants, contrary to Genesis. I have watched debates on YouTube where atheists quoted this "fact" as an example of how the Bible was erroneous. In 2011, isotope evidence was found along with fossil fragments (Strother et al., 2011) that showed that there was vegetation on land and in the water 600 million years before animals appeared in the ocean. I always wondered how could they get this right?

I always felt that the main complaint with Genesis was about the 24-hour days, and as I never believed that's what it meant, this had no teeth for me. I tell myself that the Bible is not a textbook and so, if there are scientific details that are wrong, such as the order of events, it shouldn't be a big deal. I tell myself that, but I know that I don't totally believe it. I know that this topic is problematic for many people, but as it was not a major area of my doubt, I did not go to the depth as I have for other areas. I will say that I have been very encouraged by what I learned. Candidly, I need to study more to be able to say if I believe that the Genesis record aligns perfectly with the aspects of the science in areas that we are certain about or there is a divergence. (I have heard that the *Genesis Enigma*, written by an agnostic, is a great resource) I can say with certainty that some of the details listed in Scripture are startling, especially when combined with the fact that the author(s) had no scientific insights and that their environment would imply an opposite view as to what they wrote.

> "Now we see how the astronomical evidence supports the Biblical view of the origin of the world. The details differ, but the essential elements in the astronomical and Biblical accounts of Genesis are the same: the chain of events leading to man commenced suddenly and sharply at a definite moment in time, in a flash of light and energy."
>
> *Robert Jastrow*
> *(The Enchanted Loom)*

Previously, my gut feeling was that the events in Genesis didn't really adhere to the scientific data on the order of creation, but that wasn't too bothersome as the Bible was not intended to be a scientific textbook. Maybe it's because I have seen my share of scientific theories get upended that I accept that there are still so many gray areas that occasionally, new evidence comes to light and turns the common knowledge on its head. Only 70 years ago we thought that the Earth was never covered in water and up until 10 years ago, we thought that ocean animals appeared before land vegetation. That's not a knock, that is how science is supposed to work. But these are two specific instances where the supposed defeaters of Genesis were the ones incorrect; where there has been dispute, our scientific knowledge has been in error, not Scripture. I was and am very surprised that the Biblical account seems to match what we know of the universe's, Earth's, and life's creation. I don't see any hard contradictions, but there are still so many gray areas that I can understand a theist strongly attesting that Genesis is a perfect representation of the way that the world evolved, but I can also see a materialist strongly attesting that there are clear conflicts. Making a hard determination when there is still much room for discovery isn't, in my opinion, wise but at this point. It seems like the writer of Genesis was either incredibly imaginative and insanely lucky, or he had some help.

The other side of the coin is that it seems to me that the description of God in the Old Testament is a very different one than the one of love described by Jesus in the New Testament. I have heard atheists argue that there have been wars or other evils that were justified by Bible Scripture or by the belief in God. This does not sway me as I find them to be incredibly weak arguments. This would be like blaming physics for the research that was used to create, and use of, the atomic bomb or biology and medicine for the human experiments conducted by the Nazis. Besides, in my experience, every instance where I have heard of evils having root in Scripture, it turned out to be a cringe-worthy extrapolation of the text or verses taken out of context.

What had some validity to me is that God's prescription for meting out justice seems severe by our standards. In Scripture, there are 16 offenses where death is the penalty, and that seems to me like a surprisingly high number. When I take a second and try to list the offenses that I could see possibly justifying capital punishment, I don't get very far. I come out of the gate swinging hard. Murder, sure. Rape, probably. Child molestation, okay. Then I start to hit what I would think of as gray areas. Maliciously severely injuring multiple people, maybe. Cheating old people out of their life savings? That's bad, but capital punishment bad? Tapping my inner cowboy, horse thief? Ok, I am getting desperate (partner....). Even if I go with all of these, that's only six. We need another ten to get to the full sixteen. For full disclosure, I am against the death penalty so I would assume that it is invariably harder for me to qualify offenses for capital punishment than for people who support the death penalty, but even with that consideration, 16 seems like quite a lot.

In order to make sense of this, I have had to change my mindset from a middle-class guy living in suburbia with a ready source of available food, clean water, social services, safety infrastructure ranging from road crews to fire and police, and most importantly, a functioning penal system compared to being a member of a tribe in a society with a very loose government structure 4,000 years ago. Strip away the refrigerator, flushing toilets, ability to call 911, DMV, department of transportation keeping roads in order, Starbucks Vanilla Lattes (keep calm, we're just imagining), and all the other conveniences. At that time, there was no penal system as we have today. As there were no jails or other places of incarceration, punishments were limited to financial or corporal. I

found that to be an important mental transition; you
could either make them take
a financial hit or you could
kill them—there is nothing
in between. Side note, the
Bible does not condone mu-

> "Anyone who reads all of it (the Bible) will become an atheist."
>
> *Penn Jillette*
> *(Penn Jillette Quotes)*

tilation, such as cutting off of a thief's hand, as most of the other
judicial systems of the time did.

Whenever I walk into a Quik Stop or other gas station convenience center, I invariably smirk at the signs declaring that the
maximum penalty for drinking at the store is a $250 fine. I always
felt like it might be more of a deterrent if they listed the minimum
fine and left the "or else" hanging. In the real world, we all know
that if you found yourself in some bizarre circumstance where you
simply could not wait to get home and just had to crack your beer
open right then and there, and actually got ticketed and then went
to court, there is no way that the judge is going to hit you with the
full $250 fine, unless you act like a complete jackass or are a repeat
offender. The point is that for a judge to give you the maximum
sentence, you must have done something extraordinary.

With that same idea, it turns out that there are 16 offenses
that may elicit a death sentence, but I found that 15 of them also
provide the judge latitude to only include a financial component
and remove the death sentence (remember there is no jail to sentence someone to). Like the $250 fine, execution is the *maximum*
penalty. The only crime that unilaterally earns the death sentence
is premeditated murder. Even I, who does not support capital
punishment, can understand why in a society with no penal system or jails, criminals who practice premeditated murder must be
stopped from murdering again.

I have also heard some atheists comically describe God in the Old Testament as being like an old-school mafia boss. They disobey me? Dead! I want them dead! Their families—Dead! Their kids—Dead! Their pets—Dead! Kill everything!

I was pretty disturbed when I learned that God ordered the Israelites to invade the land of Canaan. Canaan is the land extending from modern-day Lebanon to the Brook of Egypt in the south and the Jordan

> *"Kill a man, and you are a murderer. Kill millions of men, and you are a conqueror. Kill everyone, and you are a god."*
> **Jean Rostand**
> *(Pensées d'un biologiste)*

River Valley to the east. The Canaanites, named due to their descent from Noah's grandson Canaan, appear in the Bible more than 150 times and are described as a wicked and idolatrous people. This society was so corrupted that they performed human sacrifice to their god Baal in which they would place infants in the outstretched metal arms of an intensely heated metal statue, slowly burning the child to death. While they were a horrific society, the real problem for them was that they lived in part of the land promised to the Israelites at the time of the exodus from Egypt by God. God apparently ordered the Israelites to invade Canaan and kill everyone.

> In the cities of the nations the LORD your God is giving you as an inheritance, do not leave alive anything that breathes. Completely destroy them — the Hittites, Amorites, Canaanites, Perizzites, Hivites and Jebusites — as the LORD your God has commanded you. Otherwise, they will teach you to follow all the detestable things they do in worshiping their gods, and you will sin against the LORD your God. (Deut 20.16–18)

This also is not an isolated instance, all the people who occupied the promised lands received the same severe treatment.

> This is what the LORD Almighty says: "I will punish the Amale-
> kites for what they did to Israel when they waylaid them as they
> came up from Egypt. Now go, attack the Amalekites and totally
> destroy everything that belongs to them. Do not spare them; put
> to death men and women, children and infants, cattle and sheep,
> camels and donkeys." (1 Sam 15.2–3)

Honest Christian theologians are upfront about how problematic these types of verses are. On one side, we have a contin-
uous picture from multiple authors across the 66 books of the
Old and New Testaments describing a God of love and justice,
and then we have these incidences of slaughter where it honestly
seems like a group of debased people were invaded with the or-
ders to completely wipe them out. It's like when you catch something out of the corner of your eye and your head whips around
to try to understand what that was. Put to death men and women,
children and infants—whoa! What's going on here???

One Christian defense of this is that it occurred for a very
short period of time in a very specific region and it stopped a people group from committing unspeakable atrocities. I understand
doing whatever is necessary to prevent truly evil acts from being
committed. I do not understand when it extends to the children,
especially those who are not old enough to possibly have participated in these acts. Simply being in an evil society does not make
you necessarily guilty of their crimes.

First, just because it was for a short period of time is a shallow
excuse. The Nazi regime only lasted for a very short period of time,
but I condemn them wholeheartedly. My point is not to compare
God or the Israelites to the Nazis, because I don't think that's fair or
proper, but it is a good illustration that the duration of something
does not factor into the judgment of something being good or evil.

Another one of the arguments that doesn't carry much water with me is that God has precognition and knows/knew what

would have happened if these people groups were to be allowed to continue. To me, this contradicts the idea of free will and an indeterminate future. While there is good evidence that the warnings that God gave about the corrupting influence were very astute and did come to pass, I don't believe that God would punish people for something that they had not done yet. Thinking this through, how could God order the death of people who had not committed the sin yet because, eventually, they would have committed the sin? As this was pre-Jesus, during the period where people were judged by works, if these people are being killed based on precognition of evil acts that they would do in the future, then at the time that they were killed, they had not committed these acts. So, at the point of their death have not sinned. If these people are judged by God to have committed the sin, even though they have not physically done so yet, then they absolutely *had* to perform these acts—there are no other possibilities. If this is the case, there is only one future. This would mean that determinism is true and there really is no such thing as free will. In this scenario, we cannot have a relationship with God, as actors in a play have no real emotion or responsibility for what the script says. These people would presumably end up in hell for something that they did not do yet but apparently had no choice in participating in it at the later time. If they are judged to be without the stain of the sin that they were killed for, what is the justification for killing them? The whole explanation and its logical extension seem incoherent to me.

Another more compelling explanation is that the quotations above are simply using flowery war speech. When someone says "Man, the Jets got killed this weekend" I know that the players are not literally dead (if you watched the game, you may need further convincing). There is good evidence that the use of hyperbole is exactly what's going on when you really consider what is being said in context. First, the actual text directing death to anything that breathes. I seriously doubt that the soldiers raced around trying to kill literally everything that breathed. I just don't see Bronze Age warriors ripping up walls to slaughter field mice (or cats, or flies, or birds, or worms, etc.). Oh, you're just being too literal, He didn't mean things like worms (yes, while they don't have lungs, they do breathe)! Well, it specifically states "anything that breathes" so you either have to take it literally or not. And no, you can't simply say that the implication is only humans as the text specifically starts to list a hierarchy of creatures *"cattle and sheep, camels and donkeys"* and contains the all-encompassing "anything that breathes."

The second area is from the archaeological evidence that shows that the areas being attacked were military fortifications with very little to no civilian populations. There is a big difference between attacking a military outpost and a civilian center. The third area is irrefutable. Even after claiming total annihilation, in just a few verses later, they continue discussing the supposedly eradicated population and how to interact with them. Sort of the equivalent of "Man, the Jets got killed this weekend and they probably will get killed next weekend too." (Sorry, many years of bitterness from being a Jets fan has to come out somewhere!) Unless the Jets did die and were raised from the dead to play again next week, this clearly didn't happen in a literal sense. If they were truly eradicated as literally stated in Scripture, the text wouldn't proceed to then discuss permissible relations. If their real intention was genocide, they wouldn't calmly discuss the rules for intermarriage with the eradicated people group.

With all that said, I find it very problematic and frankly, I don't understand how a good and loving God could order warfare and the death of a population, even if it's only partial or purely against military targets. To be honest, I am a little disappointed. There isn't enough certainty on motive or reasoning for me to feel like this invalidates the idea of a good and just God, but it does raise some truly unsettling questions and leaves me with an uneasy feeling. I don't think this issue is a slam dunk for either side, I consider this one of the "I don't know" issues. I have come to realize that this is okay. The bigger question is if either side is true, does that preclude the ability to believe in God? To that, my answer is no.

I also feel like I need to include this for fairness:

> Again, this answer does not completely deal with all the issues. Our focus should be on trusting God even when we do not understand His ways. We also must remember that God looks at things from an eternal perspective and that His ways are higher than our ways. God is just, righteous, holy, loving, merciful, and gracious. How His attributes work together can be a mystery to us—but that does not mean that He is not who the Bible proclaims Him to be.[53]

The area that I grew up in was about 50% Catholic and 50% Jewish. As such, many of my friends were Jewish. I was fully immersed in the culture, and I went to so many Bar and Bat Mitzvahs that I knew the Jewish prayers by heart. One day in the 9th grade, we were all having a conversation during lunch. While I do not remember the topic of the conversation, I vividly remember when my friend David remarked, "Well, we are the chosen people," and the rest of my lunchmates who were Jewish all solemnly nodded in agreement. Apparently, this was common knowledge to them. I knew Jesus was a Jew, that God had always had a relationship with the Israelites, and the Old and New Testaments were stories about the Hebrews and their role in God's plan and its fulfilment in Christ. I did not know that God had chosen the Israelites to be His people above all others. Needless to say, I was profoundly shocked and surprised. It seemed remarkably unfair to pick one group out of the whole planet of people and give them preferential treatment. Also, if they were the chosen people, then where did this leave me? I got the very distinct feeling that I was a second-class citizen or even worse, on the outside looking in. If I were to spend eternity being the cosmic busboy or garbage man for the Jews, I would take it over the void, but I admit that I wouldn't be that happy about it.

As eternity is a very long time, and I didn't like the sound of what my role was to be, I did some investigating. Yes, the people of Israel were the chosen people, but they were not chosen because they were more spiritual, numerous, or "better" than everyone else. Interestingly, their sins and iniquities were frequently displayed and were regularly punished for falling short of the requirements of God. Their intended purpose was to be God's messengers for the prophesied Messiah. Once the Messiah (Jesus) came, all believers across the globe became the chosen people with the responsibility of spreading the Word. God's chosen people is all of humanity.

Passages such as Galatians 3.28–29 state that "There is neither Jew nor Gentile…. for you are all one in Christ Jesus" or Romans 11.17–24 where there is the metaphor of

> "…a people for Himself, a special treasure above all the peoples on the face of the Earth."
>
> *(Deuteronomy 7.6)*

non-Jews being grafted into the covenant, show that Jesus expanded God's promise to all believers. Once Jesus's mission was fulfilled, He expanded the covenant to include all believers who would now be "heirs" to God's promises. Matthew 28.19–20 describes The Great Commission which commands Christians to spread the message globally.

Instead of being a second-class citizen, the New Testament confirms that all of humanity is now God's chosen people and offered salvation—if I choose to accept it.

NINETEEN | *Reliability of the Bible*

The foundation of Christianity is the faith in Jesus Christ and the best source of information about His life and miracles are the Gospels. To believe the stories contained in the Gospels, you must have high confidence in the reliability of the Bible. As I started to investigate the miracle claims to figure out if there were good reasons to believe them, I found out that there are some people who don't believe that Jesus ever existed at all. They allege He is a fictional character made up to fulfill a role, and the Bible is entirely made up.

While pervasive on the Internet, I never really thought that there was much meat on this bone. The idea is regularly dismissed by scholars and thought leaders—including non-Christian ones. Besides the biographies in the New Testament, there are independent, non-biblical accounts that Jesus existed. For instance, Josephus, a Jewish historian, mentioned Jesus Christ in in *Antiquities of the Jews* (c. AD 93–94) as does the Babylonian Talmud (e.g., *Sanhedrin* 43a), which is a Jewish rabbinical compilation. It is interesting that the Talmud does not deny his miracles, instead, they attribute His works to sorcery.[54] Also, Tacitus in *Annals* from AD 116, when writing of Nero's attempt to blame the Christians for the Roman fire of AD 64, said,

Nero fastened the guilt . . . on a class hated for their abominations, called Christians by the populace. Christus, from whom the name had its origin, suffered the extreme penalty during the reign of Tiberius at the hands of . . . Pontius Pilatus, and a most mischievous superstition, thus checked for the moment, again broke out not only in Judaea, the first source of the evil, but even in Rome. . . .[55]

This clearly states that there were Christians, who derived their name from Christus (Christ) and this Christ suffered execution by crucifixion during the reign of Tiberius at the hands of Pontius Pilatus (Pilate).

The idea that Jesus never existed fell out of favor in the 1970s and virtually no serious New Testament scholar or historian agrees with it now. As F.F. Bruce notes, "Some writers may toy with the fancy of a 'Christ-myth,' but they do not do so on the ground of historical evidence. The historicity of Christ is as axiomatic for an unbiased historian as the historicity of Julius Caesar. It is not historians who propagate the 'Christ-myth' theories."[56]

I find no merit in the accusation that Jesus never existed at all, so I will leave it to the reader to dig deeper if this is of a personal concern.

If you partition off the historical and spiritual aspects of the Bible and look at it simply as a piece of literature, it is filled with what I would consider weird stories. Jonah spending three days in the mouth of a great fish, mass rising of the dead before the Pentecost, the wise men of the Pharaoh turning their staves to snakes, and Moses not only turning his staff also to a snake, but then his snake eating the snakes of the Pharaoh's wise men, and the list goes on and on. Ever since I graduated from youthful wild-eyed wonder to applying critical thinking, these Bible stories have always given me pause.

If I am being candid, my assumption was that these narratives probably started in some factual event but then, much like the children's game of telephone, they were changed with enthusiastic embellishment over time. "Oh, your god did that? Big deal, my God did *this!*"

In the game of telephone, you gather a group of children and separate them individually. The goal of the game is to pass a message to the first child who then has to walk over to the second and relate the message to them, then the second to the third and so on until the end. The final player shares the message they received followed by the original message to see how they differ. While good for laughs, playing a game of telephone shows how ridiculously corrupted stories become with each telling—and that was only among children with little incentive to exaggerate. Imagining the parallel to the Bible stories that were orally transmitted over time, yet which you are supposed to shape your worldview and life, is very troubling.

Applying this to Jesus, the original telling surely described a simple, uneducated man who became a great moral leader or teacher. As they told the next group, it changed slightly. The narrators of the stories certainly would have had a vested interest in the tale being bigger and better than its competitors, so embellishments built the myth of Jesus. "Despite countless variations …., the basic thesis of every competent mythologist, then and now, has always been that Jesus was originally a god just like any other god (….a deity), who was later historicized..."[57] says Jesus denier, Richard Carrier.

I had repeatedly heard that the story of Jesus started with a man who was a simple teacher and that story was embellished with each telling and grew to the myth that we follow today. "When Jesus is deconstructed and when it becomes clear that the

Christ of miracle, mystery, and authority never existed, it is a short step to wondering if the Jesus story as a whole is a myth .... But the historical-jesus (sic) as such never existed." Claims the Westar Institute, founders of the Jesus Seminar.[58] Their theory posits that Jesus Himself never existed and that the entire idea was created to counter the deity stories from Persia and Rome. Feeling pressure to have their own God, they borrowed from myths, cults and sects to create the Jesus that we know from Scripture.

One miracle immediately comes to mind: Jesus turning water into wine. I could easily see how maybe the wedding feast was drunk dry and Jesus showed up late with some wine. If you have ever been at a really good party in college and the last keg of beer starts spitting empty, you know what a downer it is. If you show up late with another case of beer, you are an instant celebrity. To me, it was easy to see how showing up with wine when their casks were empty was like a miracle. It changed their cups of water that they were drinking (as they were out of fermented beverages) to wine! Major miracle explained!

> "Oh man, that guy Jesus was awesome, we were down to drinking water and He showed up with more wine!"

> "Oh man, that guy Jesus was like a miracle worker. Last night, he showed up and our water went to more wine!"

> "Oh man, that guy Jesus was a miracle worker last night, he showed up and changed water to more wine!"

> "Oh man, Jesus performed a miracle last night, he showed up and changed water to wine!"

> "Jesus performed a miracle last night; he changed water into wine!"

I never thought that this specifically happened, but it's a somewhat silly illustration of how I could see a narration change with oral transmission over time. This is commonly known as the Myth Theory.

When trying to find out if Scripture fell into the category of mythification, I found that there are two major issues. First, mythical stories have specific properties and patterns, but the Scripture story of Jesus does not meet those criteria. Second, the story that we have today remains unchanged from the very beginning.

Myths have easily digestible ideas, and their heroes are attributed with sensational attributes, ignore hardships, do not include specific details, and paint the narrator and characters in a positive light. As J.P. Moreland puts it, "Legends are short on details, long on drama. Their characters are larger than life...."[59] The ideas in the New Testament demand that its adherents make significant modifications to their lifestyle, so much so that some biblical stories note that many people turned away when faced with these changes. Jesus did perform miracles, which are larger than life by definition. However, taking it a step further and looking at His life, it was filled with hardship and oftentimes scorn which is contrary to mythologization. Myths promote unbeatable heroes who easily vanquished their enemies, not ones who have to flee from mobs trying to stone them, groups who rejected His message, spat upon, beaten, and ultimately killed in the most degrading way possible. Myths also do not include details while Scripture has an abundance of details both from a time, date, and location standpoint as well as from undesigned coincidences. Undesigned coincidences are when certain elements from stories from different writers unintentionally fit together, like John 21.2 naming Nathanael which fits with the fishing context of Luke 5.1–7, that adds information and validity. Finally, it is compelling to note that there were two main audiences for Jesus's disciples, the Jews, and the Greeks and Romans. In the Jewish culture at the time, resurrection of any form was reserved for the end times when the dead would rise from the graves. In the Greco-Roman belief system, the soul was immortal, and the body was unimportant and so a resurrected body would be worthless. Creating a story where the hero rose from the dead would be contrary to the belief systems of either group and would create a barrier to belief. It is the exact opposite of the message that they would want to convey if they were trying to convert the Jews and Romans. It is clear that by simply looking at the scope of the stories of Jesus: the richness of the details, the embarrassing admissions regarding both the foibles of the disciples and the way that Jesus was treated and ultimately killed, it certainly does not look like the story of Jesus arose from mythification.

Going beyond the telephone problem, there seem to be instances where human beings could reproduce some of the Old Testament miracles and some could have a natural explanation.

In the story of Moses trying to gain the freedom of the Hebrews from the Pharaoh of Egypt, there are tales where the humans can compete with Moses divinely granted powers. The staff example listed above is a major one. In short, the magi of the Pharaoh were able to turn their staffs to living snakes (Exodus 7.10–12). Another is that when Moses turned the Nile into blood, killing all the fish (Exodus 7.20–22). Curiously, the Pharaoh's wise men were able to do the same thing with another body of water with no declared divine empowerment. In this century, witchcraft and magic have been thoroughly debunked, so I find it very hard to believe that these regular humans had the ability to transmute water to any other substance or conjure live snakes from wooden staves. If a major fact in the story is dubious at best, then it lends doubt to the entire narrative.

Okay, you're walking around jolly old England on holiday with your spouse. It's a very romantic trip that you had planned for years. As you walk along the road in the English countryside, you see storm clouds roll in. As it begins to rain, you don't worry because it's a rare warm spring afternoon and getting caught in a rain shower in the rolling hills of a foreign land is exotically romantic. You can almost hear Barry White playing and are somewhat giddy at the thought of returning to your hotel room and the adventures thereafter! Suddenly, you hear a thud and then another. A frog splatters at your feet. Then another. In a moment, everything around you are being pelted by frogs! Dodging the airborne bombardment and dancing through the gore of mutilated amphibians under your feet, you realize that it's literally raining frogs! (You also realize that after this mess, it's going to be an early evening, sorry.)

Instead of bizarre nonsense better found in a science fiction novel, it's an actual phenomena (that for some reason has a higher incidence in Great Britain). The scientific explanation is that a high-pressure system that precedes a severe thunderstorm causes a waterspout (a water-based tornado). The center of the waterspout is very low pressure (if you remember Bernoulli's principle where high speeds results in low pressure) and a high-pressure cone. On land, it can pick up cows, cars and the most notorious element, mobile homes. Since it is over water or swampland, it picks up what is in its path, namely fish and frogs. Since these aquatic creatures are very light, they stay suspended in the updraft much, much longer than heavier items. As the storm hits land and loses energy, the pressure drops, and the clouds begin to release the water they are carrying. With the rain falling, the vortex loses the last of its energy and dumps whatever it has picked up to the ground, in this case frogs. Not weird enough? There are recorded incidents of tomato rain. My point is that there are very, very weird, verging on miraculous, but scientifically explainable, phenomena.

One day I was driving and National Public Radio, NPR, had the chief meteorologist from some government agency on discussing tornadoes. I called in and asked him why they seemed to frequent developed land. I had theorized that maybe the heat generated by humans and their creations perhaps caused some sort of updraft or that the building interfered with the natural airflow. His answer was simply that there was no higher incidence over developed areas compared to undeveloped land (with weighting based on percentage of rural to urban land factored in), it simply generated more attention. This does underscore how perception can exaggerate phenomena, such as miracles.

I started digging into the miracle stories to sort out which could really have purely naturalistic answers and to my surprise, there were remarkably few. The Plague of Boils was the sixth curse that God manifested on the Egyptians trying to move the Pharaoh to free the Hebrews (Jews). There were ten curses with each having a one-month duration, the first three weeks were warnings and the last week, the proverbial hammer fell. Someone could say that something like the Plague of Boils in Exodus 9.8–12 could be easily explained medically, for example by anthrax, and that is certainly true. The fifth curse killed the livestock and so it is possible that the decaying animals gave rise to an anthrax pandemic in curse 6. I have consistently seen that God has repeatedly worked through nature. I believe that, assuming God exists, He created the laws of physics and nature and as such, they do not constrain him. Instead, they are His preferred method of action. It's like if I created a recipe and process for baking a special cake. When I started to bake the cake, I would follow my recipe. It would be folly to say that I was constrained to work within the method that I created.

While I can see that a natural explanation to the illness is possible, I have a very hard time believing that the timing is natural. The probability of someone saying you are cursed and then the population having a pandemic immediately after is a little too improbable. If there was a curse and then at some point in the future it did happen, I wouldn't give that much weight as it could coincidental. I curse you to stub your toe! Well, given enough time, I guarantee that my curse will be proven true. However, if someone warns you for three weeks and then you are hit with the plague right when they said you would, that would be an eerie coincidence but still not 100% persuasive. If for 10 consecutive months there is a different foretelling, and it comes true in every instance, in the exact same sequence, with events that could not have been created by human hands (they could have natural causes though), well, that's too hard to dismiss.

In the example of Jesus turning water into wine (John 2.1–11), when I looked directly at what Scripture claimed and not the third grade Sunday school version that I knew, I learned that the actual claim is that Jesus was at the wedding when they ran out of wine. At the behest of His mother Mary, He has the servants fill six jars with water. Now, when I think of a jar, I think of something that is approximately the size of a wine bottle or maybe a milk container, maybe a gallon at the most. The specifics are that the jars described in the bible story are stone waterpots holding two or three firkins each. Knowing off-hand that a firkin is equivalent to almost nine gallons (ok, maybe I had to look that up), that means that each jar held between 18 and 27 gallons. Also knowing that a gallon of water is eight lbs. (I actually did know that), this means that each jar weighed between 144 and 216 lbs. each, plus the weight of the stone jar itself! These were clearly stone fixtures in the house that were made for holding water for washing, to think that Jesus came strolling in with an extra couple of bottles of wine to keep the party going was childishly naive. Again, this does nothing to prove or disprove theism, but it does shed light that taking a quick view of miracle stories and drawing conclusions is unwise.

I have consistently found that while there are elements of many stories in Scripture that can be explained with natural phenomena, there are other key elements that simply cannot be. At this point I accepted that the stories could not be dismissed on those grounds, but then I had to look at if they were just embellishments over time resulting in miraculous stories. As the Old Testament spanned centuries and was based on oral tradition while the New Testament was a much smaller timeframe and was physically recorded, I will discuss each separately.

When I grew up, there were no smartphones, we had a rotary phone mounted on the kitchen wall. There was no Internet, only four channels of TV—and no remote, and no speed dial. If you were going somewhere, you found a map and memorized the route. Calling someone? You had better remember their number and so on. The point is that even with all the conveniences of the 1980s, we had to remember a significant number of things. Today, I simply say "Siri, Call Paige" to phone my wife or "Navigate to 123 Main St." to have my GPS set my directions and then it talks me through my route. I have more than 400 channels to choose from, so I only linger on a channel for a moment and if it doesn't provide something of immediate interest, I am off to the next. The technology boom has had an impact on us and especially our kids. The mail used to be days or weeks but still considered fast, then came overnight delivery, now we pound our 'send and receive' icon when impatiently waiting the five second eternity for an email! There are scientific studies that show that using smartphones at an early age rewires the developing brain. This clearly demonstrates that outward stimuli can have a physical effect. Attention spans have dropped radically in recent years. You can readily see this in TV and in movies. Films from the 1930s–1950s had an average shot length that ranged from 8.5–11 seconds which has shortened to 4–5 seconds. Television commercials have dropped from 30 seconds down to 15 seconds (don't smile, there are just twice as many commercials). When you watch a show or movie, they constantly change the camera angle to recapture your attention. Now watch an old movie and notice the difference.

The Old Testament was passed down orally from generation to generation and had edited sections. If you doubt the editing, the books attributed to being authored by Moses contain detail on Moses' death, so that part, at least, could not have been written by Moses. I think to really assess the integrity of the Scripture; I needed to try to understand society at that point in time. Thousands of years ago, written texts were rare, and the mechanism of transmission of information was primarily oral. The tuning of memory, over generations, has been proven to be able to precisely commit vast amounts of data. In ancient Jewish culture, there were three tiers of education. Just the first tier, which lasted up to about 12 years old, students were required to memorize the Torah, the first five books of the Old Testament. They used techniques such as song and "mnemonics" to make it easier to retain. Memorization was so standard that it was expected that 12-year-olds could recite the first five books of the Bible, word for word, on demand.

It is undeniable that rabbis had a significant portion or even the entirety of the Old Testament thoroughly committed to memory. Scripture was viewed as the immutable word of God, and that it was deemed too important to allow any change. Close enough may be good enough for hand grenades and horseshoes, but not God's word. Also, it seems that if you have a number of rabbis who have the Scripture memorized, it is quite the conspiracy theory to think that an instigator could convince all of the individuals who held this knowledge to only pass down a new, modified version. It is important to note that there are textual variations in the Hebrew Scriptures. In fairness, I need to note a point made by Dr. Jonathan McLatchie that the "Masoretic text of Jeremiah has 2,700 additional words than are found in the Greek Septuagint version and there are actually Hebrew copies that were discovered among the Dead Sea Scrolls of both the longer and shorter versions of Jeremiah." It is true that they are not identical, but I do not know of any textual difference that alters the message of the Scripture.

Probably the most popular claim is that the Gospels were written centuries after the fact and the large gap of time allowed humble tales of a wise and charismatic person to become the grand myths of the New Testament. I had never considered this to be an issue, and it seemed unlikely to me, but since this was so widespread a claim and so important a topic, I had to do my due diligence. I had heard some people with authoritative-sounding credentials position Jesus as a great teacher that ran afoul of the Roman authorities and was executed. The stories of Jesus were retold over generations and with each retelling, embellishments grew Jesus from simple man to deity. Since I discussed some of this issue previously and the data on this topic is voluminous, I am not going to go into all the details here; however, I will provide a summary of the facts that helped me move past this with the certainty that this is a non-issue. If this is an issue for you, there are a multitude of books, papers, and videos of legitimate scholarship on this.

To be honest, I find these facts on the authenticity of the stories to be somewhat compelling but as there is no full recorded history, there is still a part of me that allows that there may have been some embellishment, especially in the early years. Here is where it gets tricky. There is no intellectual or factual reason to believe that, it is a "feeling" that comes from fear. Combating fear-based feelings is much harder than dealing with intellectual doubt. Intellectual issues can be resolved with logic and study. They may take a while, but it is a clear and linear path to become satisfied one way or the other. Emotional doubts, like this one, are rooted much deeper and need to be addressed in a different manner.

Jesus' ministry lasted three years and started somewhere between AD 27–30 and the crucifixion in either 30 or 33. The Gospels are presented as firsthand knowledge and so must have been written within the lifetime of the authors. First, there is very compelling evidence that the Gospels were composed before 100 which is a significant threshold because it falls within 70 years of the crucifixion, well within the lifespan of the apostles or their associates. Evidence dates Mark to 60–70, Matthew and Luke to 80–90, and John to 90–100. Second, it is key that independent witnesses would still be alive to dispute any of the events accounted in the writings. As the Gospels were the basis for their preaching, and that preaching occurred directly in the region and cities where the events transpired, there would have been living witnesses to the original events present at the time of the recounting. If they were wild stories, there would be people alive to object.

This is highly significant because the group in power. who recently crucified Jesus as a threat to their authority, would be seeking opportunities to debunk or disprove the claims of the early Christians and quash this emerging "cult." Interestingly enough, there are no records of any witnesses coming forward to refute the Gospels. The only dispute that I am aware of is that the Jewish writers later in the Babylonian Talmud (e.g., Sanhedrin 43a) and, interesting enough, in the Gospel of Matthew where, in both instances, the miracles were attributed to the power of Satan instead of God. Remember that the Babylonian Talmud is a collection of Jewish writing that were compiled between the 3rd and 5th centuries AD. In Matthew 12.24 it states, "But when the Pharisees heard it, they said, This fellow doth not cast out devils, but by Beelzebub the prince of the devils." The Gospel itself testifies that the Jewish leaders of the time admitted the miracles but would not accept that they came from God.

I do find it entirely plausible that people did come forward with counterclaims that were not recorded, or the records were lost over time but without evidence, I can only say that it's possible. It may be my New York skepticism, but I would think that if there were significant objections to what was being publicly preached by the new Christians, the powers of authority that wanted to destroy this new group, especially the established Jewish leaders, would have made sure that the objections were documented, transmitted, and preserved. The silence is deafening.

During this search I was alarmed to find that dirty little secret of the church is that the New Testament was created by a meeting of a cadre of elite Christian leadership who filtered numerous books down to the four Gospels that we use today. This was known as the Council of Nicaea. It is said that they had a wide body of writings, with a variety of stories—including from Judas and Mary—but only selected a few choice works that supported their narrative of a divine Christ. Even though I came upon this circumstantially, it was alarming as if true, again, would erect a serious barrier to belief. I pictured a darkened council chamber, the large bonfire in the center of the room casting flickering shadows on the walls behind hooded figures. The head of the chamber reads aloud a "gospel" before they decry "Heresy!" and he throws the scroll to the fire! At the end of the readings, only four remained; those to become the New Testament—by the order of the emperor!

The reality is that the Council of Nicaea was ordered by the Emperor Constantine I, in AD 325. It was a gathering of 300 clergy members to address the and affirm details of the divinity of Christ and to address some escalating controversies among church leadership that were becoming problematic in the failing Roman Empire and Christianity at large. The main theological issues were the debate between whether Christ more human or more divine, created or begotten, or if He is equal to the Father. It also contained many more fine point details such as the relationship between the Father, Son, and Holy Spirit and the date to celebrate Easter. Scholarship shows that Emperor Constantine felt "called" to bring about peace, love, and unity in the church, not to diabolically omit books that were not to his liking.

> "My dear," Teabing declared, "until that moment in history, Jesus was viewed by His followers as a mortal prophet. a great and powerful man, but a man nonetheless. A mortal."
>
> "Not the Son of God?"
>
> "Right," Teabing said. "Jesus' establishment as 'the Son of God' was officially proposed and voted on by the Council of Nicaea."
>
> "Hold on. You're saying Jesus' divinity was the result of a vote?"
>
> *Dan Brown*
> *(The Da Vinci Code)*

While good drama, it's a ridiculous notion to anyone who has done the proper study. The Council of Nicaea did produce a statement of doctrine regarding items like the ones aforementioned and an affirmation of faith, the Nicene Creed (which if you had a Catholic upbringing, you know by heart).

> We believe in one God,
> the Father, the Almighty,
> Maker of all that is, seen and unseen.
> We believe in one Lord, Jesus Christ,
> the only Son of God,
> eternally begotten of the Father,
> God from God, Light from Light,
> true God from true God,
> begotten, not made, consubstantial
> of one Being with the Father.
> Through him all things were made.
> For us men and for our salvation
> he came down from heaven,
> and by the Holy Spirit was incarnate of the Virgin Mary,
> and became man.
> For our sake he was crucified under Pontius Pilate;
> he suffered death and was buried.
> On the third day he rose again
> in accordance with the Scriptures;
> he ascended into heaven
> and is seated at the right hand of the Father.
> He will come again in glory to judge the living and the dead,
> and his kingdom will have no end.
> We believe in the Holy Spirit, the Lord, the giver of life,
> who proceeds from the Father and the Son.
> With the Father and the Son he is worshipped and glorified.
> He has spoken through the Prophets.
> We believe in one holy catholic and apostolic Church.
> We acknowledge one baptism for the forgiveness of sins.
> We look for the resurrection of the dead,
> and the life of the world to come. Amen.

The four Gospels in use today were not decided upon by the Council of Nicaea but had been widely used for hundreds of years. Even the most skeptical, non-Christian scholars date the Gospels to the first century and, calling back to the importance of early dating, these four books are the only ones written before 100. Any other purported competitors to the four Gospels have a writing date hundreds of years later. In other words, the ones with dating that were within the lifetime of the apostles were included, ones that came later and were potentially subject to mythification, were omitted. While it makes for good Hollywood, there is zero evidence that the Council of Nicaea even discussed the canon of the New Testament.

The dating of the documents is critical in understanding that the New Testament was written and believed immediately after the resurrection. Even the most skeptical, non-Christian scholars agree that the date of the Gospels is within the first century. The actual dates of the four books, or Gospels, are as follows. The gospel of Mark is believed to be the first, written around 70.[60] Remember that if this was written in 70 and the crucifixion was at 30 or possibly 33, this isn't hundreds of years after the event, this is at most 40 years later, which is easily within the window of firsthand knowledge or attestation. In other words, the gospel was being preached to people who were alive for the events in question and could easily refute it. As for the other Gospels, Matthew and Luke were written between 80–90 while John was written between 90–100.

I immediately asked how it is possible to know these dates with any certainty? The first three Gospels discussed the fall of the Jerusalem Temple, which would be a momentous event as the temple was a central part of Jewish life. A good parallel would be the White House burning to the ground or the destruction of the Twin Towers. The fall of the Jerusalem Temple did happen in AD 70 but in these Gospels, the actual event is not mentioned— only the future prophecy. Therefore, I find it incredibly unlikely that someone would note the prophecy of an event but then not actually make mention of the very same event if it had already occurred.[61] Wouldn't it raise concerns if I prophesied about 9/11 or the Covid pandemic years after they occurred and never linked them to the actual events?

Also, in the book of Acts written by Luke, the deaths of Peter and Paul in 64 are never recorded, which is an extremely important detail to have missing. Luke's actual gospel preceded his writing of Acts, and it is readily agreed that Mark precedes Luke. A majority of New Testament scholars agree that Paul's epistles date between 48–60 and that Paul quotes from Luke's gospel, so again, Luke must have been written before Paul.

> "Further study.... showed that the book (Acts) could bear the most minute scrutiny as an authority for the facts of the Aegean world, and that it was written with such judgment, skill, art and perception of truth as to be a model of historical statement."
>
> **Sir William Mitchell Ramsay**
> (*The Bearing of Recent Discovery on the Trustworthiness of the New Testament*)

The Rylands Papyrus P52, found in Egypt, contains fragments of John.[62] As it was dated in approximately AD 130, John's gospel must have been written significantly before this as first it had to have been hand copied (assuming first iteration for shortest time) and then it had to traverse from Greece to Egypt. As John's gospel is agreed to be the last gospel written, that puts an endpoint of the latest time somewhere around 100. It is true that we do not have the original copies that the authors physically wrote, but it's also true that you don't have a copy of what I physically wrote and that it doesn't change its validity. By contrast, Alexander the Great's life, as was recorded in Plutarch's Lives and Arrian's Anabasis, 400–450 years after, or Tiberius Caesar with the best source of information on his life was 80 years after his death. None of these are questioned. In fairness, if we have misinformation on Alexander, it really doesn't make a major difference in our lives, but if we have misinformation on Jesus, it matters a great deal. Overall, I don't find the timing of other characters of antiquity meaningful, but I do find it important that there is good evidence of the Gospels being written within the lifetime of the witnesses.

To test if a game of telephone was what happened, there is a relatively simple method of checking for modification. If there are sufficient manuscripts from a good sample of regions and times, we should be able to do a comparative analysis to see if there is any divergence. Versions of the New Testament were hand copied and sent to burgeoning churches and then reproduced by hand again for further spread, making checking for modification over time relatively simple. There are more than 5,000 early Greek manuscripts from a wide variety of regions, providing a rich sample size and diversity of location. This includes 130–140 Greek sources from the 2nd-4th centuries. If you include early translations, letters or incomplete writings, the number jumps from 5,000 early manuscripts to more than 24,000 total textual witnesses. After analysis, none has any divergence that affects the tenets of Christianity.

For perspective, there are seven copies of the works of Plato and ten copies relating to Caesar. Even the widely quoted atheist New Testament scholar, who writes popular level books damning the Bible and highlights all the "contradictions," admits within professional circles that there are no meaningful differences. Some other food for thought:

- Fragment of Gospel of Mark estimated to late first century.
- Fragments of Acts and epistles dated slightly later than Mark.
- Clement of Rome: letter to the Corinthian church quoting Gospels in AD 95.
- Ignatius: quoted all the Gospels in his letters and was martyred in AD 115.
- Polycarp: quoted the Gospels in letters from AD 120.
- Justin Martyr: quotes Gospels material in AD 150.

An abbreviated timeline:

AD 30	Crucifixion
AD 55	1 Corinthians
AD 70	Mark
AD 80–90	Matthew
AD 80–90	Luke
AD 62–64	1 Peter

I also learned that it takes two generations, or 80 years, for legendary accounts to take root. J.P. Moreland noted that "if these books and letters were written within two generations of his death, it would have been impossible for legendary features to have crept into the biblical documents."[63] If the resurrection was at the earliest point, 30, then anything taken before 110 should be regarded as not having been tainted in this way. It seems there is very compelling evidence that the Gospels were written well before the 80-year span and well within the lifespan of witnesses. Said another way, every one of the Gospels and letters in the New Testament was written well before the earliest expected beginning date of mythologization of 110. If this isn't enough, there is a creed that is later copied into 1 Corinthians 15.3–5 (a letter to the church in Corinth) written by Paul clearly stating their belief that Jesus was divine:

[that] Christ died for our sins according to the Scriptures, and that He was buried, and that He was raised on the third day according to the Scriptures, and that He appeared to Cephas, then to the twelve.

This creed is dated to *between six months and two years* after the crucifixion. The most skeptical scholarship dates it to 41, still roughly 10 years after the crucifixion. It is clear that immediately after Jesus' death, they believed that Christ was resurrected and was divine. This creed alone, dated 32–35, makes the idea that the resurrection was invented over time impossible.

The idea that the claims of Jesus' divinity were a product of mythologization is compelling until the idea is analyzed. The New Testament bears none of the hallmarks of myth and conversely, shows depth of detail and unintended coincidences that speak to its truth. Jesus being a great teacher that had events attributed to him is shown to be false by the early dating of Scripture and by creeds that clearly attest to His divinity. It is very clear that the stories of the Gospels have remained unchanged in meaning since the period immediately following the resurrection.

I also find no contradiction and no natural explanation for these accounts. It seems that either there was great care taken to pass down the stories in exact detail or that they were written down immediately after the events. The timing was well within the window that witnesses could dispute them. It does not seem that there is any power in the concern that it was simply modification over time. Then it comes down to do I think that these stories were simply made up or do they hold up as the truth.

Another objection that I often hear is that you must dismiss the Gospels because they contain miracles. As discussed earlier, I find this to be a silly objection as this seems to be the tail wagging the dog. If there is an omniscient, all-powerful God, then of course there can be miracles. If there isn't, then there won't. It simply doesn't work to dismiss miracles out of hand and use that as a reason to dismiss theology.

Jim Jones, the leader of a cult, could apparently heal the sick and predict the future so convincingly that he had convinced his followers that he was supernatural and they believed him to be God, in a literal, not meta-

> *"Miracles are like pimples, because once you start looking for them you find more than you ever dreamed you'd see."*
>
> **Lemony Snicket**
> *(The Lump of Coal)*

phorical, way. His devotees would do anything for him: lie, cheat, steal, assist in fake healing and psychic demonstrations, or even drugging followers to perpetuate the idea that he could raise the dead. They did this because some believed that this allowed him to conserve his supernatural powers for more important matters. In some situations, belonging becomes the most important facet of the members' lives and fear of rejection and becoming an outcast outweighs everything. Once in this mental state, any act is conceivable and self-justified.

I know that I am supposed to hold the apostles with reverence, and part of me certainly does, but another part wonders about the personages. One real area of concern is directly related to the credibility

> *"Why did you follow Jim Jones?" I asked him.*
>
> *"Because I believed he was God,"* he answered. *"We all believed he was God."*
>
> **Survivor of the Jonestown Massacre**
> *(Quoted in Psychology Today)*

of the apostles and gospel writers. Throughout history, there have been groups that were fooled into thinking that their charismatic leader was divine. They believed in it so heartily that they were willing to die for their leader. A part of me secretly feared that the early Christians were like the Jonestown followers, only a cult that happened to catch on and gain traction.

If someone was perpetuating a hoax that they knew to be fake and it came time to be martyred for the cause, I am confident that the person would quickly recant to avoid death. That someone is willing to die for a person or cause does not testify to the truth of the issue, but it is strong proof that the individual sincerely *believed*. In both instances, modern-day cults such as Jim Jones and the Peoples Temple and early Christians, very often the true believers died for their faith. However, I did find that there are some very important differences.

First, cultists perform targeted overly aggressive evangelism. While everyone has been hit by that overzealous "saved" person, in my experience it's different from when I have had an interaction with someone involved in a cult. Cultists target those who are troubled, weak-minded, very young, or old while Christians try to draw in the general population. Secondly, cults deal in secret knowledge and disallow questioning while Christianity provides full access to the Bible and, as this writing is a testament to, makes an effort to answer questions. Cults use emotional manipulation to promote the leader as divine and excuse away any failings, Christianity incudes many embarrassing details of the church founders and regularly admits their own limitations and flaws. Third, cults usually involve financial exploitation where the members relinquish ownership of their possessions to enrich the leader. Conversely, Christianity is based on giving away your material goods to those that are in need. Modern cultists are often martyred by suicide ordered by their leader while Christians view suicide as a sin. When Christians are martyred, it is most often for not abandoning their faith and the killing is committed by an outside source. Cultists keep their members close so that they can reinforce their doctrine, conversely, early Christians were sent out into the world to spread the word. In summary, cults involve manipulation to keep the person in the group and empower the leader with power and money. Christianity was founded on Jesus, someone who is proposed to have died in service to people.

I also had concerns that the apostles were a group of ignorant and superstitious people. When I think of the apostles, I think of a group of illiterate and uneducated fishermen that would be easy to fool. There is the Christian argument that the workings of Christ were of a sort that needed no education or guile to verify, everyone knows the difference between a dead person and a live one or water and wine. While this is true, it also strikes me that cultists, in their belief that the leader is divine, are willing to help fabricate miracles to convince the members. I do think that Jesus' miracles extend much farther, and would be considerably harder to deceive people, but I see some limited parallels that do give me pause.

When I stop and take a moment, the reality is that some apostles were fishermen but there were also many highly educated people as well. For example, Luke was a Greek physician and a first-rate historian. I quickly dismissed being a physician as I equate medicine of antiquity to leaching or other misguided practices, but the truth is that the Greeks were the originators of modern medicine and while their medical knowledge was much less than ours today, they had established medical schools for training and the intellect required to be a physician is on par with today. Another famous example is Paul, a religious scholar who studied under Gamaliel. Gamaliel was a well-respected leader of the Jewish Sanhedrin (council of elders) who was lauded for his knowledge and wisdom, any apprentice that he took on to mentor

246 | *The Doubt Project*

would have needed to be intellectually sound. Then what struck me was why was I discounting someone because they were a fisherman. I do a bit with real estate, and I can certainly tell you that I have met many, many tradesmen who were highly rational and intelligent people. I also have a software company, and I can tell you with certainty that I have met quite a few knuckleheads with college degrees or a PhD. This was a personal judgement issue, I simply needed to cease looking down my nose at someone for their occupation and making assumptions about their intellectual prowess or ability to be fooled simply based on their line of work. Interestingly, looking at the Gospels against other early writing styles, studies have shown that Gospels are in the same genre of Greco-Roman biographies. When I removed my bias due to their occupation and actually read the text, my opinion radically changed. There is an itch in the back of my head that while it is possible that Christianity started as a cult or the members were gullible but after reading the writings of the apostles, it is hard to say that they sound weak-willed or delusional. While possible, I find it highly unlikely that they were simple dupes.

TWENTY | *Contradictions*

When I started digging into my doubts, instead of answers, I often encountered other areas for skepticism that I never knew existed. Some of these seemed intuitively false and were easily discarded, but there were some that were real eye-openers and deserved investigation. It was not long into my search when I heard the objection that the Bible is full of contradictions and so, is unreliable. A contradiction is when two things are claimed that are mutually exclusive. Both cannot logically be true. Of course, I know what a contradiction is! Yes, but what was startling to me is that if there is a contradiction in Scripture, one of the versions must be incorrect, false, erroneous—in other words wrong! If there are contradictions, then some of the Bible is wrong, if some of the Bible is wrong, then it's not divinely inspired, if it's not divinely inspired, then it must have been written by fallible human authors recounting different versions of truly extraordinary events—and that opens a Pandora's box of questions and doubt. When I first heard this, I was a bit shaken as I had always thought that some people may not believe in God, but the Bible was unquestionably sound. The claim that it originates from divine inspiration and is perfect in form is one of the pillars of its trustworthiness. Let's face it, some of the stories in there are pretty incredible. When you are asking for belief in the incredible, your details had better be airtight. If the authors were playing fast and loose with the facts and didn't even agree with each other, that would be a tremendous problem.

Doing a quick internet search will yield many proposed examples of how the Bible is rife with contradictions, some sites even boasting of the "Top 100!" After some digging, I found that the claims of contradiction in Scripture seemed to me like people taking a quick read of Scripture looking for gotchas, instead of questions arising out of sincere scholarly research. Most of them are poor examples of objection, verging on juvenile, but there are some that elicit legitimate investigation. A few of the more common examples are the women at the tomb, are we saved by faith or by good works, even things like where Moses received the Ten Commandments.

The most common accusation of contradiction is when two passages are compared, and they don't contain the same details about an event. The important part is that while they don't say the same exact thing, they do not say that something that directly goes against what the other verse attests. When I woke up early this morning, my wife was not there. When she got home, she told me all about her CrossFit workout at the 6 AM class. Later today, I heard her talking to her sister about the 5K run that she went on this morning with her friend. I caught her contradicting herself! Which did she do, the 6 AM CrossFit workout or a 5K run with her friend—and more importantly, why was she lying to me and where was she really?! Before we bring in Dr. Phil, we need to apply some logic and see if there really is a simple explanation. The fact is that she does a 6 AM CrossFit workout at the gym and then does a 5K later in the morning with her friend pretty much every day. So, while her exercise regimen is psychotic, there was no nefarious contradiction. Many of the supposed contradictions in the Gospel accounts mirror my story where differing details (e.g., Matthew 28.1 vs. Luke 24.10) complement rather than contradict each other.

If you asked my daughters, wife, mom, and friends to describe me, they would agree on many of the core elements, but each would focus on different aspects of my life and would be writing from their own perspective. My daughters would probably recount how I talk about life lessons and how I stress the importance of learning math and science. My wife would hopefully talk about what a good husband and father I am. My mom may talk about how I was as a child or stories about how my brother and I had a daily fistfight. My friend Allen would talk about how I am going through this spiritual ordeal while my other friend Don would talk about the real estate deals that we do, and how "going out for beers" with me really means that I let him drink beer while I sip club soda (I can't seem to live that down). Each of these are facets of who I am but they are just a view from a different angle and not contradictory. If you took all of these stories together, you would get a more complete view of who I am. Similarly, the Gospel authors' varying perspectives (e.g., Mark's brevity vs. John's theology) help create a fuller picture of Jesus and ironically help prove its trustworthiness.

Another common error is with timing or lack of specificity. An immediate example is that in the opening sections, I said that I was 50 years old and then later on, I said that I was 51. This is a pretty clear contradiction and so, either I am a liar, or I am so clueless that I don't even know my own age. I think any rational person would agree that if someone, or something contradicts themself, whatever they have to say should be taken with a very small grain of salt. On the other hand, if someone over the age of six doesn't know their own age, their mental competence should be questioned. Either way, we need to dismiss anything that they have to say.

If you look at it on a surface level, it is clear that at one point I stated that I was 50 and in another, I attest that I am 51. Done deal—or not so fast? If I claimed to be two ages simultaneously, I agree that it would put either my word or mental state in doubt. The problem is that the foundational assumption is incorrect, while I did claim the ages of 50 and 51, I did not claim both ages simultaneously. When I started this writing project eight months ago, I truthfully said that I was 50. Currently, I am 51 and have no idea if this project will span even more birthdays. Just like in the errors with timing, obtaining context resolves apparent contradictions.

One day, I was in the park having a conversation with another dad while my young daughters played with his son. As he was telling me that his son was 5 years old, he was indignantly interrupted with "I am five and 3 months!" I grabbed my kids and fled from the park as he clearly could not be trusted. Ok, that didn't happen. What did happen is that I immediately realized that he was speaking in general terms and rounding his son's age while his son was using a higher level of precision. Neither was lying or incorrect. I see this type of example commonly used as an attempt to defeat Scripture, but like the example above, it doesn't seem to hold water.

An example of a shallow, gotcha claim is regarding the location of Moses being given the Ten Commandments. In many verses, it specifically states that the location where God presented the tablets to be Mount Sinai. Exodus 31.18, 34.4, 34.32, Leviticus 26.46. The objection is that Scripture in 1 Kings 8.9, 2 Chronicles 5.10 and Malachi 4.4 identify different locations.

Exodus 31.18	"And he gave unto Moses, when he had made an end of communing with him upon Mount Sinai, two tables of testimony, tables of stone, written with the finger of God."
2 Chronicles 5.10	"There was nothing in the ark save the two tables which Moses put therein at Horeb."

The first problem is that in Exodus, it states that Mount Sinai is the location where Moses received the tablets but in Chronicles, it details that Moses put the two tablets in the ark at Horeb. If we stop there, it could look like two different locations were being identified as where Moses received the tablets, which would be a contradiction. Does this not simply imply that he received them at one location but performed a completely unrelated action, putting them in the ark, somewhere else? For argument's sake, let's say that they both said that theirs was location of transfer and so would be a contradiction. In my opinion, if you are making a claim like that, it is your responsibility to go further and really investigate the specifics. It took me less than two minutes to find out that Horeb is the region in which mount Sinai is located. The statements that "he proposed to her at the Lincoln Memorial" and "she got engaged in Washington D.C." are not contradictions, and neither is stating that Moses was given the commandments on Mount Sinai and at Horeb. I think that anyone who is familiar enough with this text to make claims regarding its content would either know the basic facts about their claim, like the specific location of the two points in question, and are being intellectually dishonest or are working from a position of having very little information but a very big agenda, resulting in knee-jerk claims with no attempt at being thorough.

Another type of objection that I have seen often is when the text from different authors is expressed from different viewpoints but does not include the same details. Honestly, I found most to be unworthy of comment, but the women at the tomb is one that I could see as giving a genuine concern.

Matthew 28.8	"The women hurried away from the tomb, afraid yet filled with joy, and ran to tell his disciples."
Luke 24.9	"When they came back from the tomb, they told all these things to the Eleven and to all the others"
As opposed to	
Mark 16.8	"Trembling and bewildered, the women went out and fled from the tomb. They said nothing to anyone, because they were afraid"

I had read somewhere that you should never take one "verse" of Scripture on its own. For one thing, the "verses" and numbers were inserted to make reading easier, they were never intended to be used to demarcate thoughts or ideas that were independent of each other. If you walked into a room and heard one sentence of a conversation between two people, it might pique your interest, but you wouldn't fly off the handle without context and completeness. That is exactly what we do when we take one verse in isolation. Comparing these single verses, it does sound like Mark is saying that the women never said anything while Matthew and Luke say that they do. When you read the complete sections, it seems perfectly understandable that Mark was saying that they said nothing at the immediate time while Matthew and Luke are talking about what was important to them in their gospel, which was what happened after. Mark's abrupt ending reflects his writing style, while Matthew and Luke emphasize later events. I also look at it logically, does it really make any sense that Mark thought that the women *never* spoke about this? If it's taken literally, they never would have spoken about it at all. Critics of the New Testament frequently claim that the Bible was written much later, refined and evolved, adding and embellishing the story. If that's true, do we think that these people were so clever as to be able to perpetuate a global hoax spanning thousands of years but still foolish enough to leave details like this hanging out there?

I have actually taken the time to go through the *101 Contradictions* proposed by skeptics and overwhelmingly, they fail to persuade me that they are contradictions at all. All except one relating to Jesus' return (Matthew 24.34 vs. Mark 13.32). While the supposed contradiction seems shallow, the more problematic part is that it seems to be, well, wrong.

Mark 13.32	"But about that day or hour no one knows, not even the angels in heaven, nor the Son, but only the Father."
Matthew 24.30–35	"Now learn this lesson from the fig tree: As soon as its twigs get tender and its leaves come out, you know that summer is near. [33] Even so, when you see all these things, you know that it is near, right at the door. [34] Truly I tell you, this generation will certainly not pass away until all these things have happened. Heaven and Earth will pass away, but my words will never pass away."

Mark specifically says that no one knows the time that this will happen, but in Matthew, Jesus says that it will before that generation passes away. While it is a lukewarm contradiction as it stands, the very next passage in Matthew is "But about that day or hour no one knows, not even the angels in heaven, nor the Son, but only the Father" which completely reaffirms Mark. While the contradiction aspect of this is weak, it seems clear to me that Jesus is saying that "this" generation will be alive (not pass away) when the end times come (the point of the passages). As this was roughly AD 32, the world clearly has not ended, and that generation did indeed pass. This was one of my biggest issues with the supposed contradictions in the New Testament and frankly, one that I was somewhat tentative to research.

What I have found is that the explanation is so simple and straightforward that it makes me a little angry at myself for going against one of my basic tenets of facing truth. I had heard, and I even have stated earlier, that you must not take a verse in isolation. When I stopped myself and began reading earlier in the chapter, it is abundantly and embarrassingly obviously clear that Jesus is speaking of the End Times when all of these events will happen. The lines of Scripture above state that no one knows when it will happen but when it does, it will be quick and last less than one generation. The perspective is not talking about the current generation and things that will happen during their lifetimes, the subject is the events, and they will occur within the lifespan of people of that time.

> "It is my goal here to make clear that the Bible does not contain contradictions, but rather paradoxes. A paradox is a perceived contradiction that upon further study is found to be harmonious."
>
> **Patrick Schreiner**
> (Are There Contradictions in the Bible?)

When you think about how many hours that you have dedicated to history, social studies, English or any other school topic and then compare it to how long you have dedicated to things of a spiritual nature, it really is eye-opening how we prioritize. I will guarantee that I have spent more time finger painting as a toddler than I spent reading the Bible throughout my entire life. I find that my unfamiliarity and lack of contemplation leads me to fall into assumptions that make these objections meaningful.

As with everything, I wholeheartedly recommend looking at both sides of the equation and making your own judgment based on facts. I found it to be a straightforward process to see for myself if these claims hold any water. First, find a site with the proposed Scripture contradictions and read each claim. I then read the passages myself and then follow up on the apologist's side to see what they have to say, and then I reread the Scripture. When that is complete, I evaluate both sides of the argument. Everyone will make their own determination, but to me, this test of contradictions was a simple one to decide.

| *Everything Hangs on the Resurrection*

My perspective was always that the Old Testament was for the Jews while the New Testament was for the Christians. I didn't understand that the Old Testament was really a preamble and foreshadowing for the Messiah—or as Christians believe—Jesus the Christ, until well into my adult years. As such, I didn't give much consideration to, well, anything, unless it is related to the New Testament. To me, the New Testament—namely Jesus being divine—is the central issue. Everything hinges on this one item. If Jesus is divine, then a radical transformation needs to take place in my life. If He is not, then who cares? Do what you want; it doesn't matter anyway.

Some of the common objections to the resurrection are that Jesus never existed at all, the four Gospels don't match, or that the New Testament was written much later. I discussed the Gospels not matching earlier, but a synopsis is this: If you had four witnesses tell a story of an event, the major facts should match, but many details will be different. As long as they don't contradict each other, and that is the key, then that should be expected from a truthful telling. It is important to note that a *good-faith* contradiction still would not be problematic, as there is expected discrepancy between eyewitness accounts. Police use this tactic all the time by separating witnesses so that they don't get a group-think unified story. In other words, variations are expected. And again, I find no contradictions in the stories.

I have studied the other world religions with enough depth that I can honestly say that Christianity is the only one that has a chance for me to believe in. I know that some people may say this is only because I was raised in a Christian household, but I don't believe that to be true. Detractors will be quick to point out that I do not know that I would not subscribe to a different religion if I had been raised somewhere else, and they are right. But it is also true that they do not know that I would not look to Christianity anyway, as to their point, I never lived in a household that practiced a different religion. The only real truth from that exercise is that arguing hypotheticals rarely yields useful results.

I do know that most people really don't evaluate, ask for evidence, and really seek the truth from any religion—even their own—and that includes atheists as well! I sincerely feel that I have looked at all sides and fairly questioned, even when it was painful. What I have concluded is that there are really three choices for me: atheism, agnosticism, or Christianity.

Many of my previous concerns centered on whether God exists at all. Deism is the belief that there is a God, but not necessarily a personal God; simply a powerful being that created the universe. Going from deism to Christianity hangs on the belief that Jesus the Christ was God incarnate, and much of that hangs on His resurrection being true.

I was completely satisfied that Jesus was real and not a made-up character who simply never existed. At the very least, there is an abundance of evidence that there was a real person named Jesus alive 2,000 years ago who was crucified. Religious scholars,

258 | *The Doubt Project*

including the atheistic ones, cite 11 independent sources (e.g., "Tacitus' *Annals* 15.44, Josephus' *Antiquities* 18.3.3, and Pliny's *Letters* 10.96") attesting to the crucifixion that were written within 100 years of the event. This is especially impressive, as other major events in history are considered well sourced if they appear in two other writings. Again, the attestation to Jesus's crucifixion is mentioned in at least 11 extra-Biblical writings. Finally, I do find it compelling that there are references from antagonistic sources, people with incentive the story being not true, who still attest to there being a person named Jesus.

I never doubted that Jesus was a real person, He had a following, and that He was crucified. I did not specifically doubt, but I also was not certain, that He really did rise from the dead—and Him rising from the dead is the make-

> *"And if Christ has not been raised, our preaching is useless and so is your faith."*
>
> ***Paul***
> *(1 Corinthians 15.14)*

or-break issue for Christianity; it all hinges on that!

There are four main theories explaining the supposed resurrection of Jesus. First, did the apostles really write the Gospels or were they stories that were modified over time and attributed to someone of authority? This is the mythic theory.

Most of the books of the New Testament—Romans, 1, 2 Corinthians, Galatians, Philippians, and 1 Thessalonians—are all accepted by scholars as being written by Paul. As discussed previously, Paul's letters, such as 1 Thessalonians, written around AD 50–60, roughly 20–30 years after the crucifixion, attest to early Christian belief in Christ's divinity. 1 Corinthians 15.3–8, written by Paul, is a creedal statement where it summarizes the early Christian belief in Christ's divinity.

For I delivered to you as of first importance what I also received: that Christ died for our sins in accordance with the Scriptures, that he was buried, that he was raised on the third day in accordance with the Scriptures, and that he appeared to Cephas, then to the twelve. Then he appeared to more than five hundred brothers at once, most of whom are still alive, though some have fallen asleep. Then he appeared to James, then to all the apostles. Last of all, as to one untimely born, he appeared also to me.

Some New Testament scholars, such as N.T. Wright and Gary Habermas, believe that this should be dated to within 2–5 years after the resurrection. In the passage, Paul says that he "received" this teaching which was believed to have been during his early instruction. In Galatians 1.18–19, Paul meets Peter and James in Jerusalem to discuss the first-hand accounts in AD 33–36.[64]

I am satisfied that there is an abundance of early evidence that attests to Jesus' followers believing that He performed miracles, that He was God on Earth, and that He rose from the dead. I consider the claim that Christianity was formed from evolved myths built up over a few hundred years to stand in stark contrast with facts accepted by both sides, atheist and Christian. It seems so implausible as to be dismissed.

The second idea is named the conspiracy theory; they wrote the Gospels, but they knew that it was not true. The conspiracy theory holds that the disciples wished for their group to continue, so they got together, stole the body from the tomb, and disposed of it. They agreed on a story and lived out their days promoting this myth.

As a direct rebuttal, some point out that Scripture states that numerous people had reported seeing the risen Jesus. A common critique of citing from Scripture is that you can't count it as evidence as the writers would have been the orchestrators of the hoax! I think for this objection, it's fair not to accept testimony from the accused!

However, I do feel like this objection breaks down for purely logical reasons. First, if someone perpetuates a hoax, there is always a motive, and when you get to the root of it, that motive is almost always money and/or power.[65] If you recall from earlier chapters, Jim Jones, the infamous cult leader who orchestrated a mass suicide of his followers when the FBI got close, was clearly deceiving his members. But the objective of the hoax was to gain power over his followers, especially for sexual gratification, and he was secretly enriching himself to the tune of many millions of dollars in hidden accounts. While he instructed his cult to commit suicide, he fled and tried to escape on a private plane to live out his life of luxury in a land that had no extradition to the U.S.! Conversely, if you look at the disciples who supposedly were the ringleaders of the Christian hoax, you see a very different scenario.

Picture this: You are a disciple, the leader of your group is brutally killed, and you know that you might be next. The inner group meets to discuss the future, and they decide on a grand plan where they would make up a story to deceive everyone. While being a member of the group, your personal role would be to live a life of poverty, constantly move around, and often get beaten up (or killed) when a village was not open to your message. No money. No idolization. Not even social status. Not a very compelling proposition. Personally, I would take a hard pass, wouldn't you? That is certainly not the life of money and/or power.

Secondly, unless you know different people than I do, the odds of a secret being kept become exponentially smaller with the more people who know about it. To make this work, all 11 disciples would need to hold their tongue (we don't need to worry about Judas), plus Jesus's mother Mary as well as a host of other people. Just one person at any point in their lifetime, testifying to the Jewish leadership would be enough for this to be undone.

Third and, to me, the most compelling, is that many of the apostles were martyred. Historical evidence confirms martyrdom for 4 of the apostles, like Peter and Paul, while tradition claims it for the others (Except for John who died of old age).[66] If I was in a grand conspiracy—no matter how important that I thought it was—and they were about to drive the stakes into my wrists and crucify me, or I was being lowered into a vat of boiling oil for preaching what I actually knew was untrue, and the only way to save myself was to recant, I wouldn't be able to get the words out fast enough. These same people would have been the original creators of the story, they certainly would have known it was false! I see no way that they would die for a lie.

A third possible explanation of the resurrection is if they were deceived into believing it; this is the hallucination theory. New Testament scholars agree that the disciples at least *thought* that they had an experience with the risen Jesus. Either they did have the

> "Men will die for what they believe to be true, though it may actually be false. They do not, however, die for what they know is a lie."
>
> *Paul E. Little*
> *(Know Why You Beleve)*

experience, or they imagined it as sort of a mass hallucination.

When Jesus was crucified, the apostles ran back to town and locked themselves away in a rear room in fear that they would be next. In the Jewish culture, resurrection of *any type* was reserved for the end times when everyone would rise from the grave. Conversely, the Greco-Roman world believed that the soul was immortal, but they also believed that the body was unimportant and did not have a place in the afterlife. Neither group expected a bodily Jesus to rise in three days. As they did not expect this to happen because it was a foreign concept, it is highly improbable that experiencing a bodily risen Jesus fell into "wishful thinking." Think about it, if they never expected a bodily risen Jesus, why would they all have imagined it to happen this way?

Skeptics argue the disciples experienced grief-induced visions, but hallucinations are internal to an individual and are purely subjective. In other words, different people's hallucinations will manifest in different ways. The idea of identical hallucinations goes against everything that we know about this phenomenon. It simply doesn't happen like that. The hallucination would then have had to extend to the disciples in the locked room (which happened multiple times), to Mary Magdalene, to common citizenry, and to Paul. Also, this hypothesis does nothing to explain the empty tomb.

The last real possibility is that it is true; this is Christianity.

Sure, I told myself, these guys could have been cult-like and so wrapped up in a lie that they allowed themselves to be killed, but I think that is just an emotional part of me holding out, as the logic sits on one side of the line. In re-

> "When you eliminate the impossible, whatever remains, however improbable, must be the truth."
>
> **Sherlock Holmes**
> *(Sir Arthur Conan Doyle)*

ality, everything is probabilistic, what is the probability of the first three scenarios? It seems impossibly low but then there is only one choice left.

I recall seeing an interview with a prominent atheist discussing the resurrection, and he stated that his view was that the body was simply thrown into a mass grave and eaten by wild dogs. The interviewer was taken aback and asked him if he really believed that this was what happened, to which he replied "No, it's not likely, but it's more likely than the resurrection." It was clear that he knew the scenario that he believed was ridiculous but would not accept considering any other. It really illustrated that even logical people will simply never give Jesus' resurrection consideration, even when they know that their conclusion is incredibly weak.

Running out of options, I thought that maybe He wasn't really dead, buried alive, and was able to free himself. To be honest, I knew that I was grasping at straws, but to also be honest, I believe that a part of me was happy that I was running out of options and being pinned in a corner.

The Swoon Theory is that Jesus was still alive when He was buried in the tomb and the cool air of the cave resuscitated him. He awoke, moved the stone, and escaped! To give this any consideration, you must first realize that the Roman Empire was founded on hard discipline. They used capital punishment as a deterrent and they were very, very good at it. It was taken so seriously that the executioners would themselves be put to death if they left the condemned alive. Also remember also that leading up to the crucifixion, Jesus was scourged before He was crucified. This involved a professional soldier whipping someone with a device that had leather lashes with sharp pieces of metal tied into them. These would cut through flesh, into muscle and bone, and could easily kill. The last step was crucifixion where spikes were driven through His wrists and ankles, and He hung on a cross for six hours.

I had always thought crucifixion caused death by blood loss, dehydration, or exposure. The reality is much, much more brutal. The medical cause of death from crucifixion is either from asphyxiation or hypovolemic shock. When crucified, your arms are stretched out to your side and spikes are driven into your wrists, so you don't fall forward while a spike is put in your ankles to keep you up. Your unsupported torso hangs down causing pressure on your lung cavity. To take a breath, you need to lift yourself to provide room for your lungs to expand. This, over time, causes exhaustion of the muscles used to breathe, resulting in slow asphyxiation. You finally suffocate when you are unable to lift your chest up enough to provide room to fill your lungs with oxygen. This method can take days for the subject to die. Excruciating? Well, it's so bad that the word "excruciating" comes from "ex" and "crux," means "off of" and "the cross."[67]

The other way that you can die from crucifixion is from a prolonged rapid heartbeat causing hypovolemic shock. Even after the beatings, flogging, and being hung on a cross, as a final act to ensure that Jesus was dead, they drove a spear into His side and blood and water rushed out. I had always thought that this was weird and assumed it was some attempt to claim his purity or divinity. What I learned is that with hypovolemic shock, water separates from the blood and gathers in the area around the heart, medically termed pericardial effusion. When the spear pierced His side and water ran, it was because the blade entered His heart sac.

Afterward, He was taken down and certainly inspected to verify death and wrapped in linen preparation for burial. I had always dismissed the preparation for burial as being a quick and trivial thing; just take the body, throw some cloth over it, and stick it in the grave. The actual procedure involved Joseph and Nicodemus wrapping the body with 75 pounds of myrrh and aloes (John 19.39). Just by the volume of spices being applied, it is impossible that this was a quick process. During this process, they had to be in constant direct contact with the body. If Jesus was still alive, even barely, they most definitely would have noticed!

After being placed in the tomb, a large stone was rolled in front blocking the entrance. While there is no specific record of the stone in question, typical burial stones weighed between 1–2 tons. Furthermore, a group of guards were stationed so that there would be no mischief. To that, the explanation is that he wasn't really dead and when He was placed in the cool tomb, He awoke, freed himself, moved the boulder, evaded the guards, and made off. Oh, and then the newly freed Jesus, instead of seeking medical attention, went to have a chat with his disciples. That's a tough one to swallow.

I also find it compelling that there are many elements in Scripture that are embarrassing for the apostles. For example, Jesus' brother James, who previously believed that Jesus was simply a madman, was a devout follower after the resurrection. I have occassionally thought that my brother was the spawn of Satan, but never, even once, did I believe that he was God. Of all the people in the world, I would think that convincing a sibling that you are God would be the most difficult.

When I consider the situation, I can't really believe any of the skeptical explanations for the resurrection, but I admit, I still have some trouble going over the line and being "all in." I think that this hesitancy is directly linked to the absolute fact that if you believe that Jesus was resurrected, then you must accept and believe all the other parts—and there is some piece of me that is resisting that. There is a big difference between logically accepting something and knowing it in your soul, but the first step is reconciling the facts and dismissing unworthy objections. Remove the dead wood so you can get a clear picture and the correct choice will become apparent.

TWENTY-TWO | *If God Exists, Why Is He So Hidden?*

Hello?
Is there anybody in there?
Just nod if you can hear me
Is there anyone at home?
- Pink Floyd / Comfortably Numb

One of my biggest problems with believing is that I don't understand why we've had 2,000 years of no discernible contact. If God truly exists, cares about us, and wants us to embrace Him, why is there no overt response to pleas or prayers? No outward signs? I am not saying that prayers should necessarily be granted, but it would be nice to know that they were at least heard. I am sincerely not trying to be disrespectful, but I often feel like praying is as vacuous as talking to my toaster. If eternal salvation is predicated on acceptance, and therefore belief, in God and Jesus, how is it remotely fair that earlier people supposedly had, at least in my mind, undeniable evidence—like a divine pillar of fire to lead the Hebrews out of Egypt or the personal experience and observation of the plethora of Jesus's miracles to persuade them—but I do not. I know that I am being thick headed, but the lack of personally witnessing undeniable signs like biblical miracles is a sticking point for me.

I concede that there are some reports of modern miracles, like those at Lourdes where there were confirmed reports of miraculous healings. Millions of people have visited the shrine at Lourdes, and the Catholic Church has recognized 70 visitors unexplained recoveries from severe illnesses—like cancer or paralysis—as miraculous. It is important to note that the determination of whether it was natural or miraculous event goes way beyond theologians. The criterion for consideration is stringent: the Lourdes Medical Bureau requires verifiable medical evidence, and the healings must be instantaneous, complete, and lasting, with no natural explanation. These cases received rigorous scrutiny by an international medical body and theological commissions, but modern medical science could offer no explanation.[68]

Also, some of the truth may lie in the definition of a miracle—an extraordinary event that is attributed to divine intervention that is *used to advance God's message.* As I have been provided with sufficient evidence through the Scriptures and other evidence,

> "The Church does not easily declare a cure miraculous; it demands that the recovery be inexplicable by the current state of medical science."
>
> **Ruth Cranston**
> (The Miracle of Lourdes)

there should be no need for me to have a direct experience with a miracle. I have also heard that in new churches where people need to see evidence of God's work, such as in China, the claims of miracles are abundant. Of course, being who I am, I immediately discount such claims as I envision uneducated, primitive farmers pleading to mysticism to explain the unknown—very much the same way I initially viewed the apostles. Much as I know that

I was unfairly judging the apostles this way, my rational mind knows that this also is unfair.

A 2019 Pew Research Center survey found that about 79% of people in sub-Saharan Africa and 60% in Latin America report experiencing or witnessing what they consider a miracle. Given the population sizes, there would be hundreds of millions of claims. The Committee for Skeptical Inquiry, which is, of course, skeptical of the claims, estimates that there are over 1 million faith healing claims made annually.[69] I am certain that if I looked at the details of these claims, an overwhelming majority would be easily dismissed. For example, the Lourdes shrine has had more than 7,000 claims of miraculous healings since 1858 and only 70 declared inexplicable by medical experts as of 2023. However, here is the pivotal idea: sure, most of the claims are bogus, I think everyone would agree with that. But is *every* single claim false? Of the millions of claims made by people from all walks of life, if even *one* is true, then a supernatural force exists that exerts influence on our reality—and I think that it is fair to label Him God. It does seem almost certain to me that at least some of these claims are legitimate.

I have seen claims, and even colored graphs, showing divine interaction and miracles were frequent, dropped to zero with the advent of digital cameras, and then rebounded with photo editing software. When I first saw these graphs, which I've encountered multiple times, I knew that I had to investigate them; if true, it would be quite telling. If the claim that the invention of digital cameras caused the incidence of claims of miracles to drop to almost zero but then a reemergence with the advent of digital editing software was true, then we should see many miracles, then none for 20–30 years when digital cameras were commonplace but before photo editing software, and then a boom when digital editing software became available. I always believed that miracles occurred frequently so we should see *something* within the 30-year window. I again had a knee-jerk, emotional reaction to something that I feared was true as when I investigated further, I found that these claims were not based on actual studies or had any foundation in real data. Ironically, they were created by someone with digital editing software and an axe to grind spreading unsubstantiated claims.

While I consider this to be a trivial objection, I mention it because during the investigation, I came to an important realization. I had always assumed that the events and miracles in the Bible occurred in close chronological order. It seemed to me like the miracles were frequent and almost rapid fire. I knew that the experiences happened to different people, but I thought that the stories were either occurring simultaneously at different places or immediately after with their direct descendants.

If you read a novel, when you transition from chapter five to chapter six, your expectation is that the events in chapter six happen right after the end of chapter five—unless the author goes out of their way to let you know of a significant time lapse. Similarly, when you are watching a show on King Arthur and the knights of the round table and come back from a commercial break, you don't expect the story to pick up in a battle of World War II. If you look at a chronology of the events that are called out in Scripture, they are often separated by many hundreds of years. Moving from one miracle event to the next usually spans about the same amount of time as King Arthur to WWII.

The history of divine interaction is filled with periods of revelation followed by long periods of silence. Active periods are very rare. If you look at the events of the Old Testament, the gaps between events are usually hundreds of years. Scripture suggests that it is God's plan to periodically portion out instruction and it is up to us to carry it forward. Jesus addresses this issue in the Parable of the Rich Man and Lazarus. In this parable, there is a rich man in Hades, realizing that it is too late for him, asks to be allowed to warn his brothers to have faith. He is told that if they would not listen to what Moses and the prophets had already revealed over the ages, "they will not be convinced even if someone rises from the dead." God states that the revealed Scripture is sufficient.

The position of Scripture is that throughout the Old Testament, God spoke to us using a variety of methods with all of them culminating in the arrival of Jesus, and with that complete, what we have should be enough. Additionally, since Pentecost, the Holy Spirit was sent to guide us—now it would not be in the form of a pillar of fire, burning bush, walking on water, or anything like that. It would be a gentle guide, not an overt set of miracles. Perhaps that is also what Jesus meant when he said "It is finished" right before He died; the culmination of divine interactions in the Old Testament leading up to the mission of His life on Earth. I find all of this somewhat compelling, but I still find it troubling that praying gives me the same outward response as there would be if materialism is true and God does not exist.

"I've seen miracles in answered prayers" or "Someone's cancer disappeared due to the congregation praying for them!" I have heard things like that many times in my life and when I do, I always put a pleasant smile on my face but in the back of

> "We cannot attain the presence of God. We're already totally in the presence of God. What's missing is awareness."
>
> **David Benner**
> (The Gift of Being Yourself)

my mind, I am skeptical. While I certainly do think that God can intervene and perform miracles, I do not think that God outwardly intervenes based on the volume of prayers. I know that it says to pray for what you need in a variety of books of the Bible, and I am not claiming that prayer is useless or a waste of time, but I do not feel that prayer is transactional.

When my kids were young and still thought I was cool, sometimes I used to take them to Dave and Busters, affectionately known as D&B. D&B's first half is a restaurant, but the much better half is the giant video arcade. As an '80s vidiot (video game idiot), I was more excited than they were! The kids really enjoyed playing the games, but what they loved the most was that at the end of the night, they could take the "Tickets" that they had won and go to the store where they could trade the tickets for items. How their eyes lit up when they saw the stuffed animals, rubber spiders, or any one of the myriad of options. (Of course, if you do the math, that rubber spider really cost me about $65) The night would usually end with something like–"Mister, I want the giant plush rainbow unicorn!!! Ok, let's check your tickets! Oh, sorry little girl, you don't have enough tickets. Keep playing!" If you have enough tickets, you get the plush rainbow unicorn. If you don't, well, sorry kid. Better luck next time.

If prayers can move God to action, then what could be the reason for any child ever dying of cancer? I bet that even non-believing parents, when their child is sick enough, offer a prayer for their child to get better. As they say, there are no atheists in foxholes—and being in a foxhole enduring the worst that war could offer is worlds better than having one of your children being terminally ill. If God is moved to action by prayers and the parents prayed and the child still dies, then what could possibly be the reason? The only answer that I can find is that there were simply not enough prayers to reach some threshold. Logically speaking, it's the only coherent way that it could work.

1. Assume God is moved by prayers
2. God loves and treats all of His children the same, there can be no preference of child A over child B and merit of each child is not applied
3. Prayers were offered for child A and child B
4. God saved child A but let child B die
5. Since the actions of A and B could not have justified healing, its either that God was already going to save A but not B due to a divine plan or sufficient prayers were offered for A but not for B

I have often heard of groups praying for someone as if having more prayers would at some point, trigger an action from God. It's like a divine credit system where you get points for prayers, and you create a transaction for your request. "God, please cure little Joey of his cancer!" "Ok, let's check your prayer points! Oh, sorry man, not enough prayers. Keep praying!"

It also implies that if you do enough worshipping and He will fulfill your desires like a cosmic wishing well. If praying influences intervention, then God is waiting in the wings, ready to save Joey, but will not move until you pray enough to reach some threshold. I can't see that its possible for God to intentionally withhold help based on the amount of prayers performed and still claim that He loves us. The main tenet of Christianity is that God loves us, it is central to all Scripture, and it is the entire point of Jesus and the New Testament. Since the condition of divine love is central to Christianity and it cannot exist simultaneously with withholding healing based on quota, the initial condition that God is moved to action by the quantity of prayer must be false.

I have also heard the argument that it is all God's plan. I don't put much stock in that for a variety of reasons, but from the prayer perspective, if He is acting out His plan, then your prayer isn't going to move Him one way or another. I can't imagine God saying, "Well, I was going to do it this way, but Becky really rocked her prayer this evening, so back to the drawing board!"

So, what's the point of prayer then? Is it a waste of time? Am I saying that I know more than the Bible? No. From my reading, prayer creates, builds, and maintains your relationship with God. It seems to have two main benefits. First, I think prayer is supposed to be a conversation with your creator who loves and wants the best for you. It is similar to going to a counselor or therapist where you can talk about your problems and fears without judgement or risk of it leaving the room. Having such a relationship has a multitude of benefits. Second, it is also to ask for help and guidance for the *internal* you, not to externally change others. If answered prayers directly changed others, that would invariably influence and potentially invalidate their free will. God waiting to help you make beneficial changes in your consciousness is consistent with the idea of free will. Maybe He is ready and willing to help you make changes, but as you have free will, He respects you enough to wait for permission.

I do not think that it is intended for Him to divinely intervene and make those credit card bills go away or to win the lottery, but I do think that the idea of prayer will help someone with their anxiety over those bills, their worry for the future and help them address the fundamental reasons that they overspend and get into a financial mess. There is a huge benefit to being able to get things off your chest and be open to hear and feel if God is reaching out to you. And yes, I am certain that something speaks to me. To be honest, I am unsure if it is my personal mind, conscience, or the Holy Spirit, but I know that something is there urging me to the right path. If anyone ever reads this, believer or not, I am sure that they will be certain of the source and wonder how I could be so blind. I also know that in the periods of my life where I have ignored "the voice" and shouted it down, it became easier and easier to do so to the point where it was barely a whisper.

I also have a problem with the idea of direct divine intervention whether in answered prayers or simply guiding humanity as I feel that it directly contradicts and invalidates free will. In short, I feel that the universe and humanity were created for the sole

> *"For prayer is nothing else than being on terms of friendship with God."*
>
> **Saint Teresa of Avila**
> (The Life of Teresa of Jesus)

purpose of having a relationship with God. Relationships must be based on love and love must be freely given. To be freely given, there must be choices or options. To be able to choose, you must have free will. In my opinion, free will is Boolean—it is either true or false. If you have free will up to the point that it would result in something objectionable and then are prevented from taking that action, then you in reality do not have free will. If God has His plan and when we are in risk of diverging from it, He forces your hand, then I reject the idea that we have free will. It's like you can't kinda be married, you either are, or you aren't. On the other hand, I do think that there is an endgame stipulated, at least in concept but not in detail, in Scripture. I have had great trouble reconciling the two views and am unabashedly vocal about my conflict, so much so that I think my friend Allen, a man of seemingly infinite patience, wanted to strangle me over fish tacos yesterday when we discussed it.

Last week, I was totally swamped. I was hectically busy from the moment that I woke up, all through the day. At about 4.30 in the afternoon, I had not eaten, and my stomach was sounding like a thunderstorm. I heard the kids running around downstairs, so I asked my daughter Jamie to make me a toasted bagel with peanut butter. Soon after, when she wordlessly came into my office to deliver my food to me and I looked up to that smiling face, I was shocked to realize that this was totally unfair. The reason that I usually always asked her instead of any of the others to do tasks was not because she was doing anything wrong, but ironically, because I knew that I could ask her to do something and there would be no complaining or whining. She was always open to requests so she ended up being given more tasks than would have been an equal share.

This sparked a thought: Perhaps there is a third option. It may be that when there are events that align with the grand plan, the whispering of the voice guides us to that outcome. Everyone still maintains their ability to choose to ignore the voice, but if you broadly apply the option, especially directed at people where you know their character has a predilection towards that outcome, it is entirely reasonable to see how guidance and free will would be in harmony.

While the "hiddenness of God" still lingers in my doubts, I recognize that the fault may lie with me and not with Him. My childlike impatience and desire for God to do "tricks" so that I can have my latest question of fear addressed is just that, childlike impatience. If God did have a permanent pillar of fire or audibly replied when I prayed, I have no doubt that it wouldn't be long until I dismissed it as a natural occurrence or a trick of my mind. I have asked myself, and still have no answer to, how many miracles do I see every day but dismiss as "normal"? I also recognize that it is based on fear and when I combat it with sober logical reflection, I find that God isn't so hidden after all.

| *The Light at the End of the Tunnel*

So now that I checked the boxes on the factual issues that had bothered me, I'm good to go, right? Why, then, do some of these issues still feel unresolved?

There are three types of doubt: intellectual, emotional, and volitional. Intellectual doubt is based on logic or evidential concerns. Emotional doubt is generated by, you guessed it, emotions such as fear. In my experience, the hallmark of emotional doubt is when the issue simply doesn't *feel* right. Volitional doubt is when you don't want to believe, usually because believing would challenge something that you view in a favorable light and don't want to give up. For me, my doubts were intellectual and emotional, but how does one resolve those?

The first step was to determine whether my preconditioned biases were the result of facts or, like the idea that breakfast is the most important part of the day, were just some narrative that I picked up along the way. Please note that I had biases for both Christianity and materialism, and to do a fair assessment, I needed to analyze them all. The most impactful were that science and Christianity were incompatible, that supernatural events didn't really happen, and that the truly enlightened and intelligent people were atheists. Once I overcame these naive objections, it opened the possibility to do a fair assessment and deal with the core subject of my doubts.

My emotional and intellectual sides had a dependence on each other and each side had to be satisfied in order to move on to the next level of belief. I was extremely discouraged when I would often spend a week obsessively pounding 60–80 hours of research and find that my confidence had not moved much, if at all. I felt that if I could spend so much time without bridging this enormous chasm of doubt, how much time would it really take and, honestly, would I even live that long? Even worse, it was very common to invest hundreds of hours and finally resolve an issue but later, return to doubting things that I felt that I had already settled. The process was painful and thinking that I could reasonably spend the rest of my life with this discord and then even at the end, never have resolution, was extremely disheartening.

What I found is that, no matter the urgency, these things take time. The intellectual answers would only take me so far until they were held up by my emotional side. What the factual arguments did do was to give me enough confidence to be able to resolve that piece of intellectual doubt. This resolution then provided a steppingstone to combat and relieve the corresponding part of the emotional side. It is as if each type was broken into many segments, with each piece depending on its counterpart's resolution before it could progress. Don't ask me how many segments there are; I still don't know. I do know that progress is very slow, but don't be discouraged, there is progress.

I spent hundreds of hours "spinning," jumping from topic to topic and never making any headway. After wearing myself out, I devised a bit of a methodology in dealing with my doubts. First, I diagnose exactly what I am questioning. It is entirely possible, common even, for it to be a high-level topic with many, many subtopics. That's fine and it's expected. As I went along, I would write it down. All of it. I would keep drilling down until I had listed each single point of contention. Keep in mind that the list is not static and will grow. Once I was honest and opened myself to facing my doubts, it was like a floodgate was released. When I was working on one topic, I would regularly encounter skeptical critiques or think of other things that I needed to resolve, and so these new items would be added to the list. It will sometimes feel like the list is just growing endlessly, and you will never make enough progress to even keep up, much less get through it. Relax, there will come a point where the new items slow and eventually become so infrequent that they almost stop. The focus is to just start and let the questions come. Don't worry about solving it all right now. The goal is to break down complex concepts that are overwhelming into single points, and therefore digestible and solvable, issues. We're moving a mountain one shovel at a time. Don't be discouraged by this, it will move!

Once I started listing my points of contention, I would ask myself how serious each issue was for my embracing or rejecting faith. Some topics will matter more than others. Don't dismiss or ignore any issue because it is not "critical" as I think the decision between Christianity or atheism is a cumulative case; just try to keep it in perspective. Obviously, there are a few that are critical, such as belief in the resurrection, but not many.

Early on, I succumbed to the temptation to jump topics when I encountered a new "fact" or statement. Jumping from topic to topic feeds the fear and to be avoided. It leads to "endless mental flailing" and results in very little progress. Following some good advice from my friend Allen, I listed my issues in priority order. In my opinion, the priority should be what is bothering you the most, even if it's not "critical" to Christianity being true. I needed to do it this to "get out of my own way" and stop being distracted. There is no hard and fast rule as long as there is some order to follow. Personally, I started at the highest priority and worked on that until I was confident of an answer. I also found that it helped that I would mentally note that this mini-project was my focus, but I would allow myself to diverge a bit occasionally if I needed a break or found something particularly interesting. The point is that I would return to the specific doubt that I was working on and keep going until completion. When I was able to get closure on an issue, I found that it gave me confidence which diminished the emotional doubt. I finally felt that I was making progress and that I would eventually get through this.

Now the hard part. When dealing with a specific issue, I would try to be as clinical as possible and evaluate if it was an intellectual, emotional, or volitional doubt. I found intellectual doubt to be the easiest to deal with as it is specifically regarding the factuality of the issue. Straight forward but not trivial. The cure here is research, lots of it. Personally, for me to be satisfied, I need to hear the best arguments that each side has to offer. First, some advice, be sure that you focus on legitimate sources from both sides. Second, be prepared to see lots of material that is presented as absolute, accepted fact that if true, will be a deal killer for Christianity. I won't lie, there were many times where I dreaded reading atheistic materials as I was afraid that they were going to point out something truly convincing. Fair warning, the authors may be well-known scholars or scientists but don't let their "authority" override your ability to think critically. Listen to what they have to say with an open mind, and then, take a breath.

What I have found is that there is no shortage of sensational claims. Every time that I stumbled upon one, it would be like a dagger in my chest. Save yourself some heartache, keep your emotions in check until you hear the whole story.

When I was having a major spin session and I stumbled over the proof that Christianity was just a made-up religion that copied the Persian deity Mithras, my stomach went to my throat. I felt the walls closing in, my throat closed, and I was on the verge of a panic attack. Luckily, I had now been fighting this battle for more than six months and had repeatedly experienced encountering a foundation-shattering "fact," that upon investigation, turned out to be grossly overstated or severely misrepresented. So, I stopped myself, took a breath, and researched the real story. The point is, consider all sides of the issue, but make sure that you keep calm until you have the full picture. We're looking for the truth, not to buy into anyone's narrative and for that, both sides have to be considered.

So, why did learning about the accusation that Christianity was "borrowed" from Mithras invoke such a strong response? It certainly wasn't clinical or intellectual, that would have had a calm and sober response. What I found was that many of my issues had a very strong emotional component as well. The telltale signs of the emotional component are when the reaction is out of proportion to an issue or, even more common, when data is presented that should fully satisfy the factual part of the issue but doesn't. When I was dealing with emotional doubt, I found that my question was answered, I could not dispute any of the underlying facts, nor had I found any persuasive counter evidence, but the doubt still persisted. The intellectual side was resolved but there was always another "what if....." It's the chameleon doubt; it looks like an honest question but it's really a symptom created by an underlying fear. Emotional doubt can be generated by strong feelings, such as fear, or very commonly, simply grows out of an unaddressed intellectual doubt.

Human beings require material things such as air, food, and water to survive. I suggest that we also need immaterial things as well—specifically hope. Throughout history, people were able to survive horrific conditions because they had hope for the future. Conversely, the news is filled with people giving up, even committing suicide, because they felt hopeless. It is my belief that emotional doubt is the hope killer. For reasons that have no tangible focus, they erode confidence. So many times, I felt the overwhelming dread for no "particular" reason that I did feel all hope was lost. I knew the facts, and the issue *should* have been closed, but I just couldn't let it go. I am a left brain, logical guy and so, I have always prioritized facts over emotions when making decisions. This led to a predisposition to trivialize or dismiss emotional responses; I did not consider them valid. I thought that I should be able to "will them away," but this feeling was unshakable. I finally grasped that instead of trivial, emotional doubt is immensely powerful and not easily defeated. Realizing that emotional doubt is the silent killer and is the much more dangerous adversary was startling.

The most challenging part of dealing with emotional doubt is determining the underlying emotion. For me, it was the fear that if Christianity was not true, then we live a few short years and simply cease to exist. Because I was so afraid that this might be true, it gave immense power to just about any claim, even some that I admit are ridiculous. The fear would move to terror when I would think about how if this were true, I would be powerless to change it.

What I found helpful was to first acknowledge that this fear is rational and I should not be ashamed. Accepting your feelings and building a game plan to resolve them makes it feel more manageable. I also had to reconcile the idea that as I undertook this project, I had no choice but to accept whatever conclusion I came to. This is incredibly difficult as the intensity of the fear wars with being able to accept the outcome.

I have found that "they" were right, writing things down really does help. When you write something down, it becomes tangible. There were sections that when I started writing and I had some major doubt or discomfort, but with no additional knowledge or information, simply writing down what I already knew, coalesced my thoughts and hardened them into an understanding. What was nebulous and shaky became firm and confident. Sometimes, I found claims I that knew to be false were still creeping around my head until I put it in writing. Once I formalized it on paper and could see both sides in their entirety, I became confident that the idea wasn't legitimate, and it was defanged. It seemed that once a claim was evaluated and rejected from the list, it was suddenly powerless.

Fear, by definition, deals with future events. When I was severely struggling, I changed my mindset to limit my perspective to the present to limit its influence. Once the intense period abated, I would allow myself free range of thought again. If you try this, be patient with yourself. It's very hard to focus solely on the present, but with practice, it gets easier.

Sometimes when I was experiencing irrational emotional doubt, I could see that the evidence and logic was entirely on one side, but my fear was giving it life. I found that revisiting the issues that I previously resolved was a great help. I would consult my notes on the subject—again, writing it down helps– to refresh the data that had previously given me confidence in my conclusion. If there was new information, then I would reopen this issue. If it was just fear, not having absolute certainty or, more commonly, where I could imagine some obscure scenario, I would combat it with what I knew for sure and reaffirm that my con-clusions were sound. These voices do get quieter and quieter until they go away entirely.

As mentioned earlier, the emotional side of doubt is the hard-est to overcome. It is like a wellspring that you can't see but seeps up and affects everything around, even in places where you would hardly expect it. Overcoming emotional doubt is a daunting task, if you can accept that it is going to take work and can be patient, you will find success. I strongly recommend watching videos or reading material regarding doubt by Gary Habermas.[70]

Through this process, I was able to identify that the source of one of my major areas of doubt was my pride. I was always com-fortable viewing God as the wise advisor, but ultimately, I was the one in charge. I envisioned sitting on my throne and waving over my gray bearded counselor to hear his sage advice, nodding gravely to his words, but the final decision being mine. Consider-ing the awe-inspiring events attributed to God, especially those as seen in the fine-tuning argument, I admit it more closely re-sembles a parent guiding a petulant child, who does as they please anyway—and then screaming "I hate you" when they make a mess of things! I had thought that my doubt was limited to intellectual and emotional, but I clearly was suffering from volitional doubt as well. I chose to make myself the master of the universe and in that paradigm, God has to take second seat.

To resolve my volitional doubt, I had to take a candid assess-ment of who I am and who I wanted to be. With my issue, I needed to get over the fact that I am not the ultimate being in the universe. Ok, sure, that sounds easy but to do that, I needed to both accept my role with humility and, even harder, surrender to the idea that I was not in ultimate control. I had to get secure in the feeling that I was powerless compared to God—and that

284 | *The Doubt Project*

was the root of my issue. It is hard for me to think that I have no power and no authority, but that is exactly what it is. Hard thing to face. Some people struggle with volitional doubt due to behaviors in their lives that they find pleasurable that they don't want to change. I do think there is a simple answer for this, but beware, it's not trivial. Ask yourself who do you want to be? I get it, you like doing whatever it is that you would be forced to give up if you truly accept Christ. It has become very apparent to me that God's rules aren't to be a galactic buzz kill. These rules are there to protect us and to lead us to what is truly better. I get it, that behavior feels good and makes you feel powerful, but can you really say that whatever you are doing is deeply satisfying? I can tell you with absolute certainty that my glimpses into the Christian world show one of incredible value. We're gorging on garbage when a feast awaits.

Throughout this writing, I have tried to be as forthright as possible to give a candid diagnosis of my search and my experiences. Some may be angry or upset with what I wrote and label me a heretic or disrespectful to God. I also know that some will say that this is just a Christian apologetics book in disguise. I can understand how either of these viewpoints could be reached but neither of these was my intention. The blunt truth is that I find most of the atheistic claims to be shallow. If you had to say, which side carries more water, I would very easily say the Christian side. The hard part is fully giving over to faith.

I watched an interview with an agnostic NASA physicist discussing God. He was very honest in saying that the events in the Bible were very compelling and he could find no fault, and that the things that were known by a technologically primitive people thousands of years ago defies explanation. He saw biblical Scripture as extremely persuasive, but his problem was that he was a devoted materialist and as such, he just couldn't accept it. I got the very distinct impression that he was saddened by this. As he was stuck between his adherence to materialism and what he saw as the truth of the Bible, he wouldn't move to either side from his agnosticism. While I am not a materialist or an agnostic, sometimes I feel locked in the push-pull the same way.

Early on, I noted that I didn't share my struggles and doubts with my wife because I am supposed to be the man, and men do not show weakness. I strongly encourage you not to make the same mistake that I made and talk to your spouse. If you are not married, find someone you can have these candid conversations with. You need someone to walk this path with you, and I think you will find that it brings you closer together. There are many communities, both locally and online, that genuinely care and can help you though this. Do not go through it alone.

I am becoming increasingly convinced that the rending of my soul is due to the conflict of submitting to God against the fear of faith. I am trying to understand why I am so hesitant to give in, but I do have vestiges of resistance. And no, I don't have some secret sin that I am loathe to give up. And yes, it makes no sense to me either.

I have learned that there is no silver bullet for or against theism. Do not expect to learn one thing and suddenly believe; it is a cumulative case. This journey has made me face my fears and frankly, become educated on the topics that I had made so many incorrect assumptions on. I do think that I succumbed to a version of the Dunning-Kruger effect; I knew so little that I didn't even know what I didn't know—and so, I thought that I was knowledgeable. I had so little knowledge of, and exposure to the real arguments and responses regarding God, that it formed a cognitive bias where I didn't recognize the volumes of information that I did not know existed. My crisis of faith forced me to put aside what I thought was common knowledge in lieu of a factual and reasoned approach yielding hard data. Ironically, this "Doubt Project" has removed many of my doubts and helped me gain a much higher certainty that Christianity is true.

When I started this project, I thought that for me to be able to fully commit would require 100% answers from one side or the other. It has been my experience that nothing is an absolute 100%. Are there some topics that I don't understand fully? Yes. There are even some topics, such as the problem of natural evil, where I feel that the more compelling story falls on the atheist side. The difference is that now I have a more mature view. Broadly speaking, the answers provided by a Christian worldview are overwhelmingly more satisfying than the atheist ones and it is in such proportion, that I accept that in the few instances where I have uncertainty, the Christian worldview has garnered enough "wins" to elicit enough trust to bridge the gap. In other words, don't let it derail you if there are some issues where you are not fully resolved. Again, this is a cumulative case. Is there enough evidence for you to trust?

I have also concluded that the Christian's answer to the meaning of life is that we are on this planet simply to have time to choose whether we elect to be with God or not. This is not a trivial choice that you can simply profess with your mouth and be done. It is something if truly spoken, guides every action that you do. It is an entire worldview and envelopes all aspects of your life—and I am finding that is a very good thing. At this point, I have seen glimpses into that world, and frankly, it does look like an incredible reality. My views are fleeting but are very real and increasingly common.

What I have had visages of, and am just starting to understand, is that when we are living horizontally, living in comparison to other people, we are in a constant state of turmoil. We compare ourselves and our loved ones to others and quickly see how we fall short in one area after another. While I know that others see my "perfect life," all I see is a person over there that is more financially successful than I am, or her, who is in better physical shape, that person is younger, they are better looking, or he who is smarter (Ouch! That's a hard one to admit). It is easy to see others as competition and therefore, easy to see them as an enemy. The frustration, fear, and envy can easily lead to bitterness and hatred. What I have seen is that living vertically, as described in Scripture, living for the relationship and trust with God, it is a life of peace. We are loved and we are sufficient. Every blemish or fault is accepted and forgiven. As this relationship is primary, the material comparisons fade away. It seems that this is the path to true happiness. I am hoping that I can expand my view and participate in this more, but that requires giving up the materialistic viewpoint and I admit that there is still a part of me that holds back.

Unfortunately, these kinds of episodes that we experience are justifiably traumatic and in a strange way, normal. I won't sugar-coat it; the voyage is massively painful. However, the process of trying to resolve these questions and doubts can end up being a positive thing. Accept that this will take time but be sure to make some measure of progress every day, if it's a small amount. You won't see much impact early on, but very soon, you will be amazed at how far you have gone. Coming out the other side, I find that most of my doubts have been assuaged, and I feel a closeness to God that I never have before.

If I could leave you with one thought that I know with great certainty, it is that it is very good to keep questioning, no truth has ever been weakened, or threatened, by that. But even more important, when you have a question or doubt about God, find a way to get past the fear and do the research to find the answer. There is no more important thing that you can possibly do. It has been my experience that the Christian worldview has very satisfying answers.

In order to go beyond Pascal's Wager and feel, really feel, true belief, it requires a level of certainty. I do not know the level, but I do know that now after asking these questions and digging for the answers, I am much, much closer to finding it.

I wish you success on your journey.

"Ask and it will be given to you; seek and you will find; knock and the door will be opened to you. For everyone who asks receives; the one who seeks finds; and to the one who knocks, the door will be opened."

Jesus— God Incarnate
(Matthew 7.7–8)

TWENTY-FOUR | *Epilogue*

It's been five years since my faith crisis began and three years since I wrote this book. I started writing about a year into the crisis, during the depths of what I call the "dark period"—a time when doubt consumed me. As this book nears publication, I feel compelled to share a few additional reflections. First, I deliberately left parts of the book untouched, reflecting my perspective at the time. While I now have a deeper, more mature understanding of faith, I purposefully chose not to revise those sections. My intention is not for this book to be the definitive argument for or against Christianity. Instead, it's a lifeline for truth-seekers who need to know they're not alone in their questions and that it's okay not to have all the answers. My goal is to expose the experience of the often-overwhelming experience of doubt, offering a springboard for those wrestling with their faith. To do that, I had to stay true to the raw emotions, doubts, and fears that were my daily companions for two years.

For those in the midst of a faith crisis, I wish I could offer a simple, quick resolution. For me, it was a grueling two-year battle before I began to find clarity. Those years were brutal. I neglected my software company, which I'd built from the ground up since I was 27, until it finally collapsed. My isolation also cost me most of my social connections. My wife bore an immense burden, shouldering the emotional and financial fallout while I grappled with my doubts. Yet, looking back, I see that this spiritual collapse was the best thing that ever happened to me. Without it, I would have continued in a lukewarm, distant relationship with God, never confronting the questions that kept me at arm's length and frankly, never truly believing. Sometimes, I wonder if God had been trying to reach me my entire life, and this crisis was His last resort. I still mourn the loss of my company, but as my friend Randy said, "It's worth losing the riches of this world to gain the kingdom of heaven." Five years ago, I would have scoffed at that. Now, its truth is etched in my soul.

In the three years since emerging from that dark period, I've continued exploring the arguments for and against Christianity. This book barely scratches the surface of what I've discovered. The evidence for the truth of Christianity is overwhelming, seemingly from every angle—history, philosophy, science, aesthetics, and personal experience. It's so compelling that I believe denying a spiritual reality is less about logic and more about emotional resistance. Someone may not "like" God, but claiming we live in a purely material world feels like a choice driven from emotion, not reason.

If you're wrestling with doubts, I urge you—please, ask your questions. Find someone who can walk alongside you, helping you navigate your uncertainties and seek answers. It's the most important thing that you'll ever do in your life.

Bibliography

Behe, Michael, "Citrate Death Spiral," Discovery, June 18, 2020, [online] Available at: https://www.discovery.org/a/citrate-death-spiral/

Behe, Michael, "*Darwin Devolves*," (Balaji Publications), January 1, 2023

Behe, Michael, *Edge of Evolution*. (Free Press), June 5, 2007

Bruce, F.F., *The New Testament Documents: Are They Reliable?* (6th ed.), (Grand Rapids: Eerdmans, 2003)

Collins, Francis S., The Language of God, (New York, NY: Free Press, 2006)

Copley, Shelly D., Science Direct, "*The origin of the RNA world: Co-evolution of genes and metabolism,*" [online] Available at: https://www.sciencedirect.com/science/article/abs/pii/S004520680700051X-?via%3Dihub

Corbyn, Zoe, The Guardian, "*Biologist Rosemary Grant: 'Evolution happens much quicker than Darwin thought',*" July 21, 2024, [online] Available at: https://www.theguardian.com/science/article/2024/jul/21/rosemary-grant-peter-grant-charles-darwin-finches-evolutionary-biology-princeton-one-step-sideways-three-steps-forward-memoir

Dawkins, Richard, *The Blind Watchmaker: Why the Evidence of Evolution Reveals a Universe without Design*. New York; London: W. W. Norton & Company, 1996

Discovery Science, *"Information Enigma: Where does information come from?,"* [video] Available at: https://www.youtube.com/watch?v=aA-FcnLsF1g

Egnor, Michael, Mind Matters, *"Why the Mind Can't Just Be the Brain,"* [online] Available at: https://mindmatters.ai/2020/08/why-the-mind-cant-just-be-the-brain/

Evolution News, *"Why the Royal Society Meeting Mattered, in a Nutshell,"* December 5, 2016, [online] Available at: https://evolutionnews.org/2016/12/why_the_royal_s/

Harris, Sam, *The End of Faith: Religion, Terror and the Future of Reason,* (New York; London: W. W. Norton & Company, 2004)

Jantzen, Benjamin, The Philosophers' Magazine, *"The Fine Tuning Argument Unmasked,"* [online] Available at: https://archive.philosophersmag.com/the-fine-tuning-argument-unmasked/

Lennox, John C., *Gods Undertaker: Has Science Buried God?* (Oxford, England: Lion Hudson plc, 2014)

Moreland, J.P. Tim Muehlhoff, Lee Strobel, *The God Conversation: Using Stories and Illustrations to Explain Your Faith* (Downers Grove, Illinois: InterVarsity Press, 2017)agel, Thomas, *What Does It All Mean? A Very Short Introduction to Philosophy* (Oxford: Oxford University Press 1987)

National Center for Science Education, *"Transitional Fossils Are Not Rare,"* September 25, 2008, [online] Available at: https://ncse.ngo/transitional-fossils-are-not-rare

NIH: National Human Genome Research Institute, "Ribonucleic Acid Fact Sheet," [online] Available at: https://www.genome.gov/about-genomics/educational-resources/fact-sheets/ribonucleic-acid-fact-sheet

Pearcey, Nancy, Total Truth, (Wheaton, Il., Crossway Books, 2004)

Princeton University, "*Study of Darwin's finches reveals that new species can develop in as little as two generations,*" [online] Available at: https://www.princeton.edu/news/2017/11/27/study-darwins-finches-reveals-new-species-can-develop-little-two-generations

Thanukos, A., "*Darwin's 'Extreme' Imperfection?,*" *Evo Edu Outreach* **2**, 84–89 (2009). https://doi.org/10.1007/s12052-008-0105-0

Tour, James, Inference, "*Time Out,*" [online] Available at: https://inference-review.com/article/time-out

Weinberg, Steven. "The Cosmological Constant Problem." *Reviews of Modern Physics*, vol. 61, no. 1, 1989, pp. 1–23, doi:10.1103/RevModPhys.61.1.

Witt, Daniel, "Evolution in Real Time," Evolution News, January 8, 2025, https://evolutionnews.org/2025/01/evolution-in-real-time-yeah-right/

Endnotes

1. Got Questions, "Why are so many young people falling away from the faith?," [online] Available at: https://www.gotquestions.org/falling-away.html

2. Isaiah 1.18 (NIV)

3. 1 Thess. 5.21 (NIV)

4. 1 Pet. 3.15 (NIV)

5. Miron Zuckerman, Jordan Silberman, and Judith A. Hal, *Personality and Social Psychology Review* XX(X) 1–30 © 2013, "The Relation Between Intelligence and Religiosity," [online] Available at https://gwern.net/doc/iq/2013-zuckerman.pdf

6. The Christian Myth, "Religion vs IQ," [online] Available at: https://www.thechristianmyth.com/religion-vs-iq/

7. Crain, Natasha, "Are Christians Less Intelligent Than Atheists? Here's What All Those Studies REALLY Say," [online] Available at: https://crossexamined.org/are-christians-less-intelligent-than-atheists-heres-what-all-those-studies-really-say/

8. DeMar, Gary, "Of 10 Highest IQs at Least 8 are Theists and at Least 6 are Christians," [online] Available at: https://garydemar.com/10-highest-iqs-least-8-theists-least-6-christians/

9. Pew Research Center, "Scientists and Belief," [online] Available at: https://www.pewresearch.org/religion/2009/11/05/scientists-and-belief/

10. Gleiser, Marcelo, "The priest who proved Einstein wrong<sic>," [online] Available at: https://bigthink.com/13–8/lemaitre-priest-proved-einstein-wrong/

11. BBC, "The problem of evil and suffering—CCEA," [online] Available at: https://www.bbc.co.uk/bitesize/guides/zhsjscw/revision/7

12. *Questions in Theology*, "Why Would God Allow Evil in the World?," [online] Available at: https://questionsintheology.com/why-would-god-allow-evil-in-the-world/

13. Craig, William Lane, "The Problem of Evil," [online] Available at: https://www.reasonablefaith.org/writings/popular-writings/existence-nature-of-god/the-problem-of-evil

14. U.S. Census Bureau, "About 13.1 Percent Have a Master's, Professional Degree or Doctorate," [online] Available at: https://www.census.gov/library/stories/2019/02/number-of-people-with-masters-and-phd-degrees-double-since-2000.html

15. Lattier, Daniel, "The Myth of the Pagan Origins of Christmas," *Intellectual Takeout*, [online] Available at: https://intellectualtakeout.org/2022/12/myth-of-pagan-origins-of-christmas/

16. Wallace, J. Warner, "Is Jesus Simply a Retelling of the Mithras Mythology?," [online] Available at: https://coldcasechristianity.com/writings/is-jesus-simply-a-retelling-of-the-mithras-mythology/

17. Tertullian.org, "The Roman Cult of Mithras," [online] Available at: https://www.tertullian.org/rpearse/mithras/display.php?page=MithrasandJesus

18. Nelson, Daniel, "What Are Emergent Properties? Definition And Examples," [online] Available at: https://sciencetrends.com/what-are-emergent-properties-definition-and-examples/

19. United States Geological Survey, "The Night the Earth Shook," [online] Available at: https://www.usgs.gov/news/featured-story/night-earth-shook

20. Cherry, Kendra, "What is Behaviorism," [online] Available at: https://www.verywellmind.com/behavioral-psychology-4157183

21. Egnor, Michael, *Mind Matters,* "Why the Mind Can't Just Be the Brain," [online] Available at: https://mindmatters.ai/2020/08/why-the-mind-cant-just-be-the-brain/

22. *Stanford Encyclopedia of Philosophy,* "The Identity of Indisceribles," [online] Available at: https://plato.stanford.edu/entries/identity-indiscernible/

23. *Mind Matters,* "Why Pioneer Neurosurgeon Wilder Penfield Said the Mind Is More Than the Brain," [online] Available at: https://mindmatters.ai/2020/02/why-pioneer-neurosurgeon-wilder-penfield-said-the-mind-is-more-than-the-brain/

24. Ibid

25. Ibid

26. May, Andrew Ph. D., "What is the Planck Time," Space.com, [online] Available at: https://www.space.com/what-is-the-planck-time

27. Berman, H.G., "How to Compute the Probability of a Straight or Straight Flush in Stud Poker," *Stat Trek,* [online] Available at: https://stattrek.com/poker/probability-of-straight

28. Wallace, J. Warner, "Fine-Tuning of the Force Strengths to Permit Life," CrossExamined.com, [online] Available at: https://crossexamined.org/fine-tuning-force-strengths-permit-life/

29. Lewis, Geraint F.; Barnes, Luke A. *A Fortunate Universe: Life in a Finely Tuned Cosmos* (p. 111). Cambridge University Press. (referencing the work of Fred Adams of the University of Michigan)

30. Barnes, Luke, "The Fine-Tuning of the Universe for Intelligent Life.," Publications of the Astronomical Society of Australia, pdf available at: http://arxiv.org/abs/1112.4647

31. Ibid

32. Davies, Paul. "Yes, the Universe Looks Like a Fix. But That Doesn't Mean a God Fixed It." *The Guardian,* June 25, 2007. https://www.theguardian.com/commentisfree/2007/jun/26/spaceexploration.comment

33. Wallace, J. Warner, "Fine-Tuning of the Force Strengths to Permit Life," CrossExamined.com, August, 3, 2014, [online] Available at: https://crossexamined.org/fine-tuning-force-strengths-permit-life/

34. Williams, Matt, "Is the Universe Fine-Tuned for Life?," Universe Today, [online] Available at: https://www.universetoday.com/153083/is-the-universe-fine-tuned-for-life/

35. Lewis, Geraint F.; Barnes, Luke A. *A Fortunate Universe: Life in a Finely Tuned Cosmos* (p. 170–172). Cambridge University Press. Kindle Edition.

36. Lea, Rob, "A Journey through Multiverses, Hidden Dimensions, and Many Worlds," *ZME Science,* [online] Available at: https://www.zmescience.com/feature-post/space-astronomy/cosmology/a-journey-through-multiverses-hidden-dimensions-and-many-worlds/

37. Penrose, Roger, "Before the Big Bang: An Outrageous New Perspective and its Implications for Particle Physics," [online] Available at: https://epaper.kek.jp/e06/PAPERS/THESPA01.PDF

38. Podos, Jeffery and Schroeder, Katie M., Science, "Ecological speciation in Darwin's finches: Ghosts of finches future," [online] Available at: https://www.science.org/doi/10.1126/science.adj4478

39. Butterfly Conservation, "Peppered Moth and natural selection," [online] Available at: https://butterfly-conservation.org/moths/why-moths-matter/amazing-moths/peppered-moth-and-natural-selection

40. National Center for Science Education, "Icon 4:Haeckel's Embryos," [online] Available at: https://ncse.ngo/icon-4-haeckels-embryos

41. Akre, K. and Rafferty, . John P.. "Miller-Urey experiment." *Encyclopedia Britannica,* November 28, 2024. https://www.britannica.com/science/Miller-Urey-experiment.

42. Bailey, David H., "How many scientists question evolution?," SMR Blog, November 29, 2022, [online] Available at: https://www.sciencemeetsreligion.org/2022/11/how-many-scientists-question-evolution/

43. Scharping, Nataniel, "How a 30-Year Experiment Has Fundamentally Changed Our View of How Evolution Works," Discover Magazine, November 11, 2019, [online] Available at: https://www.discovermagazine.com/planet-earth/how-a-30-year-experiment-has-fundamentally-changed-our-view-of-how

44. Kimbrough, Liz, "Droughts could change bird songs, creating new species, says study on Darwin's finches," Mongrabay, November 8, 2024, [online] Available at: https://news.mongabay.com/2024/11/droughts-could-change-bird-songs-creating-new-species-says-study-on-darwins-finches/

45. John A. Smith, *Evolutionary Dynamics and Computational Modeling* (New York: Academic Press, 2020), 145–47

46. Michael K. Richardson et al., "There Is No Highly Conserved Embryonic Stage in the Vertebrates: Implications for Current Theories of Evolution and Development," *Anatomy and Embryology* 196, no. 2 (August 1997): 91–106, https://doi.org/10.1007/s004290050082

47. Meyer, Stephen, *Signature in the Cell.* 2009, Chapter 9, (pp. 204–231). HarperOne.

48. Douglas D. Axe, "Estimating the Prevalence of Protein Sequences Adopting Functional Enzyme Folds," *Journal of Molecular Biology* 341, no. 5 (August 27, 2004): 1295–1315, https://doi.org/10.1016/j.jmb.2004.06.058

49. Stephen C. Meyer, *Signature in the Cell: DNA and the Evidence for Intelligent Design* (New York: HarperOne, 2009), 212

50. Futterman, Allison, "5 Vestigial Body Parts Found in Humans," *Discover Magazine,* April 13, 2023, [online] Available at: https://www.discovermagazine.com/the-sciences/5-vestigial-body-parts-found-in-humans

51. Quanta Magazine, "Scientists Seek to Update Evolution," November 11, 2016, [online] Available at: https://www.quantamagazine.org/scientists-seek-to-update-evolution-20161122/

52. Oakes, John Dr., "If the Hebrew word "yom" in Genesis means a 24 hour period, why do you interpret it figuratively to be a period of time?," *Evidence for Christianity*, [online] Available at: https://evidenceforchristianity.org/if-the-hebrew-word-yom-in-genesis-means-a-24-hour-period-why-do-you-interpret-it-figuratively-to-be-a-period-of-time/

53. Got Questions Ministries, "Why Did God Command the Extermination of the Canaanites?," GotQuestions.org, 2025, https://www.gotquestions.org/Canaanites-extermination.html

54. Gleghorn, Michael, "Ancient Evidence for Jesus from Non-Christian Sources," *BeThinking*, [online] Available at: https://www.bethinking.org/jesus/ancient-evidence-for-jesus-from-non-christian-sources

55. Tacitus, *Annals* 15.44

56. F. F. Bruce, *The New Testament Documents: Are They Reliable?* (6th ed.), (Grand Rapids: Eerdmans, 2003), p. 123

57. Carrier, Richard, *On the Historicity of Jesus*, (Sheffield, Sheffield Phoenix Press, 2023), p. 52

58. Galston, David, "Myth and the historical-jesus," Westar Institute, Last Modified August 8, 2014, [online] Available at: https://www.westarinstitute.org/blog/myth-historical-jesus

59. J.P. Moreland, Tim Muehlhoff, Lee Strobel, *The God Conversation: Using Stories and Illustrations to Explain Your Faith* (Downers Grove, Illinois: InterVarsity Press, 2017), p 90

60. Craig, William Lane, "Dating the Gospels," *Reasonable Faith*, [online] Available at: https://www.reasonablefaith.org/writings/question-answer/dating-the-gospels

61. Manning, Eric, "13 Good Historical Reasons for the Early Dating of the Gospels," CrossExamined, [online] Available at: https://crossexamined. org/13-good-historical-reasons-for-the-early-dating-of-the-gospels/

62. Bible Archeology Report, "The Earliest New Testament Manuscripts," [Online] Available at: https://biblearchaeologyreport. com/2019/02/15/the-earliest-new-testament-manuscripts/

63. J.P. Moreland, Tim Muehlhoff, Lee Strobel, *The God Conversation: Using Stories and Illustrations to Explain Your Faith* (Downers Grove Ehrman, Bart, The Bart Ehrman Blog, "Why Date the Gospels After 70 CE," [Online] Available at: https://ehrmanblog.org/why-date-the-gospels-after-70-ce/

64. N.T. Wright, *The Resurrection of the Son of God* (Minneapolis: Fortress Press, 2003); Gary R. Habermas, *The Risen Jesus and Future Hope* (Lanham, MD: Rowman & Littlefield, 2003)

65. Warner, Jim Wallace, "Were the Gospel Eyewitnesses Lying About the Resurrection?," *Cold Case Christianity,* April 1, 2019, [online] Available at: https://coldcasechristianity.com/writings/were-the-gospel-eye-witnesses-lying-about-the-resurrection/

66. McDowell, Sean. *The Fate of the Apostles: Examining the Martyrdom Accounts of the Closest Followers of Jesus.* London: Routledge, 2015

67. Online Etymology Dictionary, Excruciate definition, [online] Available at: https://www.etymonline.com/word/excruciate

68. Sanctuaire Notre-Dame de Lourdes. "Miraculous Healings." Accessed August 20, 2025. https://www.lourdes-france.com/en/miraculous-healings/

69. Pew Research Center. "Many People in Sub-Saharan Africa, Middle East and North Africa, and Latin America Report Religious Experiences." 2019. https://www.pewresearch.org/religion/2019/10/07/in-u-s-decline-of-christianity-continues-at-rapid-pace/

70. Habermas, Gary, *The Thomas Factor: Using Your Doubts to Draw Closer to God,* Broadman & Holman: Nashville, TN (1999)

*For a full listing of DeWard Publishing
Company books, visit our website:*

www.deward.com

DeWard™
for your journey

www.ingramcontent.com/pod-product-compliance
Lightning Source LLC
Chambersburg PA
CBHW020149090426
42734CB00008B/756